THE ORAL HISTORY AND LITERATURE OF THE WOLOF PEOPLE OF WAALO, NORTHERN SENEGAL

The Master of the Word (Griot) in the Wolof Tradition

Samba Diop

African Studies
Volume 36

The Edwin Mellen Press
Lewiston/Queenston/Lampeter

Library of Congress Cataloging-in-Publication Data

Diop, Samba.
    The oral history and literature of the Wolof people of Waalo,
northern Senegal : the master of the word (griot) in the Wolof
tradition / Samba Diop.
        p.   cm. -- (African studies ; v. 36)
    "The epic tale that constitutes the core of this study is the
first attempt of a literary reconstruction of the foundation myth of
the Wolof, the myth of Njaajaan Njaay as performed by a griot, Sèq
Ñan . . . The second text with which this study is concerned ia a
genealogy of the rulers of Waalo, also from the lips of Sèq Ñan "-
-Introd.
    English, French, and Wolof.
    Includes bibliographical references.
    ISBN 0-7734-9031-0 (hc)
    1. Folk literature, Wolof.   2. Wolof (African people)--Folklore.
3. Wolof (African people)--History.   4. Oral tradition--Senegal.
5. Folklore--Senegal--Performance.   I. Title.   II. Series: African
studies (Lewiston, N.Y.) ; v. 36.
GR352.72.W64D56   1995
398.2'09663--dc20   94-38898
                                                               CIP

This is volume 36 in the continuing series
African Studies
Volume 36 ISBN 0-7734-9031-0
AS Series ISBN 0-88946-175-9

A CIP catalog record for this book is available from the British Library.

The Edwin Mellen Press   The Edwin Mellen Press
        Box 450   Box 67
    Lewiston, New York   Queenston, Ontario
    USA 14092-0450   CANADA L0S 1L0

                    The Edwin Mellen Press, Ltd.
                     Lampeter, Dyfed, Wales
                    UNITED KINGDOM SA48 7DY

            Printed in the United States of America

To the memory of my Father, Mapaté Diop who initiated me into Oral Traditions and to Wolof History and who also taught me to respect the traditions.

To the Griots and Masters of the Word Sèq Ñan, Ancumbu Caam, and Magate Caam, the Guardians of the Traditions and the Embodiment of African Historical Consciousness.

Gratefully and in Remembrance of the Pioneer and Trail blazer of African History and Antiquity, Cheikh Anta Diop (d. 1986).

En Afrique noire, le griot, le troubadour, est souvent appelé "Maitre de la Parole."

Léopold Sédar Senghor, In *Elégies majeures* suivi de *Dialogue sur la poésie francophone*, p. 105.

TABLE OF CONTENTS

ACKNOWLEDGMENTS

I wish to thank the following persons for their comments and suggestions during the course of this study:

-Professor Joseph DUGGAN, Department of French and Comparative Literature - University of California at Berkeley.

-David GAMBLE, Professor Emeritus, Department of Anthropology - San Francisco State University.

-Professor David LLOYD, Department of English - University of California at Berkeley.

This book is a thoroughly revised and updated version of my Ph.D. dissertation from the University of California at Berkeley.

"On n'arrête pas le progrès"

Samba Diop

INTRODUCTION

I. *Scope of the Study*

The study of Wolof oral traditions from Senegal in particular and of West African traditions in general is in a way a reconstruction of a specific culture.[1] Different elements must be taken into account when reconstructing Wolof culture: customs, beliefs, superstitions, language, and the use of oral traditions as a source.

The epic tale that constitutes the core of this study is the first attempt of a literary reconstruction of the foundation myth of the Wolof, the myth of Njaajaan Njaay as performed by a griot, Sèq Ñan. Prior to this study, there were mostly historical accounts on Njaajaan, obtained from oral informants or based on previous writers.[2] The second text with which this study is concerned is a genealogy of the rulers of Waalo, also from the lips of Sèq Ñan.

The definition Jan Vansina gives of oral traditions in general can be applied to Wolof oral traditions. It reads as follows:

> Oral traditions consist of all verbal testimonies which are reported statements concerning the past. This definition implies that nothing but oral traditions -- that is to say, statements either spoken or sung -enter into consideration. These must not only be distinguished from written statements, but also from material objects that might be used as a source of knowledge about the past. It further indicates that not all oral sources are oral traditions, but only those which are reported statements -- that is, sources which have been transmitted from one person to another through the medium of language. (Vansina 1965: 19-20)

This study also deals with the tribal and national history of the Wolof.

In his study of the Kuba society of Congo, Central Africa, J. Vansina stresses the importance of tribal history:

> Tribal history recounts the migrations and the formation of chiefdoms; village and family history tell how villages were formed, how clans spread through the country and split themselves into sections. (1960: 46)

The Wolof epic tale is an indication of how the villages cited by the bard were formed even though we have to take the necessary precautionary measures vis-à-vis oral historical accounts; however, one will never stress enough that in the case of Africa, oral traditions as well as oral historical accounts constitute an invaluable source in the attempt to reconstitute and to rewrite the African past.

In our case study of the transmission of knowledge, the griot Ancumbu Caam has learned his knowledge aurally from his father, Amadu Caam. Ancumbu is transmitting that knowledge orally to his son, Magate Caam.

By the same token, one must have recourse to a variety of fields of study. It is essential to take an interdisciplinary approach to African oral texts, because the texts themselves combine literature, history, music, medicine, religion, and other elements. The unity of these fields within oral texts suggests that the method of interpretation should also be unified (K. Barber 1989: 43). The foundations of African studies are still being laid, making the need for an interdisciplinary approach all the more imperative. Thus, in this study of Wolof oral traditions, various elements coming from the fields mentioned above are combined: The literature that is orally transmitted, the history of the Wolof including their myths of genesis and of ethnic origin, the music that accompanies their oral literature, and their traditional creeds and beliefs, as well as the impact of Islam on those creeds. Besides combining these various elements, there is also the task of interpreting them.

Thus, a cultural interpretation would apply to a specific situation like that of the Wolof, namely the interpretation of customs *sui generis*. However, M. Herskovits suggests that we go further. He proposes the concept of cultural re-interpretation (1960-61: 129). Cultural re-interpretation would be conceived as the way in which we see how a people would assimilate or would be influenced by new customs. In Africa, cultural re-interpretation has a three-dimensional feature, for besides indigenous customs and traditions, one must deal with the European influence from colonialism, and the primacy of Arab and Islamic customs over the European ones, at least in sub-Saharan countries that border the southern fringes of the Sahara. On the influence of Islam in Africa, B. Kamian remarks:

> Pendant toute la période qui va de 639, conquête de l'Egypte par l'Islam, à l'arrivée des premiers navigateurs portugais, la seule influence extérieure qui s'exerça sur l'Afrique noire a été l'influence musulmane, arabo-berbère. (1971: 104)

Along these lines, I will be making use of other traditions within Africa and outside Africa for comparative purposes. Sometimes, the resemblance between Wolof oral traditions and those other traditions is striking; at other times, there are differences between them. Those differences can obviously be seen most in the idiosyncrasies that are specific to Wolof culture.

My putting an emphasis on the differences between Wolof culture and other African cultures does not mean that there is a profound gap between them.

On the contrary, there are more similarities than differences between the African cultures. There are nuances between a micro-culture (Wolof culture) and a macro-culture (the total of African cultures). Thus, Wolof culture would be a micro-culture within the total African ensemble; the latter ensemble constitutes the macro-culture. This is very well illustrated by Dr Simo:

> Les différences à l'intérieur d'une macro-culture peuvent être très importantes mais jamais fondamentales. C'est au niveau de deux macro-cultures différentes que les spécificités sont tellement opposées, qu'elles ne sont pas facilement perceptibles ou compréhensibles par des personnes du hors-groupe. (1985: 15)

This approach is also emphasized by T. Eagleton when he says that "the individual units of any system have meaning only by virtue of their relations to one another" (1983: 94).

Along the same lines, two macro-cultures can constitute two different poles but are not necessarily conflictual or antagonistic: "Il est légitime d'observer des cultures séparées dans l'espace et dans le temps; mais inadmissible d'en conclure à une discontinuité dans le genre humain" (T. Todorov 1989: 128).

Thus, the different African cultures would constitute the individual units. Those units should be analyzed together but at the same time, each one of them should also be considered separately.

The main material in this study is an epic tale that I collected in Northern Senegal in the delta of the River Senegal in December 1989 and January 1990 from a griot. That area is known as Waalo. One must note that the geographical division of the region is indeed very important and determines the economic activities of its inhabitants. On both banks of the river and for approximately 10 kilometers on either side, the area is called *Waalo Tak.* The people who live in that area have fishing as their main activity. They also cultivate rice on the flood plains when the river recedes after the heavy rains that fall roughly from June to September. Conversely, the people who live inland have mostly farming and cattle-breeding as their main occupations.

B. Barry has attempted an extensive reconstitution of the history of Waalo from 1658 to 1859 (*Le Royaume du Waalo*).

I give here a brief summary of that history. However, beforehand, it is important to point out the fact that the Wolof poet is very aware of the history of Waalo as well as of the colonization of the state of Waalo in particular and of Senegal in general by the French.

The birth of the kingdom of Waalo as a military aristocracy is parallel to the development of the Atlantic trade between Europe and the African shores of the Atlantic, most of all in West Africa; with the flourishing of the slave trade in the second half of the seventeenth century, the state of Waalo became very strong (Barry 1985: 301). Prior to 1638, there was a fierce rivalry as well as wars between the various European powers which were trying to take control of the Atlantic trade: England, Holland, Portugal, France. Eventually, France was going to have the last word as far as Senegal was concerned. In 1638 a French captain called Thomas Lambert built at the mouth of the River Senegal a settlement (Barry, p.90), named Saint-Louis in remembrance of the island of Saint-Louis in Paris. Interestingly enough, Saint-Louis in Senegal (at least the original settlement) was composed of two islands.

The kingdom of Waalo was occupied by the English until 1786. Toward the end of the seventeenth century, with an agressive colonial and maritime policy on the part of Cardinal de Richelieu, the first trading post was set up in Saint-Louis with its recapture by the French; moreover, the French had an exclusive right to trade on the River Senegal (Barry, p. 89; citing J. Boulègue's [*La Sénégambie*]) .

Thus, with the monopoly that the French had on the River Senegal, they were set to play a primary role (unlike any other European power) in the history of Waalo as well as to play much influence in that part of Senegal. The definitive occupation, colonization, subjugation, and consolidation of Waalo by the French was going to be the work of Faidherbe in 1855 (Barry, p. 304).

While most of Barry's arguments are based on written documents whose authors are French, Monteil's account of the relationship between the French and the inhabitants of Waalo is mostly based on local traditions. Briefly, Monteil gives a description of the European presence in Waalo. However, he warns that that description seems to be acquired from books (most likely through Yoro Dyao, an oral historian who was also literate in French; he also collaborated with the French) and therefore has really no link with oral traditions.

First, according to this version, the *Sinwaa* (probably the Genoese) were the first Europeans to make contact with the inhabitants of Waalo with whom they wished to trade; however, they did not get along with the Brak (king) and thus left the country. Then the *Golwa* (Gaulois, or Gauls) came. In their turn, they could not get along with the local inhabitants and then left. After the Gauls, the *Portuges* (Portuguese) came. Then, the *Angle* (English) came. The *Dyêpwa* (Dieppois, natives of Dieppe) visited Waalo for trade and stayed for a long time. Finally, a French trader named *Labeyka* (probably André Brüe) negotiated with the Brak for the transfer of the island of Saint-Louis to the French as well as their definitive settlement in Saint-Louis (Monteil 1966: 41).

There is no chronology in this account; we have rather a concatenation of events. The words in italics are originally from the French and are rendered here according to Wolof pronunciation.

In the introduction to his study of the kingdoms of the savannah of Central africa, J. Vansina gives the reasons why his study his confined to the savannah area and does not cover the forest regions:

> Notre ouvrage ne couvre pas l'histoire de toute l'Afrique centrale; il se limite à celle de la Savane au nord du Zambèze et au sud de la Forêt équatoriale. Cette limitation n'est pas totalement arbitraire, elle résulte d'un fait remarquable: tous les peuples de cette région, ou presque, ont institué des royaumes ou des chefferies, systèmes politiques dont la structure est centralisée et qui sont gouvernés par un individu. En revanche, à la périphérie de cette région, la plupart des populations sont démunies d'organisation étatique, elles n'ont pas de structure politique centralisée et très souvent n'obéissent pas à un seul chef. (1976: 8)

Vansina's remark on the kingdoms of the savannah of Central Africa can be extended to those of the savannah of West Africa, and specifically to Waalo. Also, the influences and exchanges available to a kingdom of the savannah differ from those to which a forest people is exposed.

The geographical setting of Waalo is important for, in the epic tale, the hero Njaajaan Njaay comes out of the river. During his journey, he stops in villages and settlements along the river. Thus, one can understand the associations that are made among water, man, and nature; moreover, the traditions give us useful information about the landscape in ancient times as well as about the flora and fauna. Iba Der Thiam has commented on those aspects:

Outre les indications intéressant l'histoire proprement dite, la
tradition orale peut renfermer des informations permettant de se
faire une opinion sur la faune et la flore passées, sur les variations
pluviométriques, thermiques, hydrologigues, toutes choses qui
pourront donner lieu à d'utiles comparaisons avec le présent:
sans compter que la tradition orale peut lever un coin de rideau
sur les institutions, le droit des personnes et des collectivités, sur
la médication traditionnelle. (Thiam 1980: 72)

Also, historically speaking, the epic tale gives us some indications on the
different stages of the history of the Wolof. Interestingly enough, there is a
parallel and simultaneous progression between some parts or epochs of the
history of the Wolof and the progress of the narrative itself. The epic tale is
also the representation of a political crisis; it is a historical moment in the whole
history of the people of Waalo; that community undergoes transformations by
going through various stages and progressing from one leadership or government
to another (B. Dieng 1980: 879; Dieng's study focuses on the Wolof kingdom
of Kayor in Senegal).

In her study of the African epic, Lilyan Kesteloot makes a distinction
based on the assertion that "the text will tend toward 'myth' in which only the
basic story is presented or toward 'epic' in which the same story is elaborated
with music, song, heroic exploits, struggles, all at great length" (1989: 205-6).
I am not going to analyze in detail this binary distinction. However, it is
interesting to see that the Wolof poet emphasizes the way in which the story of
Njaajaan has been handed down to him by his ancestors. Does the story of
Njaajaan actually have the two aspects delineated by L. kesteloot, namely the
'mythic' aspect and the 'epic' feature? The answer to that question is that we
probably have both aspects for Ñan narrates the story of Njaajaan in song but

he also plays the accompanying music with his *xalam* ; unfortunately, the reader cannot witness the gestures or hear the music in this print form but can do so only in a live performance.

Concerning the sources for the study of African oral tradition in particular and of African history in general, there is the usual division into three categories: the documents left by Arab geographers, historians and writers who travelled to Africa south of the Sahara desert, such as Ibn Batuta or Ibn Hawqal (or Hawcal); the sources left by European colonial administrators, anthropologists, ethnographers, and ethnologists. Finally, we have the African oral sources whose guardians in Senegalese society are the griots (Kaké 1964; Kamian 1971; Niane 1985; Robinson 1985). However, Robinson, in his article devoted to the *Jihad* of Al-Hajj Umar, proposes another method, which consists of keeping a similar tripartite division but with different headings. Thus, we have the internal testimonies (chronicles) left by native clerks who mostly used Arabic as a medium for writing down certain events of their time.[3] The literate clerks also wrote in African languages such as Wolof by using Arabic script. Then there are the mixed sources that are mostly, if not entirely, oral; they include historical episodes sung by the griots. Finally, there are the external sources that are mostly made up of writings on Africa by Europeans who lived or worked in Africa (Robinson 1985: 409-426).

The epic tale of Njaajaan is structurally analyzed in the present work and also compared to other epics in Africa and elsewhere as well as viewed in the light of the theory of oral literature. However, this study does not pretend to be a general, or much less an exhaustive treatment of Wolof traditions, which is not possible on the current state of our knowledge. More studies on Wolof literature are needed. This is well illustrated by A. Gérard, who declared in regard to

10

written literature that,

> As to Wolof, in spite of the efforts of such Senegalese scholars as Cheikh Anta Diop, Pathé Diagne, and Amar Samb, there is as yet no substantive survey of its written literature, which anyhow did not begin until the late nineteenth century. (Gérard 1980: 69)

Nor does it pretend to be a study of African oral traditions outside of Waalo.

II. Field Work, Methodology, and Treatment
of Oral Texts. The Informants

The methods of approach to oral texts are various. J. M. Foley states that:

> Lord's methodology is straightforward; he applies the personal experience of a living oral tradition in Yugoslavia to earlier literatures, illustrating by analogy the traditional oral form of those literatures. (Foley 1988: 41)

Jeff Opland has written studies on Xhosa extant oral traditions as well as on Old English poetry. According to Foley, "Opland's major thrust of much of his writing has been to provide another living analogue for comparison with medieval and other manuscript traditions." (Foley, ibid., 88). Thus, Lord uses the Yugoslav oral tradition as a tool for analogy in order to illustrate ancient traditions written in dead languages such as Greek, whereas Opland is using the Xhosa oral tradition as a tool for comparative purposes. However, one must take into account the fact that both Lord and Opland were trained first in the ancient European traditions (Homeric, Old English).

When one is dealing with a living tradition, numerous problems are to be solved when it comes to fieldwork. The usual pattern of any folklorist or specialist in modern oral traditions is to carry tape recorders and movie cameras or camcorders to the field. Philip Curtin argues that the tape recorder can change the psychological setting of an interview and that, at times, the informant will speak more fully if he knows he is speaking for posterity. At other times, he will speak far less frankly than he might have done in private conversation (Curtin 1968: 370-371). Conversely, one may also make the point that it is important to record these oral traditions on a durable medium since they will certainly disappear one day. However, certain precautionary measures should be taken, such as a classification of the data provided by the informant, and a rigorous and critical method of analysis of the oral data that was collected.

The most important step is critical evaluation. This is not so much a question of finding the best version of a particular tradition as of finding what truth it may contain. Most formal traditions, repeated from memory, were preserved because they served political ends (P.D. Curtin 1964: 17).

In the case of Wolof oral traditions, we are fortunate that the traditions are still alive. For instance, I had the chance to go back to the same griots in order to obtain additional information on the same themes. However, the griots are doomed to disappear altogether because of new forms of entertainment such as cinema, radio, television, and videotape, but most of all because of the impact of schooling and of literacy. Their disappearance is really the disappearance of the traditions: because of social changes, the caste of the griots will soon disappear. When that happens, the old way of storing traditional knowledge in the memory and of transmitting it orally will also cease to exist. In the meantime, however, new forms of tradition come into existence. J. Opland writes:

> Tradition is not a lifeless thing; it alters and adapts to new social circumstances. A differentiated approach is also called for, since a tradition is not any one thing but is made up of many things, each of which responds differently to new social forces or environments. (Opland 1983: 236)

Opland goes on to show how there can be a departure from tradition; the example he gives is the extant Xhosa traditional poem of Southern Africa that is called Ntsikana's hymn. That poem is preserved for us because it exploits the tradition to encompass the new ideas introduced by Christian missionaries; in some respects it is traditional, but in other critical respects it represents a departure from tradition. (Opland 1983: 240)

Likewise in Wolof society, because of a mass internal immigration to the city of Dakar and other large towns, people coming from the rural areas bring along with them a different way of life. However, they will certainly lose those traditional values without adapting to urban life, as illustrated by Gérard Chaliand in "A l'épreuve du temps" (Introduction to F. Fanon's *Les Damnés de la terre*, 1991, p. 32).[4]

Concerning the methodology and treatment of oral texts proper, there are technical aspects to be considered. J. Foley (1988: 109-111) suggests that certain methodological preliminaries in studies associated with oral theory be observed. He distinguishes three aspects:

A. Tradition-dependence. Idiosyncratic features that are the trademark of the specific tradition are to be observed; moreover, these features should be actively incorporated into one's critical model of that tradition. Important elements, such as natural language characteristics, metrical and other prosopic requirements, narrative features, and mythical and historical content that are peculiar to that tradition must be taken into account.

B. Genre-dependence. The critic must strive for nothing less than the closest generic fit available; any and all comparisons must be calibrated according to the exactness of that fit.

C. Text-dependence, which is simply the need to take into account the precise nature of each text. Here, it is necessary to distinguish among orally-derived texts: texts that are recorded from sung performances or dictated, recorded or written down in manuscript.

Finally, Foley emphasizes the importance of defining oral traditional *sui generis*, that is, of understanding its aesthetics on its own terms.

Features that are specific to Wolof tradition will be analyzed in the present work. For instance, it is important to see how the Wolof language can have an impact on the performance and on the structure of the memory text itself (breath units, tones, ideophones, etc.). The Wolof memory text will also be placed within its own context since it is a text derived without intermediary stages from a live performance, as opposed to texts that were fixed a long time ago in manuscript form, i.e., the chansons de geste, the Homeric epics, *Gilgamesh*, and *Beowulf*.

The Wolof epic tale that I collected cannot be analyzed in a vacuum; it must be viewed in relation to the setting that produced it. To that end, D. Ben-Amos's remark is very pertinent: "The social context, the cultural attitude, the rhetorical situation, and the individual aptitude are variables that produce distinct differences in the structure, text, and texture of the ultimate verbal, musical, or plastic product" (1971: 4). The Wolof memory text will also be compared to other traditions within Africa and in other areas. Other technical aspects to be considered are those linked to anthroponymy, the interpretation and the meaning of toponyms, and finally the problems of dating certain events that happened in the past (Iba D. Thiam 1980: 73).

Another aspect that is relevant to the field of oral traditions is the question of the teaching of orality. As pointed out by Olabiyi Yai, a teaching methodology which would generate a fresh problematics of oral poetry should be devised. Moreover, the meeting point between the natural contexts in which oral poetry is elaborated and the university world should be scrutinized (O. Yai 1989: 66).

Yet another challenge within the field of oral traditions is the hermeneutics of translation. In this regard, Yai (1989: 68-69) suggests the following steps to be taken:

1. The translator must first be immersed in the culture of the source language. Attempts to translate with the aid of special dictionaries are of little help in oral translation, as the putative translator must have 'lived' oral performances in the source culture.

2. The second step is the search for viable and orally acceptable equivalent forms in the target language.

3. Extensive experience with oral tradition is required, with a written text as an optional visual aid.

4. The performance should be non-mediated.

In the task of translation, various elements must be taken into account; for instance, one must consider the relation between the source language and the society or culture being studied and from which the translation is coming.

Along the same lines, Eno Belinga suggests the following approach:

1. Choice of a system for transcribing the African language.

2. Transcription of the oral text.

3. Use of a bilingual lexicon, if one is available, and if possible of a grammar.

4.   Word - by - word translation.

5.   Final translation, faithful to the original but at the same time respecting the rules and nature of the target language (S.-M. Eno Belinga 1978: 60; citing Pierre Alexandre's two articles entitled "Problèmes linguistiques des états africains à l'heure de l'Indépendance," *Cahiers d'Etudes Africaines*, 1961 and "Sur les possibilités expressives des langues africaines en matière de terminologie politique," *L'Afrique et l'Asie*, 1961, IV, 56).

On the same order of things, B. Sitoe comments that:

> Each language is a relational structure or system of relations in which the essence and the existence of the units we identify as theoretical constructions when analyzing a sentence of a particular language are the result of those relations and are intrinsically connected within the culture of the linguistic community. (1990: 4)

Another challenge is the cultural component itself. As suggested by B. Sitoe concerning the whole theory of translation, in the Wolof tale, for instance, one has to translate familiar or unfamiliar information meaningfully when "language" means not only the verbal system but also the whole symbology expressed by gestures, images, particular attitudes, and cultural acts, all of them integrated as cultural manifestations.

However, a problem that is rightly to be considered is that once the oral text is written down, it becomes mummified, fixed, whereas the orally performed song or tale goes on experiencing variations and embellishments as long as that song or tale is orally performed.

In an interesting article, G. Bruns discusses the questions of fixed text, of interpretation, and of translation. He gives the example of the Bible as well as the metaphor of an open text as opposed to a closed text. The concept of "text" itself refers to something which is not to be altered but which, on the contrary, must be adhered to -- scribally, morally, and doctrinally (Bruns 1980: 127). By the same token, when the Wolof epic tale is sung, recorded, and written down, it leaves the realm of the text that is only orally sung; it enters the realm of fixity, of "closure." According to Bruns, "it appears that there can be no conception of 'text' without a corresponding notion of fixity" (ibid). However, if on this spectrum we have openness on the far left and fixity or closure on the far right, we shall have to consider the space that lies between the two ends of that spectrum. Thus, through the very process of being transcribed and studied, the Wolof epic tale is subject to a new interpretation and translation. Actually, the question of openness and fixity or closure is linked to that of translation, imitation, originality, and interpretation. G. Bruns discusses three examples; I am going to sum up his arguments and then explain how those arguments can be related to Wolof literature and its translation into French or English.

The first example is Petrarch's Latin translation of Boccaccio's tale of Griselda (Bruns 1980: 117). According to Bruns, Petrarch transposes the story from the locality of the vernacular to the universality of Latin, which is a way of finishing the story and publishing it to the world. The vernacular text becomes a learned text. Bruns concludes by saying that, for Petrarch,

> A story that does not make its way into Latin is a story that goes to waste, because it acquires no institutional reality. At all events Petrarch's translation confers upon the vernacular story the authority of a Latin text, and thus we may think of the translation

as a way of enshrining the story or finding for it a permanent author. (Bruns, ibid.)

The Wolof epic tale was originally orally performed in the Wolof language, a national language with its various dialects. Wolof is the everyday language of the ordinary people of Senegal, in short a popular language. On the latter point, there is an article written by Pathé Diagne entitled "Langues africaines, développement économique et culture nationale," (1971) in which there is an outline of the main problems, difficulties, impediments, and hopes pertaining to the language question in Senegal and Africa in particular and in the Third World in general. Diagne distinguishes the European languages such as French and English that are appropriated by the educated elites (p.4). By the same token, those elites have also seized upon modern thought and political power, and no effort is made on their part to upgrade the African languages to a scientific and technological level. The national languages such as Wolof constitute the only medium for the masses who are also the majority of the population in any African country.

From performance, the tale is transcribed into written Wolof through the use of Roman characters. In a third step, it is translated into French or English. That translation confers on the text a kind of authority for the simple reason that in Senegal itself, French is the language of education, of scholarship. At this time, Wolof has not yet achieved that status. By the same token, the translation of the tale from Wolof to English confers a similar authority on the text. However, the gap between the second and third steps is very great for, without a more aggressive language policy on the part of the decision-makers in Senegal, no authority can be conferred upon the national languages. The mere transcription of the tale into Wolof should and would, in the presence of the right language policy, be enough to confer authority to the tale as it is written in its original medium of expression, namely Wolof.

Bruns's second example is Dryden's remarks on Chaucer's *Troilus*. He writes:

> In his Preface [to *Fables, Ancient and Modern*] Dryden describes translation as a 'transfusion', by which he means the transfusion of new life into an old text, or of new efficacy into an archaic or obsolete utterance; but he also means the reincarnation of the original author in a new writer. (Bruns 1980: 118)

The transcription of the Wolof text and its translation and passage from "orality" to "writing", render the tale subject to interpretation and to reassessment. On a slightly different level, the performer himself, the griot Ñan interprets the tale at each performance, for two performances of the same tale are not exactly the same, as elements such as embellishment, the griot's memory, or the audience's reactions bring about changes.

Bruns' third example concerns the *Lais* of Marie de France:

> In the Prologue to the *Lais* of Marie, for example, we are told that "it was the custom of the ancients, as witnessed by Priscian, to speak obscurely in the books they wrote so that those who came later and studied those books might construe the text and add their own thoughts." (Bruns, 1980: 120, citing Eugene Vinaver, *The Rise of Romance*, 1971)

Thus, beyond the questions of translation, imitation, and interpretation comes into play the question of beginnings.[5] However, concerning the Wolof tale, is the beginning the moment it is fixed in writing or is it when the singer performs it orally? This is a difficult question for the Wolof performer actually operates a new "beginning" whenever he sings the tale; conversely, he carries on a tradition that has been already established by previous singers whenever he performs the song.

Another complex of problems that arises out of translation is that there is a loss from the source language to the target language, namely from Wolof into English or French. In the translation of the *Epic Tale of the Waalo Kingdom* from Wolof into English, I had to consider such important matters as word choice and expressions of equivalence. Ultimately, however, the semantic resonances of words in the source language are always different from those in the target language, so that translation is always, in the last analysis, inadequate. I endeavour in my notes to the translation to compensate for the shortcomings inherent in the process of translation.

1. *About the Performers: Name, Age, Occupation and Residence*

When I recorded his performances in December, 1989, and January, 1990, Sèq Ñan was 61 years old. He is a retired truck driver and used to work for a sugar refinery called Compagnie Sucrière Sénégalaise (C.S.S.) based in Richard-Toll, about 20 miles east of Rosso-Sénégal. Ñan also told me that from 1950 to 1952 he was conscripted into the French army. This was during colonial times; he was based in Atar, Mauritania. He learned to drive while he was in the army. He also told me that while in the army he used to play his guitar (*xalam*) to entertain people. He lives permanently in a village called Xuma that is situated about 10 miles east of Richard-Toll.

Sèq Ñan is a griot by profession. This is a hereditary occupation: his ancestors were griots too. The fact that he went into the army and became later on a truck driver is the result of the French colonization of Senegal.

Since my father had a house in Rosso-Senegal, Ñan came there for the recording sessions. However, he used to visit my father frequently in Rosso-Sénégal when the latter was alive. On the opposite bank of the River Senegal (the right bank), facing Rosso-Sénégal, is Rosso-Mauritanie.

My second informant, Ancumbu Caam was 81 years old at the time of the recording. Caam is blind. He used to be a farmer in Waalo in the village of Caggo. That village is situated within the heart of the former Waalo kingdom, an area that encompasses also Rosso-Sénégal and Richard-Toll. Most villages that are mentioned in Sèq Ñan's tale are situated within that area along the banks of the River Senegal. Both Ñan and Caam are griots by birth and are attached to my family.

In his study of the role of the griot in Wolof society, E. Magel observes that "each major freeborn family [among the Wolof] has its attached *gewel* [i.e., griot] family who are responsible for knowing and recounting its particular history" (1981: 185). My family belongs to the caste of the nobles, commonly called *gèer* in Wolof.

D. Robinson describes the strategic setting of the valley of the River Senegal as well as its social organization. As we see it in the *Epic Tale of the Waalo Kingdom*, Waalo and Fuuta were closely linked and there were between them many exchanges (commercial mainly) by way of the river. The strategic setting and the social organization of Fuuta (the subject of Robinson's study) are similar to those of Waalo, for both regions share the same geographical and linguistic features. Thus Robinson remarks:

> The migration traditions and linguistic evidence point to the strategic position and economy of the middle valley of the Senegal River. It lay just beneath the Western Sahara and very close to the Trans-Saharan caravan routes which developed in the days of the Ghana Empire and the Almoravid movement. The Mediterranean geographers locate the Muslim state of Takruur [or Tekrur] in or close to the middle valley in the 11th century. (1984: 2)

Concerning the geographical features of the valley of the River Senegal, Robinson adds:

> The settlements of the middle valley developed in east-west tiers corresponding to the main channel and the edges of the flood plain. One line of villages lies close to the southern edge of the average flood. There the inhabitants could farm the flood plain (*Waalo*) in the dry season and higher or *jeeri* land in the rainy season. They could graze their cattle, sheep and goats in the *jeeri* during the wet months and in the Waalo after the flood plain harvest in February. Another line of villages lay along the

southern bank of the river; the livelihood of these people came from Waalo farming or fishing in the main stream and its tributaries. A similar line of villages dressed the north bank, while some *jeeri* settlements formed a fourth and final tier, in the north before the land gave way to steppe and desert. (1984: 3)

These migratory movements can be explained in the following fashion: In West Africa, as in many parts of the world, people tend to concentrate around areas where there is plenty of water and a sizable amount of arable land. Thus, with the increase of the population, there tends to be an overcrowding and it is only normal that people would move out of that overcrowded area and seek new areas where there is arable land and water. This was the case with the Nile valley and since Africa is a vast continent people moved westward towards Lake Chad and to the areas of the rivers Niger and Senegal; others moved towards Southern Africa. However, these migratory movements happened in successive waves. The same holds true for migrations within a restricted area such as the region around the River Senegal. Thus, starting up-river, after the dissolution of the state of Tekrur, the petty kingdoms, chieftaincies, and states that came into existence along the river were as follows: Saraxolé, Tukulor, and Wolof. In a geographical order, they went from southeast around the River Senegal to northwest of the same river. Later on, as a consequence of migrations and according to the Wolof poet, the other kingdoms of Jolof, Kayor and Bawal (or Baol) were founded inland, south and southwest of the River Senegal. Then, the Lebu republic was founded in what is present-day Dakar (also known as Cap-Vert and not to be confounded with the island and Republic of Cape Verde that lies 300 kilometers off the coast of Senegal).

Two exhaustive studies treat the migration topic at length. The first study is devoted to modern migrations in West Africa; rural-urban socioeconomic links; the impact of migration on village life and society; the employment of non-nationals in West Africa; sociological aspects of modern migration in West Africa (*Modern Migrations in Western Africa*, Samir Amin[ed.], 1974).

The second study treats the aspects and meaning of migratory movements in Africa; ancient and modern migrations; migrations of the Lobi people in the Ivory Coast; a case study of intra-African migrations focussing on the migration of "guinéens" to Senegal; migrations in sub-Saharan Africa (*Les migrations africaines. Réseaux et processus migratoires*, Jean-Loup Amselle [ed.], 1976).

Migratory movements are of course accompanied by the creation of new settlements, villages, trading centers, and towns. In that regard, the resources of ethnonymy and toponymy must be taken into account. L. Kaba makes the point that "ethnonymy is a valuable, but limited concept. Like toponymy in geography, it is relevant as far as the researcher can find enough evidence to sustain his hypotheses. It can be of great importance to the study of migration, although one should be cautious in drawing conclusions. For people, after they have moved to a new place, often adopt new names or add them to their old ones for different reasons. However, the diffusion of a name is evidence of migrations or an indication of some processes of integration within society" (1973: 329).

However, ethnonymy can be helpful when one wants to understand the origins of traditional settlements and villages. In this case, the name of the founder of a village or settlement plays a crucial role as remarked by R. Rousseau in his study of Waalo and the Saint-Louis region: "On peut constater combien est vivace dans la tradition le souvenir du fondateur de chaque village" (1931: 340).

Along the same lines, C. A. Diop (1967: 196) stresses the limitations of the concept of ethnonymy. At the tribal stage or within the clan, that concept can be useful when one is doing the study of migrations. However, when tribes and clans merge into bigger states, monarchies, or nations, ethnonymy becomes less relevant.

It is important to make a distinction among the settlements, hamlets, towns, and villages. In the case of Senegal, they fall under three categories:

-The ancient settlements such as those mentioned by the Wolof singer: Mbilor (l. 563), Mbégèñ (l. 547), Kawas (l. 562). These traditional villages were founded by inhabitants of Waalo.

-The commercial trading centers also created by the people of Waalo such as Dagana (l. 549). Trading centers and posts came to existence along the River Senegal because it was a commercial waterway. For instance, people would collect gum Arabic from Waalo-Jèèri (the hinterland) and then would come to a collecting point such as Dagana. Thus, people gradually set up houses and residences. Most of the gum Arabic was collected by the Moors and European traders.

-The third category is made up of towns such as Saint-Louis, Gorée, Rufisque, and Dakar. All these towns developed because of trade with the Europeans including the slave trade. In the case of slavery, Gorée and Saint-Louis were the shipping ports. For instance, all the slaves captured along the Atlantic coast (from Senegal to Angola) were brought to the island of Gorée; there, they were sorted out and then shipped to the Americas. In the case of Saint-Louis, all the slaves captured along the River Senegal and further inland (present-day Mali and

Niger) were transported on the river or by foot to Saint-Louis.

Most of the towns described above (except the island of Gorée) used to be small villages.

An important characteristic of a Wolof traditional village is that it is initially made of small family units that stand within 100 to 500 feet of each other. Each of those units is called a *keur* . This is how R. Rousseau describes the Wolof village:

> La plupart des agglomérations ainsi constituées s'appellent *keur Untel*, appellation équivalent au "Chez Untel" si fréquent en certaines régions de France; nous proposons de les appeler des *keurs*. Cette appellation et ce qu'elle désigne évoquent plutôt l'idée d' un hameau que d'un village: moralement, administrativement et surtout économiquement, *un village, c'est un ensemble de keurs.* (1933: 90 [author's emphases])

Another important feature is linked to the way in which the Wolof village is built, namely the scattering of the *keurs*. According to Rousseau, the scattering of the dwellings and units is due to the "grand esprit d'indépendance des Ouolofs" (Rousseau, op. cit.; p. 89 and passim).

Historians such as Abdoulaye Ly (*La compagnie du Sénégal*, 1958), Boubacar Barry (*Le royaume du Waalo*, 1985) and Abdoulaye Bathily (*Les portes de l'or* , 1989) have pointed out the ways in which slavery destabilized and changed the economy of the region extending from Bakel (Upper Senegal) to Saint-louis (Lower Senegal); slavery also upset the social structure of the various societies and ethnic stratifications of the area. In this context, it was a question of large-scale enslavement, namely the shipping of Africans outside of the continent to the Americas. This intercontinental type of slavery, also known as the "Ebony Trade," was of course different from internal slavery that was confined within the African continent and was the result of capturing people during local wars.

It is also important to note that the development of towns and villages was parallel to the progress of transportation.

In his study of the persistence of the caste system in contemporary Wolof society, O. Silla (1966: 751) states that transportation was organized around three axes: the River Senegal, the railway line going from Dakar to Saint-Louis, and tarred or dirt roads that linked the main towns such as Dakar, Rufisque, Thiès, Kaolack, and Saint-Louis. He adds that with French colonization, small market towns also known as "ports of call" (*escales* in French) sprawled along the waterways, roads, and railway lines. Exceptionally, one comes across settlements that were created by the French colonial administration as pilot farms. This was the case of Richard-Toll, a colonial farm project. Today, this is a sprawling town where there is a sugar refinery (Compagnie Sucrière du Sénégal or C.S.S.) and it therefore attracts labor from the adjoining villages as well as areas as far away as Casamance in the south of Senegal. There are also sugar-cane fields where villagers are employed as cutters.

Richard-Toll literally means "Richard's farm." It is intimately linked to the history of colonization in Senegal. H. Azan describes Richard-Toll as "un superbe jardin botanique dans lequel M. Richard s'était livré avec beaucoup de succès à l' acclimatation de différents arbres fruitiers venus d' Europe et des autres colonies, survécut à ces tentatives avortées [of previous projects] et resta jusqu' en 1840" (1863b: 608). Citing M. le baron Roger, D. Boilat (1984: 340-41), explains in detail Richard's farming project and colonial farming projects in general in Waalo during the nineteenth century. Richard was a Frenchman who started an experimental agricultural station in that area in the

28

nineteenth century. Since Waalo had fertile lands and a lot of water, it was targeted as a farming colony by the French colonial administration. In his preface to *Le Royaume du Waalo*, Samir Amin makes the following point:

> Le projet de colonisation agricole du Waalo, pour en faire un pays de plantations (coton, canne à sucre, tabac, etc.), formulé pour la première fois par le gouverneur anglais de Saint-Louis, O'Hara, à la fin du XVIIIe siècle, sera mis à l'ordre du jour pendant la Révolution et l'Empire, comme conséquence de la révolte des esclaves de Saint-Domingue. Le Waalo est "acheté" en 1819 par le gouverneur Schmaltz. (S. Amin 1985: 22-23)

Richard started his farming project after Schmaltz's action. Thus, the settlement was named after him and the actual rendering in Wolof of Richard-Toll is "Rissaar-Tòòl."

In the final analysis, the colonization of Senegal and the agricultural colonization in particular was a central and essential matter for the French. This question is very well discussed by M. Diouf (*Le Kajoor au XIXe siècle*, pp. 121-28).

When I mentioned to the Wolof griot that there are historians who say that the first Wolof kingdom was that of Jolof, he flatly and emphatically denied that hypothesis. He said that Jolof was born after Waalo. In the epic tale, he reinforces that point (lines 889-93).

In a separate instance, and during a conversation I had with the griot Ancumbu Caam, the latter got angry and was very disturbed when I read accounts of French historians such as V. Monteil who gave pre-eminence to the state of Jolof and who pointed out that Jolof was anterior to Waalo. For instance, I read to him the following passage from Monteil and translated it into Wolof; actually, I made a direct translation from French into Wolof for Caam is illiterate in French:

> Province lointaine, aride, peu peuplé, le Dyolof est, cependant, le
> berceau de la plus ancienne dynastie du Sénégal. (Monteil 1966:
> 595)

Then, citing S. Sauvageot (*Description synchronique d'un dialecte wolof:
le parler du Dyolof*, 1965), Monteil adds: "On tient le dialecte Wolof du Dyolof
pour le plus pur de la langue" (Monteil, op. cit.). For Caam, this second
statement was insult added to injury. However, in answering, Caam said that
Monteil was absolutely right in saying that Jolof was dry, remote, and sparsely
inhabited. He added that the Peul cattle herders were fond of that region. For
all these reasons, said Caam, Njaajaan was sent there by the elders of Waalo in
order to establish some kind of political and social organization. He added that
the kingdom of Waalo had been in existence for 400 years before Njaajaan
arrived, organised it, and enlarged it, annexing the territory of Jolof. B. Barry
supports both griots' arguments when he declares that Waalo is anterior to Jolof.
However, Barry bases his argument on the legend of Njaajaan Njaay and on
Wolof oral traditions, not on written sources. He claims that Njaajaan was the
founder of the Empire of Dyolof (or Jolof) and then states:

> Cette tradition, qui place ce règne à la fin du XIIIe ou au début
> du XIVe siècle, nous fait entrevoir l'existence d'entités politiques,
> tel le Waalo, avant la formation du Dyolof. (Barry 1985: 46)

Caam's point is corroborated by Ñan's (line 947); however, one must
take into account the fact that both griots come from the same cultural matrix
and may have gotten more or less similar information that is shared within the

Wolof linguistic community of Waalo.

Concerning the Wolof state of Jolof, R. Cornevin observes that:

Le Djolof n'acquiert son indépendance qu'avec N'Diadiane N'Diaye qui réussit à débarrasser le pays de l'influence toucouleur du Fouta. (1960: 265)

Cornevin's statement does not seem to corroborate Ñan's argument as to the primacy of Waalo over Jolof for the singer says that Njaajaan was sent to Jolof (in the middle of the Waalo empire) in order to organize that territory. Likewise, J.-L. Monod tends in the same direction as Cornevin:

Les Ouolofs furent pendant longtemps les vassaux des Toucouleurs. Vers le milieu du XIVe siècle, ils supportaient mal cette vassalité. Un chef Ouolof, *N'Diadiane N'Diaye* , souleva le Djolof contre le Tekrour. Il battit les Toucouleurs et assura l'indépendance au Djolof sous la dynastie de ses descendants, les N'Diaye, qui règnent encore aujourd'hui. (1931: 178)

One last testimony on this question between Waalo and Jolof is that of Dr Lasnet who writes:

L'empire djolof comprenait autrefois le Djolof, le Oualo, le Cayor, une partie du pays sérère, et s'étendait même au delà du Toro [or Fuuta] des Toucouleurs; son souverain portait le titre de *Bour* ou "grand Ouolof." On ne l'approchait qu'en rampant, la tête couverte de poussière; les rois secondaires lui devaient un tribut et au moment de son élection lui adressaient un tambour d'hommage; ces rois étaient le *brack* du Oualo, le *damel* du Cayor, le *teigne* du Baol. (1900: 111)

On the relationship between Waalo and Jolof, G. Nicolas believes that Jolof was anterior to Waalo:

Les trois états du Waalo, du Cayor et du Baol se sont émancipés de l'autorité de la vieille dynastie du Dyolof et de la tutelle peul et ont refoulé les Serer vers le sud. (1978: 364)

Overall, there is not a definite consensus about whether primacy belonged to Jolof or to Waalo.

J. Vansina defines the African kingdoms as "sovereign political groups, headed by a single leader who delegates authority to representatives in charge of the territorial units into which the country is divided" (1962: 325). However, in the bard's opinion, it is the Council of the Elders that decided to send Njaajaan to Jolof, in the middle of the empire.

Both Caam and Ñan emphasize the pre-eminent role played by Njaajaan in the formation of Waalo. The process they describe accords with I. Lapidus's views of the process of state-formation in this region:

Sudanic states had their origin in family groups led by patriarchs, councils of elders, or chiefs of villages. The state came into existence when a local elder, an immigrant warrior or perhaps a priestly ruler, established his control over other communities. (1988: 490)

In the case of Waalo, it is not an elder who is said to have founded the state but the son of an immigrant and a young man at the same time named Njaajaan Njaay. The latter has broken the gerontocratic rule, at least in the epic tale.

On the topic of internal colonization, M. Kunene writes :

There is a tendency for people in many recently occupied and colonized countries to regard the colonial experience as unique to themselves. The style and manner, the intensity and efficiency of colonial occupation was perhaps new, but the sorts of political and economic control elaborated under colonialism [European] are actually as old as the earliest human codes of power. (1992: 30)

In the case of Waalo and Jolof, and according to the Wolof singer, this is an example of inter-ethnic or domestic colonization. In Africa, the occupation and subjugation of one ethnic group by another, of a tribe by another, of a kingdom by another is a very old practice and pre-dates the advent of European colonization. Instead of colonization, J. Vansina uses the subtler term of conquest, which has a very strong military flavor. Besides pointing out the complexity of the process of conquest itself, Vansina adds:

Conquest means not only to defeat enemies, but also to integrate them, that is to make the enemy accept a loss of independence. The incorporation of enemies becomes even more complex if they themselves have not had a state structure before their defeat. For then it is not merely a matter of making the enemy accept his subjection, but also of teaching him to adopt a new political organization. (1962: 329)

Later on in the epic tale, we learn that Jolof was unsettled and that it was Njaajaan who brought some kind of political organization to that region.

For the last 32 years (starting in 1960), Ancumbu Caam has been living in the Dakar area, more precisely in Guédiawaye, which is a suburb of Dakar, situated 12 miles east from the center. Ancumbu lives with his son, Magate

Caam, who owns the house. At the time of recording, Magate was 45 years old; he is currently a caretaker in a primary school that is located in his neighborhood.

2. Sources of the Information Given by the Two Griots.

If there is a point of convergence between Ñan and Caam, it is that both are griots by birth. Moreover, they both insist on the very important fact that the knowledge they possess has been transmitted to them by their respective fathers. In their turn, the fathers learned from their fathers and so on. Ancumbu Caam attempts to go back to his lineage as he retraces the lineage of the Diop family.

The authority of both griots is acknowledged by their own communities. There is an "oral" consensus on the part of the Wolof community in Waalo, in Dakar, and in certain other parts of Senegal concerning the qualifications of Ñan and Caam.

Griots travel a lot, visiting people in many places. In her analysis of the functions of the oral narrative in West Africa, L. Kesteloot points to the fact that these functions vary from one group to the other and that "les sociétés opèrent sur des schémas qui circulent par le truchement des griots voyageurs, et d'autres modes de transmission de la tradition orale" (1986: 63). The griots and their travels in West Africa constitute one of the surest means for the spread of myths, legends, and stories across the savannahs. In his analysis of the Muslim state of Fuuta Toro and of the *Jihad* of Al-Hajj Umar in the nineteenth century, D. Robinson remarks that the griots who sang the narratives of the *Jihad* used to travel, adding new elements to their narratives. The focus in Robinson's remark is the griot's travels and movements:

Avec le déclin du pouvoir [of the Muslim state of Fuuta] et de la richesse de la chéfferie pendant la période coloniale, le griot voyageait de plus en plus loin, entretenant des relations avec une plus grande clientèle et était ainsi amené à se constituer un répértoire susceptible de s'adapter à un large public. (Robinson 1985: 419)

An important and even essential source of the information given by the two griots is the Qur'an, and Islam in general. Within the framework of a project of reconstituting an African culture such as the present one, one of my main concerns is the scholarly attitude (of my informants) toward Islam as a prestige culture. To that end, B. Kamian warns against giving too much weight to Islam as a prestige culture so as to create a bias against African indigenous creeds and beliefs:

> Les sources islamiques doivent être passées au crible de la critique. Elles font souvent preuve d'incompréhension envers tout ce qui est défavorable à l'Islam, envers tout ce qui est animiste, et de parti pris manifeste pour tout ce qui est musulman ou arabe. Elles expriment une sorte de complexe de supériorité de la culture musulmane et ont tendance à rattacher toujours les dynasties et les généalogies africaines à des origines arabes, voire chérifiennes. Dans les régions où la conversion à l'Islam a été totale, le passé anté-islamique reste difficile à saisir avec exactitude, malgré une adaptation, une africanisation de l'Islam au milieu africain. (B. Kamian 1971: 102)

In his study of the pre-colonial state of Baté in Upper Guinea (present-day Republic of Guinea), Lansiné Kaba stresses the tendency of claiming descent from an Arab genealogy:

> According to the local traditions, there was a southward migration after the fall of Ghana and the decline of Mali; this migration started in the 16th century. Within this migratory context, most Baté families claim that their ancestors originated in the northeast,

and either associate them with the Sarokolle [also known as Soninke] or accord them an Arab origin. (Kaba 1973: 330)

The griots are known within the whole community, and since they sing genealogies as well as reconstructing them, they necessarily come into contact with the people whose genealogies they are singing. The griots constitute the living chain between the contemporaries and their ancestors. Both Caam and Ñan had traveled extensively within Senegal. Ñan told me that, many years after he finished his military service, he visited many times the Wolof who left Senegal and established themselves in Mauritania for economic reasons, namely for trade reasons or to seek jobs. Ñan would sing in praise of those people; during his stay, he was given accommodation and food, and upon his departure, money and gifts. Two nineteenth-century French authors who traveled to Senegal also emphasized the gifts given to the griots by the nobles. Bérenger-Féraud wrote:

Les cadeaux qu'il [the griot] obtient des courtisans, de ceux qui recherchent sa bienveillante intervention auprès du souverain, les largesses de ce souverain lui-même, constituent des bénéfices autrement plus considérables pour sa fortune. (1882: 267)

He then added:

Dans le cayor et le oualo, le chef des griots reçoit au moment de l'éléction du Damel ou du Brak de riches cadeaux comme les autres grands fonctionnaires de la nation. L'usage veut même qu'il ait un beau cheval à sa part; et, dans ce pays; une belle monture est une des choses les plus difficiles à se procurer. (Idem, p. 268)

Along the same lines, V. Monteil cites Golberry, a Frenchman who traveled to Senegal in 1802 on the topic of potlatch:

> Golberry explique que les griots vivent de cadeaux, 'parce qu'une des faiblesses honteuses dont les hommes savent le moins se défendre, c'est celle de se corrompre avec plaisir, par le poison de la louange et de la flatterie.' (V. Monteil 1968: 774)

Both Caam and Ñan receive gifts from the nobles, for it is the griots who sing and praise the nobles and there is an obligation on the part of those being sung about to give gifts to the singers. However, Caam and Ñan do not really fit into Golberry's description; both griots have genuine relationships with my family and those relationships are based on friendship and not only on money and gifts.

Is the relationship between the griot and the noble or other person being praised of a proportionally reciprocal nature concerning gift exchange? In appearance it may not seem to be, because it is very difficult to relate the amount of gifts being given to the griot to the scope of the performance. For instance, in the case of Mandinka society as studied by G. Innes (1974), the people being praised were compelled to give more and more. In a specific case, Innes points out how the griot was able to create a competition in gift-giving among members of the audience. In Wolof society we have the same phenomenon. The griot would openly praise one person in order to compel others to give him more. However, the person being praised gains in prestige and in status in the community. Thus, in Wolof society, the relationship between the griot and the person being praised is not entirely fixed in economic terms.

On gift exchange, I can give an example based on a personal experience that I had in Senegal during a visit in 1992. An old griot who is attached to my family set up a very clever strategy, which consisted in creating competition between my elder brother and me as to who was going to give him more money. The cleverest part of that strategy was how the griot came to obtain money from both of us. Because of the Islamic influence in contemporary Wolof society, the eldest son plays the role of a father figure and that role is more greatly emphasized after the death of the father. This was the case after my father's death in 1991. Usually, at the end of the griot's visit, if either of us (my brother or I) gives him some money for his transportation home, it should be enough, for the one who is giving is doing so in the name of the whole family. However, the old griot was clever enough to ask me before approaching my brother. He did so without either of us knowing that the other was being solicited. However, this is a specific case when the griot pays a visit, but when he is performing or when there are ceremonies such as weddings, naming ceremonies, or other religious functions, the griot is entitled to receive as many gifts as he wishes, and from anybody.[6]

3. *Place, Date and Circumstances of Recording*

From January 12 to 15, 1990, I had the opportunity of recording the master of the word (griot) Sèq Ñan over a two-day period in Rosso-Senegal. This small town is located roughly 250 miles northeast of Dakar, the capital of Senegal. During the recording, an audience was present and was composed of my father Mapaté Diop and two other men, Ibrahima Mboj and Abdoulaye Gaye. At all times (except for a few breaks), Sèq Ñan, my father, Gaye, Mboj, and I were there; in addition, once in a while neighbors would come in to greet my father and me since I was the visitor coming from Dakar as well as from abroad, namely from the United States. These visitors did not stay too long. From time to time, the performer would stop singing and playing his guitar, the *xalam*, in order to greet the visitors; then, he would start singing again. He also took pauses in order to eat (the food was shared by all of us), drink tea,[7] and pray, for he is a Muslim. Actually, the prayer is a group practice with everybody in the room praying at the same time together. The recording thus took place as part of a communal experience. The session lasted from 5:00 P.M. to midnight on the first day and from 10:00 A.M. to 5:00 P.M. the next day.

At the beginning, Ñan was nervous, for he felt "invaded" by the recording devices --the camera and cassette recorder -- but that nervousness occurred only at the beginning of the recording session. After about two hours, Ñan became oblivious of the recording devices and was more at ease, singing and playing the *xalam* as if they were not there. With the passing of time, in the relaxed atmosphere, and with his being accustomed to the recording devices, the performer was performing with ease and naturalness. I can attest to the diminished impact the recording devices had on him for when I was much younger (from 1970 to 1980), Ñan used to come and visit my family in Dakar for a long period of time, on occasion singing and playing the *xalam*, naturally without recording devices. In 1990 in Rosso-Sénégal, he seemed to be as much at ease after the initial period of nervousness as he had been in Dakar one or two decades before. However, I should mitigate my personal judgment on the question: In any case, recording devices may have at least some influence, no matter how small, on the performer.

The recording session I had with the second griot, Ancumbu Caam, took place on December 27, 1989, in Dakar. When I told my father (who had come to his house in Dakar to visit, for during that time he had moved on a permanent basis to Rosso-Sénégal) of my desire to have Caam perform, he sent a messenger to Caam and consequently a day and time were agreed upon and all the arrangements made.

On the 27th of December 1989, Ancumbu Caam, accompanied by his son Magate, came to our house in Dakar. My father's house was roughly five miles away from the center of the city, whereas Caam lived in the suburb of Guédiawaye, which is 12 miles from the center of Dakar. After Ancumbu and Magate had finished lunch with us, I set up the recording devices, namely a video camera and a tape recorder.

A major difference between Ñan and Caam in regard to the impact these devices would have on them is that Caam is blind. However, he was aware of his being recorded but he was at ease and did not appear nervous at all. He merely asked me if he could start performing, and I answered positively. Later on, when my father took part in the discussion, as well as Caam's son, Magate, the performance (i.e., the interview with Caam) was more flowing and less strained by the solemnity imposed by the recording devices.

The audience was composed of Caam, his son Magate, and my father, all of us seated on chairs in one corner of the yard. Contrary to the Rosso-Sénégal session, the Dakar session took place outdoors. Since many of the activities (cooking, tea drinking, praying, gatherings) take place outdoors because of the heat, there were other people in the yard, such as my aunt, my mother, and some of my younger brothers and their friends. However, these other people were not taking part directly in the performance, but were attending to their own affairs or talking among themselves. Once in a while, they would listen to Caam. Most probably the reason why the other people who were present when Caam was performing did not pay any attention to him, or did not take part in the performance, is that there was no music, no guitar playing. When Ñan was performing, on the other hand, people would pay more attention to him because he would play the *xalam* and sing at the same time. Thus the presence or absence of music is an important additional element to be taken into account. Also, since Ancumbu and his son Magate were frequent visitors, they were no novelty to the members of my family.

During both recording sessions (Rosso-Sénégal and Dakar), there was no interpreter. Since Wolof is my native tongue and the performances were in Wolof, there was no need for one. However, when the singers (both Caam and Ñan) uttered a word that was out of usage or difficult to understand, I would interrupt and ask the meaning of that word or wait until the end of the performance to do so.

As I pointed out earlier on the subject of gift-giving, Caam and Ñan received gifts and money from my parents. That giving of gifts to the two griots was not tied to their having to perform. They found it a duty to sing and praise the genealogy of our family. Thus the payment does not affect the performances of the two griots directly, since, as part of the ongoing relationship, they always remember the numerous past occasions in which they received gifts and money without having to perform. However, my family is not the only family that Caam and Ñan are praising. They are attached to other families as well.

In contemporary Senegalese society, I have heard stories of griots fabricating false genealogies for people who are considered *nouveaux riches* or *parvenus* and who in return would pay the griots lavishly. According to the testimonies I heard, those *nouveaux riches* had an obscure past or a low status (or their ancestors or parents did); thus, with their wealth, they attempt to raise their social status as well as to enhance their prestige. This phenomenon constitutes a testimony to the changing nature of traditions in contemporary Senegalese society. It is also a proof of the griot's astuteness in adapting to new social norms. Since most people who belong to the ancient Senegalese nobility and aristocracy have only their names and titles as wealth, it is obviously not enough for the griot to sing for them alone, because he must make a living, especially in an urban setting.

The most poignant example in Senegal is that of El Hadj Mansour Mbaye a very famous griot. Momar C. Diop and Mamadou Diouf (1990: 19 and 113) describe in detail the participation of this griot in political life. Mr. Mbaye is a news and political commentator and journalist on Radio and Television. In fact the president of Senegal Abdou Diouf appeals to Mr. Mbaye. The latter praises the former and helps the president in the strengthening of his power. Mr. Mbaye is paid a monthly salary and perks; he is also given a car and assigned a chauffeur just like the other high top officials and cabinet members of the government. Griots also play a similar role to that of Mr. Mbaye in neighboring Mali and the Gambia. In Mali, we have the example of the famous griot Baba Cissoko:

> Baba Cissoko est sans doute actuellement le conteur le plus célèbre du Mali. Depuis plusicurs années, chaque lundi soir, ses "causeries" diffusées, par Radio-Mali sont écoutées avec un plaisir attentif, un peu partout en Afrique (G. Dumestre 1979: 31).

This situation is somewhat similar to that of nineteenth-century Europe, specifically in England and France after the Industrial Revolution with the consequent rise of a new entrepreneurial bourgeoisie and the steady decline of the old aristocratic; the latter had their titles to depend on and perhaps land but the whole industrial structure was the monopoly of that new bourgeoisie which went about buying noble titles in order to enhance its prestige.

I pointed out to the two griots (Caam and Ñan) the urgency of collecting and preserving the oral traditions as well as the importance of the vast knowledge they possess, for after them this art of transmitting knowledge orally would disappear. I explained the same thing to my father. All three agreed on the necessity of consigning these traditions to writing and tapes for posterity. I also explained to Caam and to Ñan that the moment a version of an epic tale or of a genealogy was written down or recorded, it became a fixed form (just like the Qur'an).[8] Both Ñan and Caam were aware of the fact that their art of transmitting knowledge orally was slowly being replaced by new forms of communication and entertainment such as television, books, and videotape. They both considered these social changes as a sign of the times.

III. *The Nature of Traditions, Their Relevance and Role in Contemporary African Societies*

In this section, I will discuss the relevance and role of traditions in contemporary sub-Saharan African societies. The reason for extending the scope of this discussion to such a vast area inhabited by peoples who speak different languages, have divergent customs, and sustain themselves through various systems of nutrition is that, behind that apparent diversity of the peoples of Africa, there is a common substratum. There is also a common recent history highlighted by European colonialism and imperialism beginning in the fifteenth century and the waves of upheavals the European domination of Africa has brought about.

The question of traditions is very complex and numerous studies have been produced by various scholars from Africa, Europe, and North America. Thus, one might be tempted to maintain that there is really nothing new to say in the field of oral traditions and of traditions in general. My contention is that there is already a necessity to redefine and focus again on traditions above all in contemporary Africa where societies and communities are faced with numerous challenges, the most salient being those pertaining to development: economic, social, political, and cultural development.

To that extent, we can extend this remark of B. Mouralis on oral literature to the field of African oral traditions:

La littérature orale n'est pas la transmission d'un héritage ancien et figé, mais une création et une recréation perpétuelles, par contamination, transfert et invention. (Mouralis 1975: 38)

Along the same lines, an interesting example of the continuity of traditions was related by James Dao in the *San Francisco Sunday Examiner and Chronicle* (June 7, 1992). The story is about Ghanaian immigrants (Ashantis) living in the United States of America and Canada who are trying to keep alive their native traditions. First, Dao remarks that "coming from the cocoa and gold-rich region of central Ghana, Ashantis have clung to traditions of royalty through British colonization, post-independence military governements and now immigration to America" (p.4). During the year 1992, these Ghanaian immigrants assembled in the hall of a New York City hotel in order to elect Nana Kwabena Brobey Dankwa of Staten Island as the new Asantefuohene (king) in America. Dao adds that "thus was a Ghanaian immigrant who is a hospital security official by day transformed into the newest Asantefuohene, or surrogate king, of the Ashantis of North America" (ibid.). No matter how symbolic this coronation was, the fact remains that a tradition that is many centuries old and which originated in Africa is being re-enacted in present-day America. This is a case of a consciousness of a past and a sense of belonging on the part of these immigrants.

The re-enactment of traditions that are very old is also present in other cultures. The most notable example is that of Britain and of its crown: changing of the guards, speech of the king or queen in front of the Parliament, yearly vacation of the royal family in Wales and Scotland.

Most African leaders and intellectuals who participated in the process of decolonization and of political independence were aware of the fact that new African states could not be grounded only in their own traditions and that contributions from other cultures were needed. Thus, citing J. Kenyatta (1962), L. V. Thomas states:

> Notre nation [Kenya] doit se développer de façon organique à partir de ce qui est indigène; tout en adaptant ce qui nous convient des cultures de l'Orient et de l'Occident, nous devons donner à notre peuple de l'orgueil et de la dignité personnelle, en conservant, comme éléments de base, ce qui est bon et valable dans notre société traditionnelle. (Thomas 1966: 56)

The most common definition of traditions is that they constitute a set of customs and beliefs that remain unchanged over a very long period of time. In this study, the question of traditions is viewed within the context of oral literature for it is Wolof oral literature that expresses the customs and beliefs of the Wolof.

I will now discuss the characterizations of traditions and of oral tradition given by various writers as well as the clash between European and Arabic values and the traditional and indigenous values of Africa south of the Sahara Desert. I will then place these matters in the contex of the debate that arose consequent to the failure of most economic programs and governmental developmental policies in post-independence Africa and the advent of structural adjustment programs brought about by the World Bank and the International Monetary Fund. That debate began in 1980, a year that coincides with the advent of those structural programs as well as with the realization of the total failure of most, if not all, African leaders and their policies that had brought corruption on a never-experienced scale with squandering and theft of public funds, illegal enrichment, and all the other corollaries linked to under-development and economic poverty.

At this stage of African history, serious African intellectuals cannot afford to confine themselves to vague or general academic theories or find refuge in a traditionalist mould.[9] In order to see the advent of real progress and better standards of living in Africa, African scholars are compelled to produce more serious and thorough works that should reflect on the various challenges facing their countries, and propose new solutions. The other challenge African scholars are facing is how to get out of the university, which is an island, and connect with their societies by bringing their thoughts to the public as well as by trying to solve the grave problems their societies are facing. To that end, the remark of the Senegalese historian C.A. Diop should not go unheeded by African intellectuals:

> Intellectuals ought to study the past not for the pleasure they find in so doing, but to derive lessons from it or, if necessary, to dissect those lessons in full knowledge of the facts. Only a real knowledge of the past can keep in one's consciousness the feeling of historical continuity essential to the consolidation of a multinational state [in Africa]. (Diop 1990: 9)

In the early 1960s, Frantz Fanon produced his famous book entitled *Les damnés de la terre* in which he analyses various aspects of colonialism and poverty. He observes concerning Third World intellectuals:

> Dans un pays sous-développé en phase de lutte, les traditions sont fondamentalement instables et sillonnées de courants centrifuges. C'est pourquoi l'intellectuel risque souvent d'être à contretemps. (Fanon 1991: 270)

According to Fanon, traditions and development or progress cannot be put in the same basket; in this sense, traditions are considered a brake on progress. For the intellectual, there is a greater risk of being cut off from the masses; thus, he would belong to that priviledged class composed of the educated elite

L.J. Calvet stresses the fact that in Africa, there is no link whatsoever between the intellectuals and the masses:

Dans l'affrontement entre le français et les langues locales, les élites africaines sont facilement du côté de la langue dominante [French]; c'est d'ailleurs pour cela qu'on les a créées et mises en place. (Calvet 1974: 135)

One of the duties of the intellectual is to reflect on the problems of his society and to try to solve them. In whatever manner, intellectuals are needed in Africa. The latter point is well illustrated by Olabiyi Yai when he says that "une communauté intellectuelle dans nos pays [in Africa] est une nécessité" (1978: 89).

The older generation of African historians and intellectuals, the first generation to go to Europe or America for higher studies in the 1930s, '40s, and '50s, have outlined the general guidelines as well as defining the framework within which the writing of African history can efficiently and rigorously be carried out. The generations that come after those intellectual pioneers must study in detail the various African cultures and societies past and present; this kind of study will lead to a synthesis and may well contribute to the political unification and economic integration of Africa. For these unifying studies, all fields are concerned: science, medicine, literature, history, sociology, agronomy, anthropology, economics.... It is only in this fashion that we can have a correct writing of African history as well as tangible progress on the African continent.

A central question for the whole project is the link between the re-writing of African History and colonization and decolonization. V. Monteil wonders if

the history [of Africa and Asia] has been decolonized and if not, what has been
done in that direction and what one can still do in order to decolonize it (1962:
3). The author goes on further by proposing some solutions:

> La première solution est, bien entendu, celle de l'histoire
> *nationale*, établie et publiée par les Africains ou les Asiatiques
> eux-mêmes, tenue, le plus souvent, par ses détracteurs comme une
> histoire *engagée* - parfois comme une 'thèse à défendre'." (Ibid.
> [author's emphases])

In Monteil's arguments, there are two aspects: the first aspect is that
African history is written by African historians. The second aspect is that that
history is considered as a "committed" history. Within the space that lies
between the two ends of the spectrum, there is the possibility to write a
non-partisan history of Africa.

In the final analysis, the challenge is up to African historians and
intellectuals to write (or re-write) the history of the entire continent. This task
is motivated by the fact that Africans have suffered a loss of collective memory
caused by European colonial dispossession. J. Ki-Zerbo remarks that "il est clair
que personne ne peut vivre avec la mémoire d'autrui. Et, dans la mesure où
l'on nous [Africans] a enlevé notre mémoire collective en nous privant de notre
Histoire, eh bien! le fait de nouer ce cordon ombilical à sa source nous
permettra, me semble-t-il, de récupérer notre mémoire, c'est-à-dire notre
identité" (1975: 42).

The reason why African historians and intellectuals had a defensive
attitude was understandable. The writing of African history by Europeans was
influenced by misconceptions and distortions and in some cases, by the lack of

linguistic competence, i.e., the mastery of African languages. It was also influenced by the social, cultural, political, economic, colonial construction and invention of the concept of Africa itself.

Along with the construction and invention of Africa, there was also the "systematic doubt which denies the historical consciousness of the African peoples" (J. Bazin, 1986: 61).

V. Y. Mudimbe notes that there is a distinction based on a theory of two types of mentality. That distinction was made by scholars like Lévi-Bruhl and his followers:

> One [theory] is rational, functioning according to principles of logic and inquiring into causal determinations and relations; the other, prelogical, seems completely dominated by collective representation and strictly depends upon the law of mystical participation. Westerners participate in logical thought." (Mudimbe 1988: 136)

In the logic of the theoricians who held onto this kind of distinction, "such peoples as the Chinese included with Polynesians, Melanesians, Negroes, American Indians, and Australian Blackfellows belong to the prelogical category" (Mudimbe, ibid., [citing Evans-Pritchard, and adding that by 1965, a scholar like Evans-Pritchard stated that no reputable remained anthropologist would accept this theory of distinction anymore]).

Among those reputable anthropologists is Marcel Griaule (*Conversations with Ogotemmêli*, 1965). Griaule had an informant called Ogotemmêli; the latter was a hunter and Griaule's fieldwork took place in what was known as the French Sudan and is present-day Mali. In thirty-three days, Ogotemmêli introduced Griaule to the profound knowledge of Dogon belief and tradition

(Mudimbe 1988: 142). It is worth quoting at length Mudimbe's remark on Griaule:

> Griaule's essay is organized around the informant's interwoven monologues. From creation to the origin of social organizations, the recitation follows two threads: a mythical decoding of the universe in its being and a symbolic interpretation of the foundation of history, culture, and society. The latter, says Griaule, defines "a world system, the knowledge of which will revolutionize all accepted ideas about the mentality of Africans and of primitive peoples in general." (1965: 2) The anthropological establishment decided that Griaule was lying. The conversations were a mystification: Dogons, as primitives, could not possibly conceive such a complex structuring of a knowledge which, through myths and rites, unites, orders, and explains astronomical systems, correspondences of worlds, calendrical tables, classifications of beings, and social transformations. (Mudimbe 1988: 142)

My focussing on African intellectuals is not meant to undermine in any fashion the important contributions of some genuine and enlightened non-African intellectuals (mostly Europeans) in the field of African studies. As I pointed out earlier, the greatest challenge the African masses are facing at this moment in history is that of economic and social development as well as how to get rid of the hold the former European colonizers and other industrialized countries have upon post-independent African countries, namely neo-colonialism.

It is important to take into account the contribution of foreign civilizations or cultures to the development and blooming of a specific culture in the process of development. A. Kabou writes:

> Le développement, même dans son acception minimale, est

essentiellement le produit d'un tour d'esprit créatif opérant dans un contexte susceptible d'amplifier les résultats de l'inventivité, de l'ingéniosité, de l'emprunt à d'autres civilisations. (1991: 24)

On the question of borrowing from one civilization to another, Greece provides another example. M. Bernal remarks that "Greek states were small and often quite poor and their national poet was Homer, whose heroic epics fitted splendidly with the 18th-century Romantic passion for northern ballads, most of which were extremely gory like the *Iliad*" (1987: 190). Greece borrowed from Egypt, and from the Middle East and then blended the whole thing in order to produce a civilization of synthesis. Bernal adds that "all in all, while Egypt, along with China and Rome, were models of the Enlightenment, Greece became allied to the lesser, but growing 18th century intellectual and emotional current of Romanticism" (Bernal, loc. cit.). Citing C. Lévi-Strauss (*Race et Histoire*, éditions Gonthier), B. Sine observes: "L'humanité ne se développe pas sous le régime d'une uniforme monotonie de sociétés et de civilisations" (B. Sine 1977: 214). In the same order of things, C.A. Diop says that "man must not be by nature impervious to any manifestation of feeling on the part of his fellow man and that his nature, his consciousness and his spirit must be capable of assimilating through education everything which is initially foreign to them" (Diop 1990: 9).

The following observations and remarks on traditions may at times seem contradictory,[10] reflecting the various methods of approach to and arguments on specific questions. Traditions, in the most extreme sense, can be assimilated to the personality and character of a specific people. A good example can be found in a passage of Ken Bugul's semi-autobiographical novel, *Le Baobab fou* in which the heroine who meets a fellow Senegalese compatriot in Brussels and invites him to her house later explains: "J'emmenai Souleymane chez moi, l'invitant à être comme chez lui. C'était sans effort, car l'hospitalité faisant partie de ce que je n'avais pas perdu des traditions qui vont, en quelque sorte, avec notre peau" (p. 90). The next step is to confront the traditions "qui vont avec notre peau" with the methods and arguments of scholarship and then derive a line of consensus and thus achieve a kind of balance.

In starting our journey through the maze of arguments and counter-arguments on oral literature and on tradition, it is good to keep in mind the observation of E. Tonkin to the effect that "much studies of oral literature are largely confined to folktales and that a lot of misleading theory has been extrapolated from such studies, excellent as many of them are" (Tonkin 1989: 41). Among those excellent studies is that of Iba D. Thiam who observes: "Les civilisations africaines sont des civilisations de l'oralité, des civilisations du verbe-parole, rythme, symbole." However, Thiam warns:

> Contrairement à ce qu'on professe souvent, cette caractéristique,
> loin d'être un handicap paralysant, ou une marque invincible
> d'infériorité, traduit tout au plus, un trait spécifique qui manifeste
> un état de différence dont il faut savoir simplement appréhender
> les vertus profondes. (Thiam 1980: 67)

Before being able to apprehend the specific characters of the oral traditions of Africa, one has to consider another feature of African oral civilizations which is the European influence. According to B. Malinowski, the whole range of European influences, interests, good intentions, and predatory drives must become an essential part of the study of African culture change (Malinowski 1961: 15).

The most salient point in the relationship between Europe and Africa is the clash between European values and African traditional and indigenous values. On that dichotomy, S. N. Eisenstadt remarks that:

> In the political realm, traditional society was thought to be based on a 'traditional' elite ruling by virtue of some Mandate of Heaven, while modern society rested on the wide participation of its population, which refused to honour the traditional forms of political legitimation and held rulers accountable in terms of secular values and efficiency. (1973: 1)

Most of the time, it is the conflict between these two worlds that is emphasized. The usual argument is that Europe came to Africa with its technology and science, thus with its superior civilization based on the machine. But Europe found no resistance whatsoever in an African continent that was too weak and unprepared for the sweeping changes and upheavals that ensued from that encounter. That point is illustred by Lanternari:

> La Dynamique culturelle et religieuse des peuples africains procède donc d'une opposition polémique à la culture dominante [European]. De là se créent les présupposés d'une transformation graduelle de la tradition indigène. Mais le processus de transformation, de choix, de développement est déterminé par les forces internes de la tradition, en opposition aux diverses pressions extérieures: en réponse et comme un dépassement de la grande crise historique déterminée par le heurt. (Lanternari 1979: 68-69)

Basically, what modern African states are facing is how to combine elements of tradition and of the past with elements of the present based mostly on consumption and on speedy technological innovations. A certain balance must be reached, or else "the development of a new society and the disruption of traditional frameworks -- be they family, community, or political mechanisms -- lead more often to disorganization, delinquency, and chaos than to a new viable modern order" (S. N. Eisenstadt 1973: 2).

Finally, on the question of the encounter between Europe and Africa, one can contemplate the most extreme points of view. Those points of view necessarily reflect a certain kind of ideology based on power, on domination. The most extreme case is the dismissal of the oral traditions (and thereby a certain kind of past attached to those traditions) altogether.[11] An example is the attitude of the British colonial writer Lugard who wrote:

> Though we may perhaps at times entertain a lingering regret for the passing of the picturesque methods of the past, we must admit that the locomotive is a substantial improvement on head-borne transport, and the motor-van is more efficient than the camel. The advent of Europeans has brought the mind and methods of Europe to bear on the native of Africa for good or for ill, and the seclusion of ages must perforce give place to modern ideas. Material development is accompanied by education and progress. (Lugard 1926: 5)

What Lord Lugard was merely saying is that Africans have no choice but to face new values and consequently to integrate them within an already existing set of traditional values. What is more, Lugard says that that past should be forgotten. However, how much weight should be given to Lugard's opinion? One should keep in mind that Lord Lugard was a British colonial administrator, a representative of the crown of England. He came to Africa within the framework of the European *mission civilisatrice*.

In the race towards modernization, V. Lanternari warns that one should pause and consider the dangers that may be brought by that full-throttle speed. He makes the point that disorder can be caused by transplanting in one go foreign values to a given society. According to Lanternari:

> Les valeurs, qui sont au fondement de la vie individuelle et sociale de chaque culture, ne se prêtent pas à des transplantations artificielles, et ne peuvent pas être déracinées du fonds traditionnel qui forme l'histoire de la société, sans déclencher les crises les plus graves et les plus chaotiques: sans que la société elle-même ne tombe en proie au désordre. (1979: 59)

Even though Lanternari's remarks are pertinent, it is important to point out that in the case of Africa, the artificial transplanting of values has in fact been carried out through the European colonization of Africa as well as through the various settlements of Europeans in East and Southern Africa. Thus, according to numerous authors, the advent of European and Arab values and influence has brought disorder to Africa. However, numerous indigenous traditions have been preserved in various parts of Africa because the guardians of those traditions, for instance the Wolof griots, did not (and generally do not still) have any direct contact with the European colonizer or traveler or tourist; they do not speak French. If they do, their mastery of the French language is not very well developed. For instance, Ñan was a conscript in the French army but he did not have any direct contact with the French officers, who gave their orders to the illiterate troops through a Senegalese sergeant.

From a different angle and coming from a totally different school of thought from Lugard, R. Deniel illustrates the advent of materialism and of new values in traditional Africa. In his study on the Ano people of the Ivory Coast, he states:

> Un bon niveau de vie repose par conséquent sur l'argent -- "c'est l'argent qu'on appelle le développement" -- et sur les biens matériels auxquels il donne accès: vêtements, voitures, et *surtout* maisons pourvues d'eau et d'électricité. (Deniel 1976: 185-86 [emphasis by the author])

However, other opinions point to the fact that an excess of materialism brings a civilization based only on repetition, in which there is little room for intellectual creativity and spiritual fulfillment. This excessively materialistic modern civilization is the one that exists in most parts of the world. In his preface to *Les intellectuels et la démocratie*, Michel Prigent writes:

> La rupture entre l'idée de tradition et le concept de progrès est une rupture factice. La valeur de notre culture [French] est essentiellement de construire un univers où les forces de tradition et de progrès soient alliées et non ennemies. L'esprit de progrès protège la tradition de la sclérose. Le respect de la tradition garantit le progrès contre l'aventure. (1980: 8)

Citing C. H. Dodd (*Political Development*, p. 12), J. A. Ayoade states that strictly speaking, modernization is not the eradication of the old and its replacement by the new, but rather the effect of the new on the old. (Ayoade 1980: 158)

S. N. Eisenstadt emphasizes the fact that "the processes of modernization are unique in comparison with other historical movements of change, because they have been grounded on the assumption that it is possible to create a new sociopolitical order, an order based on premises of universalism and equality"

(1973: 6). Moreover, even in the process of modernization, there is still an attachment to customs and ways of the past or a combination of modern elements with elements of the past. Thus, there is no actual rupture between past and present. Among notable examples are present-day England or Japan, where there are still forms of political organization---a monarchy, an empire---that have been in place for centuries, although they are much less powerful than in the past. Eisenstadt concludes by saying that "modernization has given rise to the continuous reconstruction of other aspects of tradition" (1973: 6).

Along the same lines, T. Melone makes the following remark about the Nigerian novelist Chinua Achebe:

> Le privilège d'Achebe, c'est d'avoir réussi à transposer dans la modernité nigérianne une mythologie séculaire et qui n'apparaît plus telle à travers les voitures meurtrières et autres mammy-waggons. Au lieu de consacrer la rupture entre l'ancien et le nouveau, il a jeté le pont entre les deux, dans son voeu désespéré de réaliser l'unité de l'être, en montrant la part respective du vieil et du nouvel ordre, en même temps que l'extraordinaire harmonie qui ici soude l'un à l'autre. (1973: 8)

Kabou (1991: 94) shows that the supposed break between modernity and tradition is a false one. She states that some African intellectuals are made to believe (or believe) that tradition and modernity constitute two poles of conflictual values and that out of that conflict came hybrid, alienated, and uprooted Africans, who endeavor to re-enter their lost and petrified culture.

A more mitigated point of view is that expressed by J. A. Ayoade who, citing Claude Welch and the latter's study on communalism, tribalism, and national unity in Africa, states that a solution to the problem of the antagonism between tradition and development is to exploit favorable aspects of traditional beliefs in order to change these beliefs in a gradual fashion (Ayoade 1980: 160).

The following remarks or basic assumptions by Chinweizu et al are very pertinent when it comes to this nagging question of modernity and tradition in present-day Africa:

> This cultural task [mapping out new foundations for an African modernity] demands a deliberate and calculated process of syncretism: one which, above all, emphasizes valuable continuities with our pre-colonial culture, welcomes vitalizing contributions from other cultures, and exercises inventive genius in making a healthy and distinguished synthesis from them all. (Chinweizu, Onwuchekwa, Madubuike 1983: 239)

Once again, concerning tradition, A. Kabou observes: "Le rôle historique le la tradition est de fournir des réponses adéquates aux défis que rencontre inévitablement toute culture vivante, et non de siéger dans un musée" (1991: 162). What Kabou is emphasizing is really the rethinking of traditions as well as the remoulding and refashioning of those traditions in order to answer to challenges posed by development.

My stance in this introduction is with those of Ayoade, Prigent, and Kabou. Like them, I reject the notion that a radical rupture separates tradition and modernity. One of my goals in this work will be to observe and analyse the relationship between traditional values and the elements introduced by European colonization, by Arab traders, and by the forces of economic development. [12]

There are previously collected versions of the legend of Njaajaan Njaay (see Appendix II).

1.   There are previous attempts at reconstruction of African cultures. However, numerous problems face the scholar who is attempting that reconstruction, the two most notable being methodology and sources. An example of those tasks of reconstruction is described by K.O. Dike and F.I. Ekejiuba in their study of the Aro of Nigeria:

> Our aim in this study is to reconstruct Aro history based largely on internal evidence. For no study which ignores the Aro view of their past can hope to throw much light on a subject at once obscure and elusive on some vital issues.   In spite of the very difficult problems of methodology and chronology, we persevered in probing any surviving evidence which might contribute to the understanding of the Aro.   In order to use the existing sources, internal and external, objectively, it was necessary to carry out an exhaustive sociological and symbolic analysis of the indigenous sources; oral testimony from eyewitness informants; iconographic material; Aro religion, rituals and belief systems in the perspective of the insights gained form fieldwork that was conducted in 1964-63, 1965-66, and 1970. (Dike and Ekejiuba 1976: 277)

Dike and Ekejiuba add:

> A study of the Aro oral history during the past 250 years therefore reveals that without viewing the traditions as an ideology of conflict and change and without a detailed sociological analysis, little sense can be· made of the conflicting versions of the Aro past that have come down to us. (Idem, 286)

In our specific case study of the Wolof of Senegal, it is also useful to quote H. Gravrand who did extensive work on the Sereer of Senegal, on the latter's customs, religion, language, beliefs, and social structures.   Gravrand admits:

> Loin d'être un danger pour l'unité nationale, les traditions ethniques lui apportent un soutien, puisque, grâce à ces traditions,

nous découvrons la Nation en gestation depuis l'Antiquité. (1980: 53)

Some similarities between the reconstruction of Aro history by Dike and Ekejiuba and this project on the Wolof is that in both cases little or no work has been done on the nature and structure of the state (as pointed out by Dike and Ekejiuba) because of the lack of archival sources; therefore any reconstruction has to be made from internal evidence. Thus, Dike and Ekejiuba suggest indigenous sources in general, and specifically oral traditions, be discussed and their role in the historical reconstruction of the Aro recognized in any attempt to probe major themes in the Aro past. Another similarity both projects share is the extensive use of oral sources and of fieldwork in Africa. However, in this study on the Wolof, the reconstruction is not only historical but also literary. Moreover, a specific methodology has been tailored for this project. That methodology is based on an interdisciplinary approach in attempting to reconstruct the Wolof past and present by including sociological, anthropological, literary, economic, ethnographic, medical, linguistic, religious, and philosophical elements.

In his study on the pre-colonial state of Baté (Guinea, West Africa), Lansiné Kaba uses a similar approach in his reconstruction of the history of that state, mostly emphasizing the role of Islam and of politics. Kaba observes:

This research is based on my personal knowledge of the oral tradition of Baté, and on textual interpretation of 19th and 20th century French travellers and military officers. (1973: 323)

Overall, the historiography of pre-colonial West African states requires the use of various sources, among them oral traditions. However, in putting together sources that are so diverse a methodology based on rigor and caution is to be adopted.

The oral informants tend to be very reliable. Thus, on her fieldwork among the goldsmiths of Senegal, M. A. Johnson remarks that "significantly, the interviews I did in Senegal were later confirmed by sources on the *Teugue* [smith] I found in the archives. The information I gained from interviews was accurate in almost all instances." ("An American in Africa: Interviewing the Elusive Goldsmith," *International Journal of Oral History*, 10 2 (1989): p.122; [author's emphasis]).

In the same order of things, the systematic collection of the African oral traditions must be a priority, for the professional caste of the keepers of these traditions (griots, bards, singers, minstrels...) is fast disappearing. Camara Laye observes: "Il serait urgent que chacune de nos générations [African] participât activement à la collecte de ces légendes, avant qu' il ne soit trop tard, car celles-ci constituent les fondements mêmes de notre histoire, et, il faut le dire, de nos civilisations traditionnelles particulières." (Camara Laye, *Le Maître de la Parole* [Paris: Plon, 1978], p. 13.)

2.   H. Azan (1863, 1864), D. Boilat (1864; the 1985 publication is considered in this study), H. Gaden (1912), R. Rousseau (1931), J. Robin (1946), C. A. Diop (1949), D. Gamble (1957), R. Cornevin (1960), V. Monteil (1966), A. Samb (1974), V. Bomba (1977), L. Sall (Mémoire de maîtrise. Lettres. Université de Dakar, 1983), B. Barry (1985), L. Kesteloot and B. Dieng (1989), E. Makward (1990). For a more detailed bibliography on the Wolof in general, see D. Gamble's "Bibliographies" in his *Wolof of Senegambia* , 1957).

3.   On this topic, see V. Monteil, "Sur l'arabisation des langues négro-africaines," *Genève-Afrique*, 2, (1966): 12-19.

4.   The same observation has been made in Jean-Pierre Dozon's analysis of the phenomenon. In sociological terms, that phenomenon is called *double-urbain*; its most apparent manifestation is the existence of associations and clubs in most African capital cities. Usually, people coming from a single village and most of the time belonging to the same ethnic group or tribe establish these associations. In Dozon's example, the Bété of Ivory Coast have village associations in Abidjan, the capital city. The same can be said about Senegal, where various ethnic groups coming from the rural areas into Dakar create associations such as the Sereer, the Saraxolé, and the Diola. Members of the associations support and help each other, financially as well as in other ways. Moreover, they bring goods (electronics, cars, clothing) and money back to the villages. Along with those goods, they also carry with them new urban values which threaten the traditional way of life. Along the same lines, Peter Worsley remarks that "village society does adapt perforce: the tribe becomes dependent on the cash earnings of the young men [and women] in the towns" (1977: 153). For more details on the phenomenon of the *double urbain*, see Jean-Pierre Dozon, "Les Bété: une création

coloniale," In *Au coeur de l'ethnie-ethnies, tribalisme et état en Afrique*, 1985, pp. 74-76. See also L.V. Thomas' "Réfléxions sur un problème d'actualité: urbanisation et développement," *Notes Africaines*, 131 (1971): 72-81.

5.   This question is discussed at length by E. Said (*Beginnings. Intention and Method*, 1985). The author argues that the novel is an institutionalization of the intention to begin (p. 100). Said also points out the fact that there is no tradition out of which modern Arabic literature developed; the latter was being established in the middle of the 20th century. E. Said probably used literature under its written form as a yardstick when he made this comment on Arabic literature.

6.   See Guy Nicolas' study on gift-giving in Hausa society in Niger: "Une forme atténuée du potlatch en pays hausa (République du Niger: le Dybu)," *Economies et sociétés*, (1967): 151-214. On gift-giving see also Nicholas' article entitled "Développement rural et comportement économique traditionnel au sein d'une société africaine," *Genève-Afrique*, 7, (1969): 26-27.

7.   Tea drinking is very widespread in Senegal. It was the Wolof in the Waalo area who started this practice, but the other ethnic groups nowadays also drink tea. This is a very important social custom whereby people gather at a house or under the shade of a tree in order to drink tea. There are three services and they go from very strong to very sweet with mint leaves. People take tea usually after lunch and dinner. Tea drinking is called *ataaya* in Wolof; however, the custom of tea drinking is a practice gotten from the Berbers and the Arabs. One can see here the influence of Islam and of exchanges between North Africa and Africa south of the Sahara Desert.

8.   On the question of fixed forms and of different versions, see the article of D. Robinson, "Sources pour l'étude du *Jihad* d'al-Hajj Umar," *Revue française d'histoire d'outre-mer*, 72, (1985): 413-16. D. Robinson points out the fact that there was a first version of the *Jihad* written in Peul with the use of Arabic. Then, there were other versions of the same *Jihad* that were a little bit different from the first. For instance, the French traveler and writer, E. Mage, wrote another version of the same *Jihad* in 1867. Robinson tells of at least three other versions of the

same *Jihad.*

9. The dilemma and confusion brought about by the clash of African indigenous cultures and beliefs on the one hand and the European way of life on the other are a difficult problem. For instance in Senegal, the average uneducated person, illiterate in French, does not reflect too much on the mixing of values from different cultures and civilizations, most of all Arab and European. Apparently, it also seems as if one were trying to reconcile two diametrically opposed cultures. However, only the educated and intellectuals worry about the false dilemma for, as pointed out by other numerous scholars, no civilization has an isolated development; there are always borrowings from one civilization to the other and no one human civilization has the monopoly on technology, science, and of the arts. Thus, in one of his novels, Tchicaya U'Tamsi, a writer from Congo, comments:

> Quand nous [Africans] voulons justifier nos carences devant la modernité, nous nous réfugions dans la fierté que nous avons de vivre selon nos traditions. Quand celles-ci nous gênent, nous n'avons d'alléluia que pour la modernité. (*Ces fruits si doux de l'arbre à pain,* p. 57)

It is also important to note that there had been a revival of oral traditions in many African countries when the latter attained their independence from various European powers in the 1960's. This revival follows the long night of colonial occupation and dispossession. The scientific process that consists in collecting, transcribing, translating and, analyzing oral material is paralleled by the revival of these same traditions I mentioned above. The following remark concerning Egypt can also be applied to our case study:

> In Egypt [contemporary] the revival of oral traditions took two forms: a scientific process of collecting, recording, indexing of oral as well as visual traditions, that is epic poems, stories, proverbs, wisdom as well as dances and art. That scientific process was accompanied by another movement for the revival of these traditions.
> (Mursi Saad El-Din 1984: 65)

Within the context of European colonization, T. Ranger has discussed the meetings of African and European customs and traditions. He states:

> The invented traditions imported from Europe not only provided whites with models of command but also offered many Africans models of 'modern' behavior. The invented traditions of African societies - whether invented by the Europeans or by Africans themselves in response - distorted the past but became in themselves realities through which a good deal of colonial encounter was expressed (Ranger: 1987: 212).

In his book entitled *Impérialisme et Théorie Sociologiques du Développement*, Babakar Sine puts forth a brilliant and enlightening Marxist analysis of the concept of tradition and modernity. In the chapter entitled "Tradition-Modernité Une fausse dialectique," the author points out that it is useless to blame the traditions for Africa's underdevelopment problems. The real culprit is colonial and neo-colonial capitalism (together with the weak African bourgeoisie) which strangulates any move toward real progress and development. (See B. Sine, *Impérialisme et Théories Sociologiques du Développement*, and more specifically, the critique of the Western school which has been spreading unworkable theories on the sociology of development and the dual concept of tradition and modernity, pp. 77-127).

10.   These sorts of contradictions are also reflected in a specific context: Senegal. H. Gravrand remarks: "Je n'ignore pas que le peuple sénégalais représente un enchevêtrement de 19 ethnies, dont les traditions sont souvent contradictoires et ne permettent pas souvent une datation dans le temps" (Gravrand, "Fondements historiques et anthropologiques de la nation sénégalaise," p. 46).

11.   Thus R. Lowie declares: "I cannot attach to oral tradition any historical value whatsoever under any conditions whatsoever" (Cited by B. Kamian 1971: 107-8). Lowie's attitude is part of the broader attitude that the European colonizer had vis-à-vis African literatures expressed in indigenous languages. For instance, in the French colony of Senegal, the French imposed their language, literature, and culture. Within the frame

of the policy of assimilation and of the *mission civilisatrice* , any attempt on the part of the local people to write or think in Wolof, Sereer, Hal pulaar, or Mandinka was discouraged. That can partly explain the reason why there is such a poor body of literatures written in national languages in Senegal.

Overall, we cannot rule out oral tradition as a source for historical reconstruction in Africa. Contrary to Lowie, R. Horton's point of view on this subject matter (as well as on the status of oral tradition vis-'a-vis writing) is carefully balanced:

> We *cannot* take oral traditions at their face value. Written records, it is true, can be suspect for all sorts of reasons. But at least what has been written down on a piece of paper does not change itself spontaneously so that when someone looks at it five years later it says something different. Yet this is precisely what *does* happen to things written on the human memory. (R. Horton 1976: 73 [author's emphases])

Still on the interaction between writing and orality and the reliability of oral traditions, the example of the Qur'an and the hadiths (words and deeds of the Prophet Muhammad) is very pertinent:

> Although writing was used in the transmission of hadith from the very beginning, a lot of this came also from the oral tradition. Those who undertook to assemble them in collections make the kind of enquiries which are always very taxing before recording accounts of past events. They nevertheless had a great regard for accuracy in their arduous task of collecting information. This is illustrated by the fact that for all of the Prophet's sayings, the most venerable collections always bear the names of those responsible for the account, going right back to the person who first collected the information from members of Muhammad's family or his companions. (M. Bucaille 1978: 242)

12.   Besides A. Kabou's essay (*Et si l'Afrique refusait de se développer?*), there are other interesting essays on the questions of identity, of nationalism, of tribalism, of ethnicity, of tradition, and of modernity in Africa. These essays also develop other interesting themes such as the relationship between Europe and Africa since the dawn of colonization, and between the white man and the black man, and the problem of corruption and nepotism in modern Africa; they also treat topics such as the image the African (or European) has of himself (and of each other) as well as the image of the contemporary African elites. Generally speaking, these essays develop theses pertaining to under-development, to poverty, hunger, lack of health and schooling facilities, as well as the continuing accusation against Europe and the white man as being responsible for all the ills cited above. Conversely, one essay tries to dissect the guilt factor that the white man feels obliged to carry all the time because he was made to believe that the only contribution he made to human civilization was colonialism, imperialism, and domination. However, still according to these theses, the other side of the coin has not been shown, namely all the help being given to Third World countries by richer countries. Which help (no matter how small, cynical, and insignificant) is diverted by the African politicians, governments, leaders and, the elite in general for their own personal gain and usage. (See Pascal Bruckner, *Le sanglot de l'homme blanc. Tiers-monde, culpabilité, haine de soi.* Paris: Éditions du seuil, 1983 and Tidiane Diakité, *L'Afrique malade d'elle-même.* Paris: Éditions Karthala, 1986.)

CHAPTER I

PART ONE

THE EPIC TALE OF THE WAALO KINGDOM JALORÉ NJAAJAAN NJAAY

1   Yalla tabaraka wa talaa dafa ni Nô
    "Bës bu mbënde mi di ñëw mi ngiy jogé
    Si bës bi sa jabar taalè,
    Sa bos ba.
5   Bos bay tëyé kawdiir ga.
    Bos ba dina daanu,
    Nga wara uti gaal ga ak kula gëm."
    Mbënda ma ñëw.
    Ñu daw uti gaal ga, jabar ja ak doom ya toppe ci.
10   Nèna ñu
    Ci gaalu Nô nak, xèt wu né, ñaaram ma nga sa woon:
    Béne gôr ak béne jigènu xèt wu né.
    Nèna ñu
    Gaalu Nô nak,
15   Kén daanu ka joow;
    Dafay di dém rék,
    Lolu di katanu Yalla.
    Yonént Yalla Nô yoni
    Picce muñuy wox raf-raf.
20   Picce ma naaw
    Ba jégé jiifu kor ka
    Daadi délusi.
    Ñaaré lu yoon wi,

Picce mi nika:
25   "Gis naa dog wu tuuti."
Nô nika:
"Fu mu nékke?"
Picce mi nika:
"Mi ngi fii."
30   Nô dawal gaal gi
Ci katanu Yalla.
Gaalu Nô nak, nékana ci mbënde mi ñénfukki fan ak béne.
Nèna ñu
Asamaan si nène Suuf:
35   "Su ma Yalla téyé wul woon,
Da naa la soti ndox
Yow Suuf.
Ba kén dotu la gis."
Suuf tontu Asamaan, nika:
40   "Su ma Yalla téyé wul wôn,
Da naa la sotti suuf
Ba kén dotu la gis."
Kon nak,
Mbindum cofaalé yoyu ñoy takku Aduna.
45   Takku Aduna,
Ñaar la:
Li wès ak liy ñëw.
Béna bi wès na,
Bi si dés mom la ño séntu.
50   Si mbënde mi nak,
Nè nañu ñëppe dugge nañu si gaal ga
Ba mu dés Iwèt.
Iwèt rék mo duggul,
Nèna ñu da fa lap.
55   Gaalu Nô nak, da fa tèr si Dundogi.
Nèñu amon na jurôm ñéti fukke sa biir gaal ga.
Wanté tèré bu ñuy wox Gadaawu Sor nèna dèdèt.
Tèré bi nèna jurôm béne fukke la won.
Bañ fa sañcè sa Dundogi,
60   Amna fa xèr wu mak.
Ñii dañu sancc sa pénku docc wa,
Ñëlé sancce sa sowu docc wa,

Ñii sancce nañu sa walu ndéyjor ba
Ñëlé sa camoñu docc ba.
65 Wanté,
Ñëppe ñu sañcon sa docc ba,
Dañu dè
Bamu dés Nô,
Ak ñéti domam
70 Ak sèni ñéti jabar.
Béne domu Nô mi ngi tudde Saam,
Kénèn ki mi ngi Aam.
Ki mujje ki mi ngi tudde Ibn Nô.
Nèna ñu nak,
75 Nô dafa tëdde,
Di nélaw.
Aam di rètaan.
Saam ni ka:
Loy rè?
80 Xanaa suñu baay ngay rè?"
Si bërëb bobu,
Nô jog,
Ni lèn:
"Bës ni ki téy,
85 Yaw,
Aam,
Yaw la nit ku ñuul di donne, yaay jur ay nit ñu ñuul.
Yaw,
Sam,
90 Nit ku wèxalay donne, nga jur ñu wèx."
Lolo tax Saam méñe Yaajojo ak Maajojo.
Aam jur na dom bu ño wox Anfësédé.
Anfësédé nèna Aam:
"Nô moy sa ma maam,
95 Yaay sa ma baay.
Dama bëgon nga ñaanal ma."
Anfësédé momu, jur na dom ju ño wox Misrayé.
Misra momu,
Nèna ñu mo sancce dëkke bu ño wox Misra.
100 Aam nak, jur na ñaari dom yu ñuul:
Béne bu gor ak béne bu jigèn.

Aam nak da fa gadaay
Ak waa kërëm,
Dém si boru déx gu ño wox Nil.
105 Bi miy gadaay nak ba aksi Nil, da fa né jabar ji:
"Ñii daal juru malèn."
Jabar ji tontu ka: "Aah!
Yaa lèn jur kéñ.
Maak yow ño jur ñaari dom yi."
110 Aam gadaay.
Fofu la xètu nit yu ñuul dorè.
Kon nak, Aam da fa gadaay,
Dém si boru déx gu ño wox Nil.
Yaga na fa lol
115 Domu Aam magge,
Ba mat sëy,
Gisu ñu sèn baay.
Ñuné sèn yaay:
"Yaay, fu suñu baay nékke?"
120 Sèn yaay tontu lèn:
"Sèn baay dé gisu maka."
Ñaari dom yi jog ñom tamit
Anda di dém rék,
Ba aksi si boru déx buñuy wox Nil.
125 Ñu daadi dox ba aksi si boru déx gi.
Ñu dajèk sèn baay, mu laac lèn: "Yèn! fa ngèn jëm?"
Ñu né ko: "Ñun dé déñ don toppe su ñu baay."
Mu né lèn:
"Sèn baay nu mu tudde?"
130 Ñu tontu ko:
"Ñun dé suñu baay lañuy sèt.
Ñin kay wox Aam.
Nèna ñu Nô mo ka jur.
Nèna ñu bi ñu judô,
135 La su ñu baay gadaay.
Lègi nak, ay mak lañu.
Ñu kô sèti ba xam ndax da nañ ka gisam dèt.
Lolo waral su ñu yon wii."
Mu na lèn:
140   "Man mii,

Maa di sèn baay Aam."
Fofu la Aam sancce,
Tuddé ko Nobara.
Aam daa di sëyël domam yi.
145 Mo waral bi ñi amè ñaari dom,
Ñu fap kii may kii, fap kè may kè.
Fa la Xaabil ak Haabib
Jogè.
Nonu la domu Nô yi méñè,
150 Ba sancce rèw mu ño wox Sordan.
Sordan nak, moy rèwum nit yu ñuul yi.
Ñi nak, si kër Aam lañu bok:
Saxéwil, amna Batèrés ak Mayaasin, amna Sanaaf.
Lègi nak,
155 Bu ñu jogè fofu, maa ni laa bugge nétali mbirm rèwum Gana.
Baalaa bobu,
Damay délu si ci rèwu Sordan.
Rèwu Sordan dé, yaga na lol.
Yonént bi (sala laahu taala aléyhi wasalaam)
160 Oté na fi bë ñu gëmke,
Mu dundë fi jurom bén fukki at ak ñét.
Abaabakar Sadèx moka done ci xilaafa gi.
Déf ñaari at,
Umar Bun Xataab done Ababakar Sadèx.
165 Yor na ka fukki at ak jurom.
Amna ñuné,
Yor na ka fukki at ak ñaar
Bubakar Umar ak Umar Bun Xataab xèx nañu jihaar,
Tuubël ñudul julit, dugël lèn si lislaam.
170 Ñom ñaar da ñu xalaat né ñi dul julit bèw nañu lol.
Lolu mo tax Bubakar Umar jogé Sordan
Sordan, rèwum nit yu ñuul yi.
Mingi andak ku ño wox Mbaarik Bô.
Mbaarik Bô momu, néna ñu manga dëkke fu ño wox Masaasi
175 Mom Mbaarik Bô jaaro bu dijje
La daan sol si bakañ bi.
Nèna ñu bu mësaan tange,
Jaaro bi déy wékèku.
Bu daan tange,

180 Jaaro bi day tawè ku,
Daadi wodde.
Mbaarik Bô anda na ak Bubakar Umar
Ñu xèx ci Gana fukki wèr ak ñéte.
Dorè Sordan ba aksi Gana, maanaam xèx nañu fukki wèr ak ñéte
185 Si fukèlu wèr ba ak ñéte,
La ñu fal
Buur bu ño wox Gana Kamara.
Gana Kamara momu,
Mo jox turëm Empire dé Gana
190 Wanté bu jëkke,
Tudul won Empire dé Gana
Ñing ka daan wox rèwum Sordan,
Rèwum nit yi ñuul yi.
Bi ñi xèxè fukki at ak ñénte,
195 Tuub lo lanu ñu baré, maanaam mom Mbaarik Bô ak Bubakar Umar.
Mbaarik Bô si la né Bubakar Umar:
"Sériif, fo jëm ?"
Muné ka:
"Man, fu ma jëm ?
200 Da ma dége béne buur bo xamné mi ngi fu soré
Bunék fu soré si sowu
Mom laa bugge dugël ci diiné lislaam."
Mbaarik Bô niko:
"Man Sérif, buge naa ngangtèk yow,
205 Wanté damaa buge falu.
Waayé yow mii, kom Sériif nga,
Té man da maa bëge néke buur,
Lolu rék la bëge, té kom Sériif nga,
Soma ñanélè,
210 Suma amè nguur,
Nguur gi di na barkèl
Ndax séy ñaan
Lolo tax Mbaarik Bô andak Bubakar Umar,
Baayu Njaajaan,
215 Jappantèk mom bu baax.
Mbaarik Bô nak,
Laac na Bubakar Umar:
"Fo jëm ?"

Bubakar Umar daadi ko tontu:
220 "Yalla dé woxa guma
Fuma jëm.
Waayé won na ma
Ci biir kèmaan nam
Né dañu jogaat
225 Topa yon wi."
Nèna ñu
Mbaarik Bô ak Bubakar Umar jogé na ñu Gana.
Ñu topa yon wi,
Di dox, di dox,
230 Ba aksi Mudèri Jaawara.
Fala ñu fékke Abram Sal.
Abram Sal nak, da fa yaakaar ni Bilal mo ñëw.
Lolo tax xèxul ak Bubakar Umar ak Mbaarik Bô.
Kon nak, Njaajaan Njaay mo njëke falu ci Waalo.
235 Sèn maam,
Yèn ñii sante Joob
Ño fal Njaajaan.
Sèn maam
Ño don Jogomaay ci Waalo.
240 Li ma wox,
Sa baay Mapaaté Joob mii tok
Xam na ka.
Njaajaan Njaay,
Sèn maam mo ka fal.
245 Jogomaay yi
Ño ko fal,
Mu lèn di jox warèf.
Waayé niñ ka falè ni la démé.
Bi baayi Njaajaan, maanaam Bubakar Jogè Sordan,
250 Ba aksi Gana ak Mbaarik Bô,
Andon na ak
Béne sérif
Bu tude Hawaat.
Ñu jogé Gana
255 Ba aksi Mudèri Jaawara.
Mbaarik Bô ceddo la won;
Bubakar mo ka tuubel.

Hawaat momu,
Ku ño wox Aali Gaye mo ka jox santum Gaye
260 Ndaxté amul won sante.
Bubakar tamit amul won sante.
Bubakar ak Hawaat, Aydara la ñu santon.
Kon nak, Mbaarik Bô modon bëkke nègu Bubakar.
Biñi tojè Gana,
265 Si lañu aksi fii
Ci rèwum Sénégal,
Si boru déx gi.
Fii lañu fékke Abram Sal,
Daadi ko tuublo.
270 Abram da fa yaakaaron ni
Bubakar moy Bilal,
Andano Yonént bi.
Lo lo tax xèxul ak mom.
Abram Sal moy maamu
275 Ñu sante Sal ñëppe.
Lamtoro yi, mo lèn méñe.
Kon nak, bubakar
Mo tuublo Abram sal.
Abram mo jur Fatumata Abram Sal.
280 Fatumata Abram nak,
Baayam daf ka may Bubakar,
Mu néke jabaram
Bubakar nak, tuublo na Sèrèer si
Ba aksi sa Godo...
285 ...Ba aksi ci Dogo, ci Bakel,
Sa wala wa, sa Ganaar ga.
Fofu fénxu késé la won;
Dañu ka tata.
Namu ñëwé, daa di toppe Sérèer si, di lèn tuublo
290 Ba aksi si Sèrèer bu mak.
Mi ngi tude Hamar-gëdde-mak
Hamar-gëdde-mak nak, da daan gëdde mak ñi.
Lolo tax ñu dika owè Hamar-gëdde-mak.
Mbaarik Bô mi andak Bubakar,
295 Mi ngi si ganaaw nèk bi
Lal déram, ték si tèrèm di jange,

Ndax tuubna,
Mi ngi jange Alxuraan.
Bubakar nak ñëw si Hamar-gëdde-mak.
300 Muni ka:
"Ñëwel nga watu
Té tuup!"
Hamar-gëdde-mak ni ka:
"May ma ma dém si ala ba bôk té ñëw."
305 Hamar-gëdde-mak ni ka: "May ma ma dém si ala ba bôk té nëw."
Bubakar ni ko:
"Démal bôk."
Hamar dém si taatu béna garab.
Daadi fap fétte gi
310 Ratax koko fii,
Si kow loxo bi.
Mu lox, mu lox, mu lox.
Daal di ñëw, woc ka,
Tala tuko
315 Bubakar daal di ñëw
Si jabar ji, Fatumata, ci biir nèk bi.
Muné Fatumata:
"Ñëwel ñu woxtaan."
Mbaarik Bô mom rékke dége woxtaan bi,
320 Ma nga sa ganaaw nèk bi,
Kén gisu ko, mi ngi tok ci déram.
Mom réka dégge woxtaan wi.
Woxtaan wi am
Diggënté Bubakar ak jabaram
325 Bubakar ni jabar ji:
"Maa ngi buge délu pénku.
Xam naa ni danaa dè.
Man danaa dè
Ndax sama gôm bii
330 Ndax féttum Hamar-gëdde-mak
Fétte wi dañ ko posson.
Bugu ma dèwè fii.
Maa ngi délu pénku.
Bëge naa délu pénku.
335 Waayé bul sëyak gôr gô xamnee

Di nga gis yaramam buy sangu.
Bul sëyak gôr gô xamné,
Buy dém alla nga janok môm
Bula nè nañ sëy,
340 Na lal bi daanu njëke,
Balaa ngèn sëy. Yoyu ñaar nga am."
Bi Bubakar di woxtaan ak jabar ji
Si biir nèk bi,
Mbaarik Bô mi ngi si ginaaw nèk bi, dége na woxtaan wi.
345 Boba Fatumata mi ngi ëmbe Njaajaan Njaay.
Mi ngi tudôn Muhamadu.
Turem bu njëkke du won Njaajaan.
Fatumata ni ko:
"Lolu daal nga buge am
350 Balaa may sëy ?"
Bubakar ni ka: "Waaw." Mbaarik Bô dége na waxtaan wi.
Bubakar fabu, dém.
Dém uti pénku.
Agul pénku
355 Si diggénté bi la dèwé,
Si dëkke bu ñuy wox Singiti.
Bamèlam mi ngi Singiti,
Sa ganaaw Ataar.
Bi lolu amè,
360 Mbaarik Bô daal di sol dalam,
Sol ay yëré yu wèx.
Daal di jël satalaa njapom, muuru.
Bu démam alla jotè,
Dafay dém ba sèna tuñ ko,
365 Mu dém alla ba,
Daal di délu si.
Fatumata yèk
Si tôj gu mak,
Di séntu gôr ñi.
370 Gôr ñi, ku siy dém alla ba,
Bo agè
Si ginaaw tata gi rék,
Daal di jonkan.
Mbaarik Bô nak, dafay déma, déma, déma, déma

375 Ba sèna tuñu ko,
Mu dém alla ba, ñëw.
Fatumata ni:
"Man daal jaaxlénaa. Xalaas!"
Bi Muhamadu judô,
380 Ba am fukki at ak béne at,
Si la xèxak Hamar-gëdde-mak,
Daadi ko dôr;
Ak ganaaw loxom,
Tocc noppe bi, daadi ko réy
385 Fatumata nak,
Kuka doxaan rék, mu bañ
Ndax lika Bubakar woxon;
Gisul kéne kuka déf.
Mu tok, tok ba Mbaarik Bô jogé fa, ñëw
390 Fékke Muhamadu amna fukki at ak béne.
Mu ñëw tabbi si biir nèk bi.
Fatumata mi ngi don togge
Si biir waañ wa.
Xam nga ñom,
395 Buñu daan togge,
Daanu ñu géne
Fi ñiy toggé
Ba liñiy défar paré.
Mbaarik daadi tabbi,
400 Fab goba gu mak,
Goba yi nga xamné
Si lal bi lay tégu,
Mu ñëw lal tagaraam.
Daal di jappe goñ wi
405 Di ka xatan, di ka xatan,
Di ka xatan
Ba mu dés tuuti.
Mu up ka,
Dém.
410 Fatumata yëgul dara
Ndax mi ngi si biir waañ wi.
Mbaarik tok bamu xëp
Ba takusaan gi tocc,

Mu aksi, ñëw
415 Fofa
Mu féka fa Fatumata
Daadi ko nuyu.
Fatumata féy ko.
Mbaarik dém tok fi mi xétéñon.
420 Ño woxtaan, di woxtaan ba yagge Mbaarik niko:
"Waay, soxna si
Dëme bugge sa mbuum gii nga jox maka."
Ñuné nii rékke,
Lal bi daanu,
425 Mu géne dém.
Fatumata né:
"Laa i laaha ila laa ! man dé lii manatumaka wox."
Bi lolu amè,
Waa këram ñëw ni ka:
430 "Da nga sëyi !
Kula bugge rék,
Nga bañ."
Muné lèn:
"Man kat,
435 Lama gôr gi woxon,
Gisnaa ka si kéna.
Muy bëkke nègam bii.
Mom mo ko déf.
Mom moy ko xamné,
440 Balaa muy daadi tôk,
Lalbi daadi daanu.
Bu fèkè né
Mi ngè dém alla,
Doko sèn."
445 Ñuné ka:
"Kon ñu mayla ka."
Ñu may koko.
Bi lolu di am,
Féke
450 Njaajaan Njaay mi ngi andak ay moromom
Di sangu si déx gi.
Ñi ngè sangu si déx gi.

Di sotanté ndox
Si boru déx gi.
455 Xalé yi dika toñ,
Nika:
"Démal fëlé !
Sa yaay amul
Kukay dénce
460 Ludul sa bëkke nègu baay."
Lolu rus loko.
Xam nga
Tukulër ak Waalo-Waalo ño yém jikko,
Ño yém si réy.
465 Njaajaan dafa réyon.
Bimu dégè lolu,
Mu mér nak.
Daadi fap jaasi;
Fap kajje;
470 Fap xèj gu mag;
Fap xèj;
Fap kas;
Fap fitte;
Fap fétal;
475 Daadi dém,
Dém sa déx ga,
Daanu si déx gi
Ni dafaa xaru.
Nuuru, munul dè.
480 Xam nga né ku mana fèy,
Su bugè réy bopam,
Duné déy lap.
Dan ñi
Njaajaan ci déx gi la dëkôn.
485 Dèdèt.
Dafa sôbu si déx gi
Ndax méram.
Mu dém jala sa wala wa,
Fap mbubëm boxe.
490 Mu tabbi si ñax mi,
Ñax miy sax si boru déx gi.

Mu nëbbu si biir ñax mi,
Baña géne.
Ñu sèt funé,
495 Yaakaar né dafa dè.
Bu xiifè,
Dafay jappe si jën yi ak loxom.
Tallal lèn si janta bi.
Mu ñor.
500 Mu walbati daadi lékke.
Yalla ak mbirem
Mayna ko lolu.
Mu nékka fa ba amfa ñaari at.
Bu bëcce gè, mu laxu si biir ñax mi.
505 Bu gudè, mu yèk si kow garab yi.
Fofu
Falay fanaan.
Amna ñaari at si Gédé,
Si boru déx gi.
510 Si biir ñax mi.
Béne bës,
Mu tok ba takusaan,
Njaajaan fitti
Si diggu déx gi
515 Nit ñi, Tukulër yi
Sow sa kow:
"Uuuh!"
Xam nga Naar ak Tubaab
Ño nuro xonxaay.
520 Njaajaan nak,
Lu séde la daan léke,
té fu séde la daan tëde
Lolo Tax yaram bi baré karaw.
Yaram bi yëppe karaw la,
525 Ba mu dés
Li wër bët yi
Ak loxa yi.
Yage si alla bi itam
Tax na mu mél nonu.
530 Bi ka nit yi gisè,

Di sow.
Mu nuur,
Duge si biir déx gi.
Dém si bénèn wala wa.
535 Fofu
Mu fap mbubôm
Yi mi laxon,
Bëge ñëw
Fèy ba Lamnaajo, mu juuru fa.
540 Amna ñaari at si Gédé.
Wanté amna si déx gi jurôm ñaari at ak jurom ñaari fan,
Si boru déx gi, si biir ñax mi.
Mu ñëw Lamnaajo amna fa at.
Bëge fèñ,
545 Jaar kow,
Daadi fèy.
Dém ba Mbégèñ.
Si jamono yoyu,
Dagana mi ngi
550 Si boru daxaaru Jaalawaali
Mu ñëw ba Mbégèñ am fa at.
Lolu yëp
Mi ngi nëbëtu
Si biir ñax mi
555 Si boru déx gi.
Bu bëce gè, mu laxu si biir ñax mi.
Bu gudè, mu yèk si kow garab yi.
Fofu, mu fanaan fa.
Bëgge fèñ,
560 Jogé Mbégèñ
Jaar kow.
Dém ba Kawas,
Si xay yoyu.
Si digénté Dagana ak Mbilor.
565 Xay yoyu si boru déx gi.
Amna at Kawas,
Bëgge fèñ
Jaar kow.
Dém

570 Ba aksi Xéwéw Gaal.
Amna fa ñaari at,
Si xéwéw gaal.
Bo bolè lép,
Mudi jurôm ñaari at.
575 Bëgge fèñ,
Jaar kow.
Dém
Ba aksi Mbégèñ Bôy.
Amna fa jurôm ñaari fan.
580 Bi ñéti fan ak jurôm ñaari fan jalè,
Mu géne.
Ci jamono yoyu ci Waalo,
Xalé yi bu ñu mësè nappi,
Ku jappe jën,
585 Da kaa sani si kow.
Bobu,
Xamu ñu
Kala.
Bu ñu wacè,
590 Tojjonté boppe yi,
Di xèx.
Kii ni:
"Maa mom
Jën bii."
595 Kè ni:
"Momu loko."
Ñu tojjon té
Boppe yi,
Xèx
600 Bi Njaajaan sènè xalé yi,
Mu géne si déx gi,
Daadi ñëw si ñom.
Bi ñi ka gisè,
Bëgge daw
605 Mu né lèn ni,
Ñu taxaw.
Bi ñi xamè ni dulèn déf dara,
Ñu taxaw

Naka ñu taxaw,
610 Mu fap
Jën yi.
Sédélé lèn,
Ba ñu yém,
Déf lèn si kale,
615 Saam lèn
Ba saam yi yém.
Sa ma baay
Nèna ma
Dafay xol béne xalé,
620 Daa di joxoñ
Béne saam
Koku jël
Saam bi ka jagé
Daal di dém
625 Mu joxoñ kénèn,
Mu jël jënem,
Daal di dox ñibbi.
Nonu la déf.
Di sédélé jën yi.
630 Muy déf lolu bamu dè ñétti fan,
Féki ñéti fan yu njëke yi mudé jurôm béni fan
Mak ñi jaxlé ni lèn: "Waaw, yèn bu ngèn mësè nappi,
Da ngè ni xèx,
Tojjénté boppa yi.
635 Lègi nak, dé ngè ni ñëw fii ak jam.
Kuné tëyé ay jënem.
Lu xéw ?"
Goné yi ni:
"Ñun dé, béne gôr mô di jogé si déx gi
640 Aki njoram,
Di ñu sédelé jën yi.
Yaram wi yëp karaw la
Ba mu dés loxo yi ak bët yi."
Mak ñi jaaxlé
645 Né: "Haah !
Nañu ka jappe
Ba xam

Kumu.
Na ngèn dém uti ay bantte
650 Sa déx ga,
Ñak bunte bi.
Bu ngèn ka ñagè ba mu dacc,
Bu tabè dilèn sédelé jën yi,
Fap lèn tax ték si bunte bi.
655 Bu dè garmi,
Du saxi ñak."
Ay gôr
Dém déf ligéy bi.
Bi ñi parè,
660 Ñu laxu nè si taatu sèp gi, di xaar.
Bi xalé yi nappé ba paré,
Dém si biir ñak bi, indi sèn jën ték.
Tabbi xèx.
Njaajaan ñëw ubi taxas gi, féréylaayu di lèn xol.
665 Bi lolu amè,
Njaajaan daal di wacc,
Dém sédelé jën yi.
Dém fa taxas ga nékke,
Ték ca bunte bi.
670 Mu sédelé ba noppi,
woñèku,
Bëgge délu nak fa mu nékon.
Mu jok di lèn sédelé jën yi,
Ñu jok jappe ko.
675 Bi lolu amè,
Mak ñi ñëw.
Sa ma baay nèna
Réy na si ñétti gôr
Ci ñi ko dèm jème jappe.
680 Ndax dolé waliyu ja.
Ñu jappe ko,
Yèw loxo yi.
Laac ko:
"Nda nga tudde ?'
685 Muné patte rék.
Woxul dara.

"Yaadi kan ?"
Muné patte rék,
Woxul dara.
690 Daño wox né
Bata Bôy
Mo ko wox lo.
Waayé sa ma baay wox na ma ni
Béne Pël bu tudde Maramu Gaaya
695 Moy ki nga xamné
Mo woxlo Njaajaan.
Sa ma baay nèna ma
Maramu Gaaya ci Sirabawar
La bokke,
700 Pël la.
Maramu Gaaya ñëw, né:
"Man bu ngèn ma bolèk mom
Si biir nèk bi,
Jox ma ñaari bos
705 Ak ñaari géwél yi ñoy togè,
Ak bolle, moy sunguf,
Ak ndox,
Ak safara.
Da naa ka woxlo."
710 Ñu déf ko, jox Maramu li mi laajon.
Njaajaan tok nii si lal bi,
Ni dëñe di ko xol rék.
Ñu déf ko, mu tok di xol rék.
Maramu ñëw di araw rék.
715 Ngake naanu bi,
Di tox,
Di araw.
Bi mi tégè ñaari bos yi
Ba paré
720 Mu taal safara si
Ndax muna toge.
Jël kawdiir gi sol ko ndox;
Ba paré
Ték ko si ñaari bos yi..
725 Bi kawdiir gi tégo,

Mu daanu
ndox mi tuuru.
Bu tégè
Ñaari bos yi rék
730 Kawdiir gi daanu
Ndox mi tuuru.
Aah ! xiif nga dé
Njaajaan ni ko si pulaar:
"Maramu Boya Gay,
735 Bos ka tati.
Ñéti bos ay jappe cin, waayé ñaari bos du jappe cin."
Muné ko:
"Han ?"
Daal di fap bénèn bos
740 Ñëw ték si, muy ñétte.
Jël kawdiir gi
Sol ka ndox.
Ték si ñétti bos yi.
Kawdiir gi tégu.
745 Mu xambe
Ba mu bax.
Mu laax
Araw gi.
Muy déf rët, rët, rët.
750 Xam nga laax bu ñorè,
Da fay rëti rëti
Muy déf rët, rët, rët, rët, rët, rët, rët, rët.
Ba yaga,
Njaajaan niko:
755 "Maramu Gaya,
Yakkal laax bi,
Ñor na."
Muné ka:
"Ha !"
760 Daal di yakke,
Ték.
Xam nga Pël
Da faa uppe.
Mu ték fëlé di uppe;

765 Laax bi.
Ngake naanu bi
Di uppe laax bi.
Munutu ka muñ,
Njaajaan ni ka:
770 "Maramu Gay Gay,
Raccal laax bi.
Mi ngè séde
Té soti si sow mi."
Maramu Gaya daal di géne
775 O nit ñi ni lèn:
"Ñëw lèn nak
Ñëw lèn,
Ñëw lèn déglu ka.
Nèna naa ték
780 Ñéti bos.
Nèna naa yakke laax bi
Ñor na.
Nèna,
Naa racce laax bi,
785 Mi ngè séde.
Ni ma naa soti sow mi."
Mak ñi laac nak
Mu wox
Lu ka naxadi
790 Yèn sèni maam, ñi sante Joob,
Bokke si Jogomaay
Ñoka laac nika nak
Mu wox nak
Warèf yi yëp.
795 Ñu jappe ko.
Bi ñi ka jappè nak, ah!
Mak ñi yabal ndaw
Sa Maysa Waali Jon Fay,
Buuru Sèrèer yi.
800 Ñu jappe jurôm ñétti waxambaané
Yabal lèn sa Maysa Waali Jon.
Boba santul Jon.
Jaxaté la santon.

Bi ndaw yi dikè,
805 Ñëw ni ko:
"Maysa Waali Jon,
Waalo ñu yoni.
Nèna ñu jappe nañu ko xamné daal,
Jaaxal na lèn."
810 Maysa Waali ni lèn:
"Lolu dé njaajaan la."
Njaajaan Njaay, fa la turu Njaajaan jogè.
Njaajaan si sèrèer moy lu umpe nit.
Turëm du won Njaajaan, Muhamadu Aydara la tudôn.
815 Maysa ni lèn:
"Bu ngèn démè,
Ték lèn ka si sèn kanam, di na mun néka kilifa.
Ngèn fal ko."
Mu ñëw nak ñu fal ko, ñu fal ko mu daal di falu nak.
820 Bamu falo
Ba am fukki at,
Féke rakke ji
Juddu na,
Na ka Mbarak Barka.
825 Yaay ji mang kay yaral fas.
Bi Mbarak amè fukki at at jurôm ñaar,
Mbarak ni yaay ji:
"Yaay! xanaa awma mak?"
Yaay ji nika:
830 "Ahan kéñ, Am nga mak.
Ma nga sa sowu, si takko ga.
Kaay nga nuyul maka.
Waayé bo démè,
Na nga yaru."
835 Na nga yaru.
Na nga yiw.
Mu daal di ñëw.
Bi mu ñëwè ba Mbégèñ,
Mu fékke fa mag ji.
840 Bi mu jubè Njaajaan, ni:
"Jamolo jara kéw!"
Non lañ daañ nuyo buur.

Muné waat:
"Jamolo Njaay jara kéwe!"
845 Njaajaan ni ko:"Bismilaa."
Mu wèsu ñëp
Ñi togon sa biir.
Ñëw
Ba si mom
850 Ni ka yéy loxo bi.
Njaajaan ni ka ñëkke tëyé.
Mu né ka:
"Waaw! fo jogé?"
Muné ko:
855 "Gédé."
Muné ko:
"No sante?'
Muy bugge wox Bô,
Né Mbôj.
860 Ñi sante Mbôj ñëp,
Mbarak moy sèn maam.
Mbôj, si Bô la jogé.
Njaajaan ni ka:
"Na sa yaay sante? Kudé sa yaay sa Gédé?"
865 Muné ka:
"Fatumata Abram moy sa ma yaay."
Njaajaan né:
"Ana sa ma yaay?"
Muné ka: "Ma nga fa."
870 Mu yëkëti ko ak dolé ji,
Ték si kow lal bi.
Dér yi won si suuf
Mu talal lèn,
Tok si.
875 Ba paré,
Wo Waalo gëp.
Ba ñëp dajè,
Mu ni lèn:
"Kii sa ma rakke la.
880 Ño bokke béne ndéy.
Bu ma fi jogè,

Na ngèn ka jox sa ma palaas.
Guné la waayee am na jom ak fit."
Ñu né ka:
885 "Salaaw Njaay."
Waayé santul Njaay,
Aydara la sante.
Sèni maam, yèn ñi sante Joob,
Jogomaayi rèwum Waalo
890 Ño jëlé Njaajaan Waalo, yobu ka Jolof.
Ni dañu kay dëc si diggu rèw mi.
Ndax mu mën até rèw mi yëp.
Mom la
Tubaab biy roy ba téy.
895 Ñom la ñoy roy
Ndax fii, féke nañ fi nguur.
Nguur gu ñu sédelé ba mu mat.
Féke nañ fi xèx kat
Yu mak.
900 Njaajaay moy Baraak bu njëk.
Mo jité won xèx kat yi.
Njaajaan mo jur Gèt Njaajaan,
Saara Njaajaan,
Dombur Njaajaan
905 Nafaye Njaajaan,
Fukili Njaajaan.
Amna
Jurômi dom.
Fukili dém Saalum.
910 Njaajaan bayi Gèt Tundu Gèt
Daal di dém wuti Jolof.
Ñu ñëw ba Warxox,
Fas wi xox.
Mu tuddé ko Warxox.
915 Ba mu ñëwè
Fanaan si Yang-Yang,
Mang fa aksi
Takusaan.
Fofa
920 Ñu may ka fa

Pël buño wox Këyfa.
Pël bobu lé, ñu fanaan
Bë bër sét,
Génelu ko.
925 Mu jogé Yang-Yang, bayi Këyfa.
Bayi ko né du ko am né jabar.
Ndéké jappa na biir.
Biir bobu mo méñe Pël yi sante Njaay.
Ñoñu sante Njaay mo lèn méñe.
930 Modi Saajo Njaay mëlé
Sa Xuma
Si wétu Risaa-Tol
Fa la jogé.
Gèt Njaajaan momu néka fa jappanté ak baayam.
935 Mér, né Njaajaan:
"Géda naa sa sante wi.
Lègi Joob la sante.
Këri Njaay yi nak,
Bokku lak kërru Njaajaan Njaay, boku ñu
940 Njaajaan Njaay santul won Njaay.
Aydara la santon.
Wanté,
Njaajaan nak fal nañu ko fukki at ak jurôm béne si Waalo
Do ka yobu Jolof.
945 Balaa muy aksi Waalo,
Bobu rèwum Waalo
Amna ñénti tèmèri at ak fanwèr Njaajaan soga aksi.
Njaajaan amna Waalo fukki at ak jurôm béne
Ñu sokafi jëlé yobu Jolof.
950 Fofa,
Sa Jolof,
Mu méñe fa Biram Njèmé Kumba ak ñom Alburi Njaay.
Alburi momu, mo dém jiité Jolof.
Ba Njaajaan aksè Jolof,
955 Boba, alla rék la won.
Kiliifté
Amu fa won.
Nguur amul won.
Lamaan na amon.

960 Njaajaan mo indi kiliifté si Jolof.
    Si méñe wala wi,
    Bawol,
    Kayor,
    Jolof ak Siin yëppe si Waalo la ñu bokkon.
965 Waalo ma nga tambalé won Atar, sa Ganaar, ba Kaasamaas.
    Man dé, mbirum Njaajaan
    Non la ma ka sa ma baay
    Joxè.
    Non tamit la jangé cosaan,
970 Aada,
    Xéw xéw,
    Ak cosaanu Waalo.
    Nii la ma
    Sa ma baay tamit woxè
975 Mbirum Njaajaan Njaay.

CHAPTER TWO

The Epic Tale of the Waalo Kingdom

1   God the Most High said to Noah:
"The Great Flood will originate
From that day when your wife is cooking.
It will come from one of the stones
5   That support the cauldron.
That stone will fall off;
You then must proceed to the ark."
The Great Flood came.
Noah took his family to the ark.
10   It is commonly said that,
In Noah's ark, there were two of every kind of creature:
One male and one female that survived the flood.
Tradition says that,
No paddle was used
15   In order to move Noah's ark.
The ark floated on the waters
Thanks to the grace of God.
The Prophet Noah sent a bird
As a herald of good news.
20   The bird flew for a long time over the rough waters;
The bird came back.
Noah sent the bird a second time;
The bird came back.
The bird said to the sender:
25   "I saw a small path opened inside the waters."
He replied:
"Where is it?'

"Not too far from where we are."
30 Noah started moving the ark,
Thanks to the grace of God.
The ark remained for forty-one days on the waters.
Tradition says that
Heaven said to the Earth:
35 "If it were not for the help of God,
I would pour water over you
Until you're completely flooded.
Nobody will be able to see you."
The Earth replied to Heaven, saying:
40 "If it were not for the help of God,
I would pour so much sand over you
That you would disappear under that weight."
Thus,
The foundation of life was laid during the Great Flood.
45 That foundation itself
Is governed by two dialectical rules:
The Past and the Future.
The Past is gone, it is memory
The Future is yet to come.
50 During the Great Flood,
It is said that everybody entered the ark,
Except a man called Iwet.
Iwet was the only one not to enter the ark;
He drowned in the Flood.
55 Noah's ark landed in a place called Dundogi.
There were eighty people on board.
But a book called Gadaawu Sor denied that number.
That book put it to sixty.
When the people settled in Dundogi,
60 Where there is a big rock as a landmark,
Some of them settled north of the rock,
Some settled south of the rock,
Some settled east of the rock,
Some settled west of the rock.
65 Later on,
All the people who settled around the rock,
Died,

Except Noah,
His three children
70 And their three wives.
One of Noah's sons name is Sham.
The other is named Ham.
The last one is Ibn Noah.
Tradition says that,
75 One day,
Noah fell asleep;
Ham the eldest son was laughing.
Sham asked him:
"Why are you laughing?
80 Are you laughing about our father?"
Right at that moment,
Noah woke up.
Noah said:
"From today on,
85 You,
Ham!
You will be the precursor of the black race.
You,
Sham!
90 You will beget all white people."
Thus Sham begot two persons called Yajojo and Majojo.
Ham begot a son called Anfésédé.
Anfésédé addressed Ham his father in these terms:
"Noah is my grandfather,
95 You are my father.
I am asking for your grace to fall upon me."
Anfésédé himself begot a son called Misrae.
Misrae himself is the founder
Of a town called Misrae.
100 Ham also begot two black children:
One male and one female.
One day, Ham went into exile.
He arrived at the shores of the river Nile
When he went into exile,
105 Ham said to his wife:
"These two children are not mine."

The wife replied: "What? You are the father.
Remember that it takes two people
To make a child: me and you."
110 Ham went into exile.
That was the beginning of the black race.
Thus, Ham went into exile.
He arrived at the banks of the river Nile.
He stayed there for a very long time.
115 Ham's children grew up.
They became very strong.
They didn't know their father.
They asked their mother:
"Mother, where is our father?"
120 The mother replied:
"I don't know where your father is."
The two children left in their turn.
They journeyed for many many months
Until they arrived at the banks of the river Nile.
125 There they met Ham.
The latter asked them:
"Where are you going?"
They answered: "We are looking for our father."
Ham said: "What is your father's name?"
130 They replied: "Our father's name is Ham;
We were told that Noah is Ham's father;
Noah is then our grandfather.
We were also told that
Our father went into exile;
135 He went to exile just after our birth.
Now we are fully grown up.
That's why we are journeying;
We want to find him."
Ham replied:
140 "The man you have in front of you is your father.
I am Ham."
Ham created a settlement on the banks of the Nile.
The settlement was called Nobara.
Then, Ham married his children.
145 When they had two children,

The two were married in their turn.
Two men called Xaabil and Haabib
Descended from that lineage.
This is how Noah's children multiplied in number.
150 Some of them created Jordan.
Jordan means the country of the Black people.
The following people belong to Ham's clan:
Saxewil, Bateres, Mayaasin, and Sanaaf.
From there, I want to tell you
155 About the history of the Empire of Ghana.
Beforehand, I would like to come back
To the region of Jordan.
Jordan is a very old country.
The prophet Muhammad (peace upon him)
160 Had called upon people to follow him.
He lived to be sixty three years old.
Ababakar Sadex succeeded him.
He ruled for two years.
Umar Ibn Xatab succeeded Ababakar Sadex.
165 He stayed in power for fifteen years.
Some sources said that
He stayed in power for twelve years.
Bubakar Umar and Ibn Xatab fought a jihad.
They converted people to Islam.
170 The two of them considered the pagans to be very arrogant.
The jihad is the reason why Bubakar Umar left Jordan
Jordan the country of the Blacks.
He was accompanied by a man called Mbaarik Bô.
Mbaarik Bô was originally from Masaasi.
175 Mbaarik Bô had his nose pierced.
He wore a big ring in it.
It is said that when it was very hot,
The ring used to fall off.
When it was very hot,
180 The ring used to expand like rubber;
It would then fall to the ground.
Mbaarik Bô and Bubakar Umar arrived in Ghana.
They fought in Ghana for fourteen months.
Actually, they fought for thirteen months.

185 In the fourteenth month,
    A new king came to power.
    His name was Gana Kamara.
    The Ghana Empire was named
    After that king called Gana Kamara.
190 But before that,
    It wasn't called the Empire of Ghana.
    It was called Jordan,
    The country of the Blacks.
    Mbaarik Bô and Bubakar Umar fought for fourteen years.
195 They converted many pagans to Islam, namely Mbaarik Bô and Umar,
    Mbaarik Bô asked Bubakar Umar:
    "Chief, where are you heading now?"
    Bubakar Umar replied:
    "Me, where am I heading?
200 I've heard of a king living in a far away country;
    A far away country in the West.
    I want to make a Muslim of him."
    Mbaarik Bô said to Bubakar:
    "Chief, I am more than willing to accompany you;
205 But I want to be king;
    I want to be crowned;
    Given the fact that you are a wise man,
    And that you have a lot of spiritual power,
    I would like for you to pray for me.
210 Pray for me to God so I can become a king.
    If I become a king,
    That crown will be fruitful.
    It will be fruitful because of your prayers."
    That's the reason why Mbaarik Bô
215 Was of very good company to Bubakar Umar, Njaajaan's father.
    Mbaarik Bô was very close to Bubakar.
    One day, Mbaarik Bô asked Bubakar:
    "Where are you leading us?"
    Bubakar replied:
220 "God hasn't told me yet the path
    I will take for the remainder of our journey.
    But thanks to his grace
    I had a dream.

In the dream, I clearly saw that we are going to leave again.
225 We are going to journey to a far-off land."
Thus, tradition says that
Mbaarik Bô and Bubakar Umar left Ghana.
They journeyed westward for many months
Until they arrived at a village.
230 That village was called Muderi Jaawara.
There, they found a man called Abraham Sal.
Abraham Sal thought that Bubakar was Bilal.
That's why he didn't fight Bubakar Umar and Mbaarik Bô.
Njaajaan Njaay was the first ruler of the Waalo empire.
235 Your ancestors, the ancestors of the Diop family,
Were among those who chose Njaajaan,
As a ruler and a chief.
Your ancestors were the Jogamaay.
They were the chiefs of the Waalo empire.
240 Your father Mapaté Diop, sitting next to me,
He knows very well what I am talking about.
He can attest to it.
Njaajaan Njaay was crowned by your ancestors;
The Jogomaay were the ones who chose him as a ruler.
245 In his turn, Njaajaan yan was under obligations.
He was under obligations to your ancestors the Jogomaay.
I am going to tell you
About the process of the crowning of Njaajaan.
Bubakar Umar, Njaajaan's father left Jordan;
250 He arrived in Ghana with Mbaarik Bô.
They fought on the way;
They converted people to Islam.
There, they found Hawaat, another chief.
Then they left Ghana.
255 They arrived in Muderi Jaawara.
Mbaarik Bô was a pagan;
Bubakar converted him to Islam.
Hawaat was given the family name Gaye.
He was given that name by a man called Aali Gaye,
260 For Hawaat didn't have a family name.
Bubakar too had Aydara as a family name.
He was given the family name Gaye.

Thus, Mbaarik Bô was Bubakar's personal secretary.
After they left Ghana,
265 They arrived in this region;
They arrived in the river Senegal area.
More precisely, up the river.
There, they found Abraham Sal;
They converted Abraham to Islam.
270 Abraham thought that Bubakar was Bilal.
Bilal himself was the companion of the prophet Muhammad;
(Peace upon him)
That's why Abraham didn't fight Bubakar
Abraham Sal is the ancestor
275 Of all the people bearing the name Sal,
Among the Lamtoro, the Tukulor people.
Thus, Bubakar was the one,
Who converted Abraham to Islam.
Abraham begot Fatumata Abraham Sal.
280 Fatumata was Abraham's daughter.
Her father gave her in marriage to Bubakar.
She became Bubakar's wife.
Thus, Bubakar converted the Sereer people.
He came to Dogo...
285 ...He came to Godo [Gédé] in the Bakel region,
On the left bank of the river Senegal.
That area was empty;
Only a fortress was there.
Thus, Bubakar converted the Sereer,
290 Until he came to face a big Sereer chief.
That chief was called Hamar-the-Scolder-of-Old-People.
Hamar used to scold old people; that's why he was called that name.
Mbaarik Bô was Bubakar's companion.
He went behind the compound.
295 There, he spread his prayer rug.
He started reciting the Qur'an.
Remember that,
He was converted to Islam by Bubakar.
Bubakar called on Hamar-the-Scolder-of-Old-People.
300 He said to him: "Come here!
I am going to shave your head;

I am going to convert you to Islam."
Hamar-the-Scolder-of-Old-People replied:
"Can you let me go to the outhouse first?"
305 Bubakar said:
"Yes, you can."
Hamar-the-Scolder-of-Old-People did not enter the outhouse.
He went behind a nearby tree.
His bow and quiver were hanging there,
310 With many arrows inside.
He took the bow;
He adjusted an arrow;
He then hit Bubakar on the forearm.
The latter quivered, quivered, and quivered;
315 He was in pain.
He went to his wife Fatumata and told her:
"Let's go inside the room.
I want to talk to you."
Mbaarik Bô was sitting on his raw sheephide prayer rug.
320 He was outside the room;
Nobody could see him;
He was the only one to hear the conversation;
That conversation that took place
Between Bubakar and his wife Fatumata.
325 Bubakar said to his wife:
"I want to go back East;
I know that I am going to die;
I am going to die,
As a result of the wound
330 Caused by Hamar-the-Scolder-of-Old-People.
The arrow is poisoned;
I don't want to die here.
I want to die back East where I am from.
I am going back East.
335 You shouldn't marry a man whose body
You would see when he's washing himself.
You shouldn't marry a man whose body
You would see when he is in the outhouse.
If the man asks you to sleep with him,
340 The mattress must fall first on the floor,

340 The mattress must fall first on the floor,
    Before you can sleep with him."
    While Bubakar was saying these lofty words
    To his wife Fatumata inside the room
    Mbaarik Bô heard all the conversation.
345 At that time, Fatumata was pregnant with Njaajaan Njaay.
    His given first name was Muhammadu;
    It wasn't Njaajaan.
    Fatumata said to her husband:
    "These are the things
350 You want me to do before marrying any man?"
    "Yes," replied Bubakar.
    A few days later Bubakar left the village.
    He headed back East to his native homeland.
    He didn't make it back East;
355 He died halfway through his journey;
    He died in a settlement called Singiti.
    His grave is in Singiti;
    It is near the town of Ataar.
    After that happened,
360 Mbaarik Bô put his shoes on.
    He put on a white robe.
    He then took the jar he used for his ablutions.
    He went to the outhouse;
    He went very far from the village,
365 Until nobody could see him anymore.
    He then went inside the outhouse.
    He came out of the outhouse.
    Fatumata erected a high pillar;
    She would stand on it;
370 She would watch the men going to the outhouse.
    When the men wanted to go to the outhouse,
    They would just go behind the fortress.
    Only Mbaarik Bô would go far away,
    Until nobody could see him anymore.
375 There,
    He would relieve himself.
    Fatumata said to herself:
    "I am really puzzled. What a shame!"

380 When he was eleven,
  He fought Hamar-the-Scolder-of-Old-People
  In a very celebrated combat;
  Njaajaan smote him with his swift hand behind the ear;
  He smashed both jaws killing him instantly.
385 Fatumata refused to marry all the men
  Who courted her
  For none of them fulfilled the conditions,
  Those conditions her late husband dictated to her.
  When Muhamadu was eleven,
390 Mbaarik Bô came into the room;
  He found Muhamadu in there.
  Fatumata was cooking inside the kitchen.
  You know,
  In those days,
395 When women were cooking,
  They stayed inside the kitchen.
  They stayed in to watch the food,
  Until it was ready.
  Mbaarik went into the bedroom.
400 He brought with him a strong piece of wood;
  It was the kind of wood
  That would make a frame,
  A frame on which to rest a mattress.
  He took out his knife.
405 He then started cutting the piece of wood;
  He narrowed both ends of the piece of wood.
  He then placed the piece of wood beneath the mattress;
  He then gathered up the chips.
  He left the room.
410 Fatumata didn't see any of this,
  For she was inside the kitchen.
  When the sun went down behind the horizon '
  When twilight covered the land,
  Mbaarik came back to the house.
415 There
  He found Fatumata inside the bedroom;
  He greeted her;
  Fatumata returned the greetings.

Mbaarik said to her:
420 "My dear lady,
I really would like to marry you."
While pronouncing those words,
He gave a quick and unnoticed push to the mattress.
The mattress fell on the floor;
425 He quickly left the room.
In a state of bewilderment, Fatumata said:
"Good God! This goes beyond my ken."
After that,
Her family members came to her.
430 They told her: "Fatumata, you should get remarried.
Many suitors came to see you,
But you wouldn't choose any of them as a husband."
She replied:
"I am going to tell you that,
435 The conditions set down
By my late husband for my remarrying,
They have been fulfilled.
The man who fufilled them is Mbaarik Bô,
My late husband's personal secretary.
440 He came here;
Before he sat down on the bed,
The mattress fell down.
The other condition had been fulfilled.
When he went to the outhouse,
445 Nobody could see him going there."
The family members replied in unison:
"You should marry him then."
Fatumata was married to Mbaarik Bô.
While these events were happening,
450 Njaajaan Njaay was playing in the river.
He was with his young friends.
They were splashing water on each other;
They were running after each other,
On the bank of the river.
455 The playmates started teasing him;
They said to him:
"Oh! Poor boy!

Your mother couldn't find any man to marry;
That's why she fell back on the man
460 Who accompanied your father.
What a shame!"
You know that
A Tukulor or a Waalo-Waalo is very hot-tempered.
A Tukulor or a Waalo-Waalo is very proud.
465 Njaajaan didn't escape this rule.
When Njaajaan heard those words from his playmates,
He flew into a terrible rage.
He grabbed an ax;
He grabbed a pitchfork;
470 He grabbed a broadsword;
He grabbed a spear;
He grabbed a bow;
He grabbed arrows;
He grabbed a gun;
475 He then left.
He went to the river.
He plunged into the river;
He attempted to drown himself;
He wanted to commit suicide.
480 But you know that a good swimmer
Cannot drown himself that easily,
Unless it is an accident.
Some people said that
The river was Njaajaan's abode.
485 That isn't true;
He went to the river
Because of his pride and hurt feelings.
He then crossed to the opposite bank.
There, he took off his clothes.
490 He hid himself among the reeds,
Those reeds growing on the banks of the river.
He stayed among the reeds.
Nobody could see him.
The people searched both banks.
495 They feared he had drowned.
When he was hungry,

He would catch a fish with his hand;
He would put it under the hot sun;
He would let it roast;
500 He would then eat it.
God gave him this power.
Nature gave him the same power.
He stayed among the reeds for two years.
In the daytime, he would hide among the reeds;
505 In the nighttime, he would climb up a tree.
There
He would sleep.
He spent two years in Gédé
On the left bank of the river,
510 Among the reeds.
One day,
At twilight,
Njaajaan emerged from the waters
In the middle of the river.
515 People standing on the right bank of the river saw him.
They all let out a murmur:
"Uuuuh!"
You know that a Moor and a white person
Look almost the same in paleness.
520 Njaajaan was pale,
For he ate only cold food.
He slept only in cool and shaded areas.
Not because he was a white person.
This was the reason why,
525 His whole body was covered with hair,
Except around his eyes and his palms.
He also spent too much time in the wilderness.
That contributed to his hairy appearance.
When the people standing on the right bank saw Njaajaan,
530 They started talking about him.
They spread news.
Quickly, Njaajaan plunged again deep into the river.
He disappeared.
He went back to the left bank of the river.
535 There

He took the clothes
The clothes he had hidden among the reeds.
He started swimming down the river.
Until he arrived at Lamnaajo.
540 He spent two years in Gédé
But he spent seven years days in the river,
On the left bank among the reeds.
Njaajaan also spent one year in Lamnaajo.
When people were about to discover his presence,
545 He left Lamnaajo.
He swam down the river,
Until he arrived at Mbégèñ.
In those days,
The village of Dagana was near
550 The big tamarind tree of Jaalawaali.
Njaajaan spent one year in Mbégèñ.
During all this time
He was hiding among the reeds,
The reeds that grew all along the course of the river
555 On both banks.
In the daytime, he would hide among the reeds.
In the nighttime, he would climb up a tree.
There he would sleep.
When people were about to discover his presence,
560 He left Mbégèñ.
He swam down the river,
Until he arrived at Kawas.
Kawas was between Dagana and Mbilor.
In Kawas, there were a lot of mahogany trees;
565 They grew not far from the banks of the river.
Njaajaan spent one year in Kawas.
When people were about to discover his presence,
He left Kawas.
He swam down the river,
570 Until he arrived at Xéwéw Gaal;
He spent two years in Xéwéw Gaal.
All together,
He spent seven years in all the villages
Where he stopped during his journey.

575 When the people were about to discover his presence,
He left Xéwéw Gaal.
He swam down the river,
Until he arrived in Mbégèñ Booy.
He stayed in Mbégèñ Booy for seven days.
580 After seven days and three days,
He came out of the river.
In those days in Waalo,
The children went fishing in the river.
When one caught a fish,
585 He would throw it several feet away from the bank.
In those days,
They had not yet learned the technique
Of taking a rope,
Of running it through the gills of each fish,
590 Of linking all the fish onto a single rope.
After they finished fishing, they would gather the fish;
They would start fighting,
For no one would recognize his fish.
595 One would say: "This is my fish;"
Another would say: "No;
It's not your fish,
It's mine."
They would keep quarrelling and fighting.
600 When Njaajaan saw the children quarrelling;
He came out of the river.
He walked toward them.
When the children saw him,
They were scared.
605 They started running away.
He raised his hand;
He signaled them to stop.
He reassured them that
He wouldn't do them any harm.
610 When the children stopped,
Njaajaan came.
He took all the fish;
He divided them in equal piles.
After that, he took a rope.

615 He ran it through the gills of the fish of one pile;
    He then put it down.
    He did so until all the piles were done.
    My father told me that,
    He would look straight into the eyes of one child;
620 He then would point to a pile;
    The child would grasp the rope;
    The rope from which the fish were dangling.
    He would then walk away.
    He would do so
625 Until all the children had their fish
    And peacefully walked home.
    For three days,
    He divided the fish in this manner.
    He did so after the children had finished fishing.
630 If you add the three days to the previous three,
    You come to a total of six days.
    The older people were amazed at the children's behavior.
    They asked: "Well! Whenever you went fishing,
    You used to quarrel and fight about the catch.
635 Now, you come back here in peace,
    Each one holding an equal amount of fish.
    What's happening?"
    The children answered in unison:
    "There is a man who comes out of the river
640 He equally divides the fish among us.
    He has been doing so for the past three days.
    He has hair all over his body,
    Except on his palms and around his eyes."
    The older people held a council.
645 One of them said:
    "We are going to set a trap;
    We should catch that man;
    We want to know more about him.
    Some of you are going to take reeds.
650 Get them from the river bank.
    Then make a round fence near the fishing place.
    When he comes to divide the fish among the children,
    You should step inside the fence.

He will certainly follow you.
655 If he is a noble man,
He will not jump over the fence
Once he steps inside it."
A few strong men were chosen to do the job.
After setting up the fence,
660 They hid behind a nearby tree.
After the children caught some fish,
They went inside the round fence;
Then they started quarrelling.
Njaajaan was watching them.
665 After a while,
He stepped inside the fence.
He calmed the children down.
He then proceeded to divide the fish.
He wanted to divide them equally among the children.
670 After he finished,
He was walking back to the exit door.
At that moment, a gang of men jumped on him;
They immobilized him.
After that,
675 The old people were called to see the prisoner.
My father told me that,
Njaajaan had killed three men among *
Those who were trying to catch him.
He was a very strong man;
680 He had supernatural powers.
After they caught him,
They tied his hands behind his back.
A man of the Council of the Elders asked him:
"What's your name?"
685 Njaajaan didn't answer;
He was silent.
The man reiterated his question:
"Who are you?"
Njaajaan was still silent;
690 He did not say a word.
Some people say that Bata Booy was the man
Who succeeded in making Njaajaan talk.

But my father told me that
A Peul man called Maramu Gaaya
695 Was the successful one
In making Njaajaan come out of his silence.
My father said that
Maramu Gaaya was a Peul;
He belonged to the branch of the Sirabawar
700 Of the Peul people.
Maramu Gaaya came to the council and said:
"If you give me this man,
I'll take him to the kitchen.
If you give me two stones,
705 A cauldron,
Some flour,
Water,
And fire,
I'll make him talk."
710 What Maramu asked for was given to him.
Njaajaan sat on a low stool;
He was staring at Maramu.
Maramu mixed the water and the flour;
While mixing the flour and the water,
715 He had a burning pipe clenched between his teeth,
Smoking.
After he finished the mixing,
He took the two big stones;
He then put them half a foot apart.
720 He then lit the logs
In order to make a cooking fire.
He then took the cauldron;
He filled it with water;
He then put it on the two stones.
725 But as soon as he put the cauldron down,
It fell and the water spilled out.
He started again;
He filled the cauldron with water;
He then put it on the two stones;
730 But the cauldron fell on the ground;
The water splashed all around.

Njaajaan was very hungry.
He said to Maramu in Peul:
"You need three stones,
735 Not two,
In order to hold the cauldron straight above the fire."
Maramu replied:
"Oh, really?"
He then took a third stone;
740 He joined it to the two previous ones;
He lit the logs and made a fire.
He then took the cauldron;
He filled it with water;
He then put it on top of the three stones.
745 This time, the cauldron stayed in place.
When the water was boiling,
Maramu poured the flour inside the cauldron.
When the porridge was cooked,
It made a noise: ret, ret, ret, ret, ret, ret, ret.
750 You know, when porridge is done,
It makes that kind of noise.
The porridge was still making that noise.
Njaajaan became impatient.
He said to Maramu:
755 "Maramu, take the porridge out of the cauldron
And put it in the calabash;
It is ready."
Maramu, feigning surprise, said:
"Ha!"
760 He then emptied the porridge out of the cauldron.
He put it into the calabash.
You know that the Peul people
Always fan the porridge in order to cool it off.
Maramu started fanning the porridge;
765 The porridge
Was inside the calabash.
He continued to fan the porridge.
Becoming ever more impatient,
Njaajaan said:
770 "Maramu Gaye, Gaye! Stop fanning the porridge;

It is going to be cold.
Now pour the fermented milk over it."
Maramu Gaye left the kitchen.
He ran out;
775 He called the people and said:
"My dear villagers, come here;
Come and witness the man speaking.
He first told me that
I needed three stones in order to hold the cauldron,
780 Not two.
After that, he told me to empty the porridge out of the cauldron
And put it inside the calabash because it was done.
Finally,
He told me to stop fanning the porridge,
785 Otherwise it would be too cold,
And that it was time to pour the fermented milk over it."
The Council of Elders asked Njaajaan
To tell them what was bothering him.
Your ancestors,
790 Those bearing the family name Diop,
As well as the Jogomaay title talked to Njaajaan.
They questioned him about his past.
They questioned him about his itinerary.
Your ancestors were the ones who caught him.
795 After they caught him,
They sent messengers
To King Maysa Waali Jon Fay;
Maysa Waali
Was the king of the Sereer people.
800 Eight strong and valorous men
Were sent as messengers to Maysa Waali.
Then, Maysa Waali's family name wasn't Jon;
His name was Jaxaté.
When the messengers got there,
805 They said to him:
"Maysa Waali Jon, we have been sent
By the Council of Elders of Waalo.
They said that they have caught a man
Who is very puzzling."

810 Maysa Waali answered:
    "That is very strange."
    The name Njaajaan means "strange" in Sereer.
    That's where Njaajaan got his name. His name was not Njaajaan.
    Maysa Waali continued:
815 "Return to Waalo!
    When you get back,
    Tell the elders to elect Njaajaan as a chief of the army,
    Tell them to elect him as a ruler."
    Thus, Njaajaan was chosen as the chief of the army by the elders.
820 Ten years later,
    Still chief of the army,
    Njaajaan's younger brother planned to visit him.
    He was born after Njaajaan's exile from Gédé.
    His name was Mbarak Barka.
825 His mother was raising a horse for him.
    When he was seventeen,
    Mbarak came to his mother and said:
    "Mother! Do I have an elder brother?"
    His mother replied:
830 "Oh yes. You have an elder brother.
    He lives in the west, up the river.
    In fact I want you to go and pay him a visit on my behalf.
    But when you get there,
    Behave yourself,
835 Be polite,
    Be courteous."
    Mbarak left Gédé and started his journey.
    When he came to Mbéngèñ Booy where Njaajaan lived,
    He found his older brother there.
840 As soon as Mbarak saw Njaajaan, he said:
    "Hail to the chief of the army!"
    That was the way kings and rulers were greeted in those days.
    Mbarak said again:
    "Hail to the chief of the army!"
845 "Come in," answered Njaajaan.
    Mbarak walked in;
    He walked past all the aides and counselors
    Who were sitting inside the compound.

When he came to Njaajaan,
850 He extended his right hand.
Njaajaan grabbed the hand and shook it.
Njaajaan asked him:
"Where are you coming from?"
He answered:
855 "From Gédé."
Njaajaan said again:
"What is your last name?"
Mbarak was going to say Bô.
But he said Mboj was his last name.
860 All the people bearing the last name Mboj,
Got it from Mbarak.
Bô was changed to Mboj.
Njaajaan asked him:
"Who is your mother in Gédé?"
865 Mbarak replied:
"My mother is Fatumata Abraham Sal."
Njaajaan asked:
"How is my mother doing?"
"She is fine," answered the younger brother.
870 He lifted Mbarak with his two strong arms.
He then seated him on top of the bed.
He then took his rugs made of cowhide;
He spread them on the floor;
He then sat on them.
875 Next, he called a meeting.
The elders and all the villagers,
All gathered inside the compound.
Njaajaan addressed them in these terms:
"This lad is my younger brother.
880 We come from the same mother.
If I am killed in battle,
I want him to succeed me as chief of the army.
He is valorous and brave.
All the people present at the meeting answered in unison:
885 "As you wish, Njaay."
But Njaajaan's last name was not Njaay,
It was Aydara.

Your ancestors, the Diop,
The Jogomaay of the Waalo empire,
890 Decided to send Njaajaan to Jolof, from Waalo,
Into the middle of the empire.
From the middle,
He could better maneuver with his army in all directions.
When the white Europeans came here long ago
895 They found here, in Waalo,
A true model of government,
A democracy.
They also found here a well-organized
And very efficient army headed by the Barak.
900 Njaajaan was the first Barak;
He was the first chief of the army.
Njaajaan begot Gèt Njaajaan,
Saré Njaajaan,
Dombur Njaajaan,
905 Nafaye Njaajaan,
Fukili Njaajaan.
All in all,
He had five children.
Fukili went to the Saalum region.
910 Njaajaan left Gèt in Tundu Gèt,
On his way to Jolof.
When he arrived in Warxox,
His horse was very tired;
That's why he named the place Xoox.
915 He named the place Xoox.
After that,
Njaajaan arrived in Yang-Yang.
He got here at sundown
At the time darkness was covering the land.
920 There
He was given in marriage a Peul woman called Këyfa.
They spent the night together.
At the break of dawn,
Njaajaan left the room.
925 He left Këyfa and Yang-Yang.
He really did not want to have her as a wife.

But Këyfa was pregnant.
She is the ancestor of all the Peul people
Who bear the name Njaay.
930 A man called Saajo Njaay,
In the village of Xuma
Near Richard-Toll, is from that lineage.
Gèt Njaajaan and his father Njaajaan Njaay got into a quarrel.
935 Furious, Gèt declared to him:
"I am going to drop the name Njaay;
From now on I am going to adopt the name Diop."
The clan of the Njaay is different
From the clan of Njaajaan Njaay. Remember:
940 Njaajaan's original last name was not Njaay.
It was Aydara.
Thus,
Njaajaan had been chief of the army for sixteen years in Waalo
Before he was transferred to Jolof.
945 Before he came to the Waalo region,
The Waalo Empire had been in existence
For four hundred and thirty years, before Njaajaan came into existence.
Thus,
Njaajaan spent sixteen years in Waalo before being taken to Jolof.
950 There,
In Jolof,
He begot Biram Njèmé Kumba and Albury Njaay.
Albury was later going to be ruler of the Jolof kingdom
But when Njaajaan got to Jolof,
955 It was unsettled.
There was no authority,
No chiefdom,
No kingdom,
There was the 'Lamanat' system.
960 Njaajaan installed authority in Jolof.
In the same order of things,
The region of Bawol,
Of Kayor,
Jolof and Siin were part of the Waalo Empire.
965 That empire covered a vast area going from Ganaar to Casamance.
This is how the story of Njaajaan Njaay

Was handed down to me
By my father and my ancestors.
This is also how I learned the traditions,
970 Customs,
Events,
And history of the Waalo Empire.
This is exactly
How my father narrated to me
975 The story of Njaajaan Njaay.

Personal Observations on the Recording of *The Epic Tale of the Waalo Kingdom* **and**
The Genealogy of the Rulers of Waalo **as performed by Sèq Ñan and**
The Interview **of Ancumbu Caam and his son Magate Caam**

In this section, I will be dealing with the contribution of my father Mapaté Diop to the performances as well as the impact he had on them.

First, I will recount a conversation I had off the record with Mapaté and the griot Ancumbu Caam. They were complaining about the distortions that were being made to the genealogies of Waalo as well as to the history of that region by some professional griots. Both Mapaté and Ancumbu gave their opinion and their stand vis-à-vis the accurate recounting of history. An important aspect of their position is that they both agreed that historical events should be told as they happened whether they are favorable or unfavorable to a party. According to them, history is not composed of only pleasant items. They were making these remarks in regard to the false genealogies created by certain professional griots for *nouveaux riches* or *parvenus* in return for gifts. It is doubtful that the recounting (written or oral) of historical events can be flawless, impartial, or untainted. Partisanship is always bound to intrude and influence the process of the telling or writing of history. The upshot of Mapaté and Ancumbu's argument is that one must do one's best to be faithful to the accuracy of historical events, to family and royal genealogies, and try *to tell them as they did happen*, whether they are advantageous or not. They were also aware of the fact that there is no such thing as a "true history," insofar oral traditions are concerned for these are prone to distortions and manipulations for various purposes.

In appendix II (Sèq Ñan's List of the Rulers of Waalo), I point out the way in which heads of families in Senegal constitute safety-valves. Many heads of families know the genealogies of their families. When Mapaté was growing up, he used to listen to his father and mother recounting the various genealogies of our family, the genealogies of other noble families, and the links between all the families and clans of Waalo.

Mapaté was present during both performances: *The Epic Tale of the Waalo Kingdom* and *The List of the Rulers of Waalo* as recited by Ñan; he also took part in the *Interview* with Ancumbu Caam. Mapaté had an impact on all these occasions but more so on the recital of the genealogy. During the performance of *The Epic Tale of the Waalo Kingdom* by Sèq Ñan, Mapaté intervened mostly when Ñan was trying to elaborate on kinship ties. I should point out that the performance of the *List of the Rulers* took place in Rosso-Sénégal whereas the *Interview* took place in Dakar. They were both recorded in December of 1989 and January of 1990.

Both Ancumbu and Ñan praised Mapaté for his extensive knowledge of the genealogies and history of Waalo. They said that Mapaté knew more on the history of Waalo than themselves. Thus, the griots were less likely to distort or modify the genealogies in Mapaté 's presence. During the performance of the *List of the Rulers* and the *Interview*, Mapaté interrupted both Ñan and Ancumbu Caam in order to rectify certain mistakes the griots made during their recitations. In the *Interview*, Ancumbu recites a genealogy. I also remember that both griots stopped during their recitation of the genealogies in order to ask Mapaté questions. Since the genealogies were very long, the griots could not remember all the names; additionally, the two griots would sometimes link two or more people that were not related. Whenever that happened, Mapaté would explain in detail and with a lot of patience how people were related, the marriages or unions that took place between various families, and the kinships by alliance. Mapaté' s knowledge of the history of Waalo underscores the general knowledge, strength, and social role of the elders of that area.

Note on Orthography and Terminology

The Wolof language was until recently only a spoken language. However, over the last thirty-five years or so, commendable efforts have been made by various linguists and scholars to attempt to develop a writing system for the transcription of Wolof. At this time, there is not yet a single convention for the transcription of Wolof. That is the reason why one can see in various manuscripts, handbooks, and dictionaries the different ways of transcribing the same word. A telling example is the word *Wolof* itself. This word is invariably transcribed as *Oualof, Ouolof, Walaf, Ouolove,* or *Wolof* . In this project, I chose the spelling *Wolof* because it seems that in the most recent studies there is a consensus among the various specialists on this spelling. Since this project is written in English (except the texts in Wolof and the facsimile in Arabic), I did my best to transcribe and translate Wolof words into English so that they would reflect the genius and spirit of the target language. Additionally, I transcribed words into English following the closest approximation of sounds in the original Wolof language.

Thus, I chose to write *Sèq* instead of the French form *Cheikh, Peul* instead of *Peulh, Sereer* instead of *Sérère, Caam* instead of *Thiam, Njaay* instead of *N'Diaye, Saalum* instead of *Saloum, Siin* instead of *Sine, Waalo* instead of *Oualo, Njaajaan* instead of *N'Diadiane, Ñan* instead of *Niang, Jolof* instead of *Djolof,* and *Bubakar* instead of *Boubacar*, so on and so forth.

The name *Gaye* is also spelled *Gaaya* or *Gaya.* During the performance, Ñan variously says *Gaye* and *Gaaya*, depending on the context and the events being narrated at that stage of the tale. In the study, I use the form *Gaye.*

In the tale (and in the mind of the audience and of most Wolof people), Waalo is conceived as an empire for it encompassed many other kingdoms such as Jolof, Bawol, and Kayor. The griot Ancumbu Caam stated that the Waalo Empire went as far south as Casamance thus including the Sereer kingdoms of the Siin area and the smaller kingdoms or chieftaincies of Saalum. However, according to historians such as B. Barry (1985) and V. Monteil (1966), Waalo was more a kingdom than an empire. (See also J. Vansina 's definition and differenciation of African kingdoms, states, and empires in *Les anciens royaumes de la savane,* 1976.)

Finally, I use the terms *poem* and *tale* interchangeably throughout the study in referring to the *Epic Tale of the Waalo Kingdom.* Both terms are relevant in the specific context of Wolof oral poetry. If it is impossible to separate African oral poetry from singing, likewise it would be difficult to separate entertainment and poetic aspects of *The Epic Tale of the Waalo Kingdom* .

CHAPTER THREE

Notes to the Epic Tale of the Waalo Kingdom

1 - 58   That the master of the word begins with a retelling of the flood myth and the fall of man is significant. That account of man's degradation is of great concern in sacred literature. In his book entitled *The Babylonian Genesis*, H. Heidel draws a parallel between man's condition in Gilgamesh (the Babylonian account of how the universe was conceived) and the Book of Genesis in the Old Testament. Heidel writes:

> In the first chapter [of the Book of genesis] God speaks, and it is done exactly as he had commanded, everything turns out in full accord with his will. Hence man could not have been morally imperfect, for God does not will moral imperfection. (1942: 122)

The flood myth is found in *Gilgamesh* as well as in the Old Testament (Genesis 1, 2). The master of the word is a Muslim; he has been exposed to the Qur'an, and consequently to the Old Testament. In present-day Africa, the flood myth is still strong. All the people who believe in the Old Testament have the flood myth as part of their belief. On the interplay between Islam and indigenous creeds as well as on the influence of the former over the latter, D. Henige observes:

Few societies have managed to escape the attention of Christian or Muslim missionaries, so it is not surprising that the Bible and (to a lesser degree) the Qur'an are by far the most common and influential sources of outside information. Most often oral societies have borrowed materials directly, if sometimes obscurely, from the scriptures themselves or from missionary teachings based on them. (Henige 1982: 82)

Studies carried out by historians and anthropologists in America have shown how the Bible has influenced local oral traditions. Thus, one should not be surprised to find Biblical stories, myths, and legends even in Maori and Hawaiian oral lore and beliefs and among other Pacific Islanders. D. Henige adds:

This enthusiasm for the printed word manifested itself quickly in the traditions of the area [Oceania]. Figures representing Adam, Noah, and other Biblical personages soon found their way into genealogies collected later in the [twentieth] century. So too did the idea of a creator god. Needless to say, the ubiquitous flood story made many appearances in oceanic traditions, as did original sin and Garden of Eden-like morality tales. The large numbers of travellers from one island to another only accelerated this propagation and assimilation of Biblical motifs. (Henige, loc. cit.)

In the case of West Africa and of Senegal, it was also a matter of propagation and assimilation, this time of Islamic motifs, but instead of missionaries, the Arab and Berber traders coming from North Africa across the Sahara Desert brought Islam.

Needless to say almost all traditional societies have a concept or an explanation of the origin of the universe, of the earth, and of man. Yusuf Ali remarks that:

> The story of the Flood is found in some form or another among all nations, and not only among those who follow the Mosaic tradition. In Greek tradition the hero of the Flood is Deukalion, with his wife Pyrrha. In Indian tradition, *Shatapatha Brahmana* and *Mahabharata* it is the sage Manu and the Fish. The Chinese tradition of a great flood is recorded in *Shu-King*. Among American Indians the tradition was common to many tribes. (*The Holy Qur'an, Text, Translation, and Commentary* by Y. Ali 1983: 1201)

In his study of the Yoruba *alasuwada* (myth of creation and body of creation doctrines in oral poetry form), A. Akiwowo cites a Yoruba text that contains the *alasuwada* myth. In that text, there is

> a passage [that] deals with the ontology of Error, or moral offence, in the world, which began when *Yankangi* strayed away from *Iregbogbo* in order to steal *iru* (a kind of seed), from the Divine Mother called *Olugamo*. The true meaning of these metaphorical statements elude one at this point. Is the allusion to the stealing of *iru* analogous to the act of eating the forbidden apple in the mythical Garden of Eden in the Hebraic myth of creation composed by Moses? It is probably an analogous doctrine of the first sin in the Christian religion, except that *iru* is a seed and food condiment, which is sometimes used to symbolize 'assortment', separation into lots, differentiation and fragmentation. (A. Akiwowo 1990: 111)

One may be tempted to assimilate *Yankangi* to Adam, *Iregbogbo* to Eve, and *iru* to the apple in the Garden. Another important element to be emphasized in Akiwowo's passage is that *Yankangi* and *Iregbogbo* are not gender-bound. We do not know whether *Yankangi* and *Iregbogbo* are male or female. Not all human societies perceive things in conflictual, in gender terms, or in paired oppositions: traditional/modern, oral/written, precolonial/postcolonial, local audience/wide audience, homogenous/hybrid (K. Barber 1993: 7) .

Even though Ñan, the Senegalese singer, is a Muslim, he is nonetheless influenced by indigenous creeds. There is an interplay between Islam and indigenous religion; the two kinds of beliefs also have different aims when it comes to temporality. R. Dilley (citing Lewis and Bravmann), comments on the idea that Islam cannot convey a sense of immediate relief compared with the concerns for the "here and now" of indigenous religious cults (Dilley 1989: 151).

The flood myth is a myth of origin but also a story of beginning. Y. Ali states that the Great Flood can be conceived as a necessary purgation (*The Holy Qur'an, Text, Translation, and Commentary* by Y. Ali 1983: 1613). Each human culture and civilization needs to establish a beginning. Thus, in the Wolof tradition, the master of the word starts his tale with a story of beginning, for the history of the Wolof could not come out of a void. A singer who was not exposed to the Qur'an or the Old Testament might have begun his story in a different fashion, but it is likely he would have started a tale of this type with some kind of story of beginnings.

5 The cauldron is not associated with the creation myth in the Old Testament but is rather an embellishment of the singer. The presence of the cauldron in the fall of man is symbolic. The cauldron surfaces again beginning at line 722 in the section in which Njaajaan is tricked into speaking. As a technological tool, the cauldron may give us some indications about the technological level of Wolof society as well as information on the pre-colonial mode of production.

There are strong indications that the cauldron is a cooking utensil the Wolof have gotten from European traders and most of all from the French. The latter established the first trading posts in the first half of the seventeenth century near the mouth of the River Senegal. The French traders bought slaves and gum Arabic and sold cloth, spirits, and guns to the local aristocracy. B. Barry (1985: 104) stresses the predominance of iron as an import (as far as firearms are concerned) from the French.

In her study of a mode of production in pre-colonial and pre-capitalist Africa, C. Coquery-Vidrovitch establishes the fact that the African continent was marked by apparently contradictory phenomena: the mobility of the population and the escalation of long distance commercial exchanges (within sub-Saharan Africa as well as between North Africa and Africa south of the Sahara desert). Thus, on one hand, we have country subsistence farming and on the other international trade (C. Coquery-Vidrovitch 1969: 67-70). In the tale, the main activity of the villages is fishing because of the proximity of the river (ll. 583-629). Thus, a semantic classification can be established between the two activities: fishing (subsistence) and the cauldron (cooking).

18   The singer employs only the generic term for bird (ll. 18, 20-24, 28). In Genesis, 8, however, a raven and a dove are mentioned.

32   In Genesis 6, the ark floats for 40 days rather than 41 as in the tale.

34   The dispute between Heaven and Earth is not mentioned in Genesis; it is an embellishment on the part of the master of the word. He refers to tradition (1. 33) meaning that he has received earlier oral accounts of this episode. However,

the Qur'an mentions both the sky and the earth: "O earth! Swallow up thy water, and O sky! withhold [the rain]" (5, XI, 44).

46 These dialectical rules are superbly introduced by the singer. He does so by using the sky and the earth (l. 34 to 42) as two opposing, yet complementary forces. They threatened each other with the heavy-handed deeds of the sky pouring water over the earth, and the earth threatening to pour sand over the sky. Only God prevents strife. At a different level of interpretation, these dialectical forces are symbolic.

52 Iwet is not mentioned in the Old Testament and must also belong to the stock of earlier oral accounts within Wolof society. However, the Qur'an (Sura XI: 42), mentions that "Noah called out to his son, who had separated himself [from the rest]" and then "the son was among those overwhelmed in the flood" (S. XI: 44), without naming the son. "Iwet" is certainly for Ñan the name of Noah's son.

55 Dundogi, like many other names in the lines relating the flood myth, is not in Genesis. Dundogi's equivalent in Genesis may be found in the vicinity of Mount Ararat where Noah's ark is said to have landed, according to Genesis 8. The Qur'an mentions a Mount Judi on which the ark settled. 'Gudi' is a variant form of 'Judi'; by metathesis, it would give 'Dogi'.

56 Neither the number 80 nor 60 (l. 58) are mentioned in Genesis.

57 This book is probably an embellishment on the part of the Wolof singer,

designed to add the authority of a written source to his account.

Over the summer of 1993, I went back to Senegal. There, I had the chance to meet Ñan again. I asked him about this book. He answered to me that that book exists and that if I go to the book shops in Dakar, I would find it. I set out to do that. I visited the vendors of Islamic theological and religious books and writings in the streets of Dakar. Most of these vendors do not know about the book. They, however, showed me another book entitled *Al-Akhdari*. The latter is a famous small book that contains Islamic prescriptions pertaining mostly to prayers and cleanliness. Thus, I was unsuccessful in my search.

Ñan may be talking about a book that really exists. The problem may be that the rendering of the original Arabic title into Wolof has been considerably altered (as is often the case) to the effect that it is often difficult to find these kinds of books.

60 This big rock is probably a reference to the mountain of Dundogi.

69 M. Bucaille summarizes the story of the Biblical flood as follows: "Man's corruption had become widespread, so God decided to annihilate him along with all the other living creatures. He warned Noah and told him to construct the Ark into which he was to take his wife, his three sons and their wives, along with *other* living creatures" (1978: 33 [My emphasis]). The number of Noah's children (3) coincides with the number given by the Wolof poet on line 69. However, in Bucaille's passage, it is stated that Noah took on board of the Ark other living creatures whereas the Wolof poet is more specific for he states that in Noah's Ark, there were two of every kind of creature (line 11).

71-73   The Old Testament mentions Shem, Ham, and Japheth as Noah's sons. Ibn Noah is probably the equivalent of Japheth.

76-90   Noah's cursing of Ham is found in the Old Testament (Genesis 9:20-27); however, Ñan does not mention Noah's drunkenness and his lying uncovered (Genesis 9:20), the incident that gave rise to the curse.

86-92   This racial division by color is not found in Genesis. The Wolof singer uses this racial distinction as a parable, which does not necessarily introduce a dualism between white and black peoples. On the concept of dualism, R. Dilley analyzes the system of beliefs of the weavers and craftsmen in Tukulor society. However, Dilley warns that it would be mere speculation if he were to suggest whether the body of lore of those craftsmen antedates the introduction of Islam or not. Citing Needham (1973), Dilley observes that:

> It is not really about a duality of beliefs between Islam and non-Islam, but a duality implied by two opposing conceptual categories of thought which divide up and classify the world in contemporary Tukulor belief. These two categories are referred to in Pulaar under the rubrics *gandal balewal* and *gandal danewal*, literally 'black lore' and 'white lore'. (Dilley 1989: 142)

K. Barber and M. Farias (1989) refer to that classification as the idea of "oppositive unity" or of "seemingly intractable ambiguities."   Discussing Trimingham (1959), Dilley comments on

the association of certain Timbuctu craftsmen's relationships with spirits concerning *gandal balewal.*. Trimingham discusses different classifications of spirit being in various West African societies, illustrating that they distinguish between 'black' and 'white'. He [Trimingham] concludes that 'following the practice of ideological antithesis Islam splits them into categories of good and bad'. The simple identification of white with good and black with bad cannot be sustained among the Tukulor. (Dilley, idem)

In the Luba myth of origins, the distinction is not a color distinction but a parallel between the Luba myth of Ilunga Luala the founder of the Luba state and the Book of Genesis in the Old Testament:

> Soon, they [the midwives] heard the baby's cry and there was this wonderful baby, black like Mbidi Kiluwe. He was named Ilunga after his father together with a praise name Luala Misaha, that is, the divider of streams or nations. (Mudimbe 1991: 92, citing Womersley, 1984)

On the Tukulor craftsmanship, Dilley concedes that "white lore is the specialism of the socially superior and politically dominant Islamic clerics and some other freemen categories, whereas black lore is the specialization of the socially inferior 'men of skill'" (p. 143). Dilley's final remark can be applied to the Wolof poet's color distinction that "these bodies of lore ought to be considered as categories of thought which are held in a relationship of complementary opposition to each other" (p.142).

91-92 The following personal names -- Yajojo, Majojo, and Anfésédé -- are not in Genesis. Once again, this is an embellishment on the part of the singer; it may also be a question of additional beliefs added to the original story by previous singers and guardians of oral traditions. However, there is a name in

Genesis (10:2), Magog, that is very similar to Majojo. The problem in trying to establish a relationship between the two names, however, is that Magog is the son of Japheth, whereas in the Wolof tale, Majojo is Shem's son.

97-99 In Genesis (10:6), Egypt is the son of Ham. In Arabic, Egypt is called *Misra* . The biblical *Egypt* is Ham's son, whereas he is Anfésédé's son in the tale. Elaborating on Egypt in the Qur'an, Y. Ali declares that "the declension of the word *misr* in the Arabic text here [S. II: 61] shows that it is treated as a common noun meaning any town, but this is not conclusive, and the reference may be to the Egypt of Pharaoh. The *Tanwin* expressing indefiniteness may mean 'any Egypt,' i.e., any country as fertile as Egypt" (*The Holy Qur'an, Text, Translation, and Commentary* by Y. Ali 1983: 32). Egypt, like Jordan, may also designate another country in Africa that has geographical features similar to those of the country of the Pharaohs.

100-142 This story about Ham fathering two children (one male, one female) is not in Genesis. Neither is Ham's going into exile. However, in Genesis (10:6, 8-11) we have the account of the story of Nimrod, son of Cush and therefore Ham's grandson. Nimrod also created the kingdoms of Babel, Erech and Accad. In his notes to *The Book of Genesis* and in the section devoted to the sons of Ham, H.E. Ryle remarks that "the races described as 'the sons of Ham' are first traced in the most southerly regions. If the name has any connexion with *Kamt,* the native name of Egypt, it is noticeable that it is here applied to the parent stock of peoples, not only in Egypt, but also in South Arabia, Phoenicia, and Syria. 'Ham is used as a synonym for Egypt in Ps. lxxviii, 5I, cv. 23, 27, cvi 22" (1921: 134). As for the sons of Cush, "the names given in this verse [Genesis X. 7, 8] are usually identified with the names of tribes, or places, on the African coast, or on the opposite shores of Arabia" (op. cit., p. 135).

Concerning the origin of the name Ham, C.A. Diop wonders where Moses could have found that name and then writes: "Right in Egypt where Moses was born, grew up, and lived until the Exodus. In fact, we know that the Egyptians called their country *Kemit*, which means "black" in their language" (1974: 7).

What we see in most of these stories is a kind of likeness between the story as it is sung in the Wolof tale and as it is in the Old Testament or the Qur'an. What happens is that the singer mixes up certain names in the genealogies of the Old Testament and since there are so many names in Genesis, it is understandable that one may link a name to the wrong genealogical line. Moreover, the singer is receiving the names and stories, not from the Bible or from the Qur'an, but from an oral source.

103 The master of the word constantly refers to the River Nile in the text (ll. 103, 113, 124, 142). During the talks I had with Sèq Ñan and Ancumbu Caam, as well as with my father, they situate the origin of the people (and particularly of the Wolof) living in present-day West Africa in East Africa, and more specifically in Egypt. Also, in the traditional lore, many traditionalists talk about the peoples of West Africa coming from the East. In most of those oral accounts, reference is made to a very large body of water situated far in the east of the continent; this must be the Nile, for, between the shores of the Atlantic Ocean and the Nile there are only two significant bodies of water, namely the River Niger and Lake Chad. Both are less extensive than the Nile and are closer

to the western edge of the African continent.

Besides the Wolof, the Mande, or Malinke, or Sos [Sosé] claim they originated in the east; they were the founders of the empire of Mali. They include the Saraxolé, who founded the empire of Ghana and who are among the most ancient people to settle in West Africa. The Mande live in present-day Mali, Guinea, Gambia and in the south and southeast of Senegal. The Saraxolé live mostly in the north-eastern part of Senegal, near the River Senegal; some of them also live on the other side of the border, in present-day Mali. On the Malinke, H. Gravrand writes:

> La tradition orale commence avec ces peuplements Sos ou Mandé. Le problème est de savoir qui sont ces Sos. La tradition orale dit simplement qu'ils viennent de Penku, de l'est. Il ne peut s'agir que de deux groupes, les Soninké et les Malinké. (1980: 48)

In a study devoted to the formation of the empire of Segou in present-day Mali, L. Kesteloot cites a singer of the Segou tradition named Taïrou, who declares that Masakoulou brought fetishes from Cairo, Egypt. Masakoulou is the ancestor of Biton Koulibaly, the heroic-mythical founder of the empire of Segou (Kesteloot 1980: 593). However, the period that Taïrou refers to may be related to the African Middle Ages and thus to the period when Islam was just coming into contact with Sub-Saharan Africa and not to the ante-Islamic period of ancient Egypt.

Another West African ethnic group which claims its origins from the East is that of the Igbo of Eastern Nigeria:

> The Igbo came from the East. It was speculated that the Igbo were either one of the lost tribes of Israel or Egypt and that for

some unspecified reasons they left the East and wandered across
the Sudan until they finally came to their present abode. (J. Okoro
Ijoma 1989: 68).

Besides the fact that most peoples of West Africa situate their origin in
the east, certain attempts have been made to establish a link between the people
of the Nile valley and the peoples now settled in other areas of the African
continent, above all those in the western part. Thus, the Senegalese historian
and Egyptologist C.A. Diop states that the founders of the Pharaonic
civilizations in Upper Egypt and the delta area actually came from farther south,
from Nubia and Ethiopia, thus from the heart of the African continent.

A. Appiah writes: "Ancient Egypt was a Negro civilization.....The moral
fruit of their civilization is to be counted among the assets of the Black world"
(1992: 101; citing C.A. Diop's *The African Origins of Civilization*, 1974). Thus,
according to Diop, there were much earlier civilizations in Nubia and Ethiopia
(present-day Sudan) and it is the founders of very refined civilizations like
Meroe who went up north and consequently created the Pharaonic civilization
of Egypt. Finally, Diop remarks: "What is noteworthy is the southern origin
of the inhabitants of the Nile Valley, which Nubians and Egyptians have always
accepted" (1974: 180).

Frank Snowden cites textual evidence on the origin of the ancient
Egyptians in the works of Greek authors such as Herodotus and Aristotle.
Citing Diodorus, Snowden oberves: "The majority of the Ethiopians, especially
those who dwelt along the Nile, according to Diodorus, were black-skinned,
flat-nosed, and wooly-haired" (Snowden 1970: 6). Citing Aristotle's
Problemata, Snowden adds: "Ethiopians were the yardstick by which antiquity
measured colored peoples. The skin of the Ethiopian was black, in fact blacker,

it was noted, than that of any other people" (ibid., p. 2). C. A. Diop relies heavily on the textual evidence left by ancient Greek and Roman authors such as Diogenes, Herodotus, Lucian, Aeschylus, Strabo, and Ammianus Marcellinus, and on the French authors M.C.F. Volney and J. J. Champollion Figeac. Most of these writers wrote on the peoples of ancient Egypt as well as on the crossbreeding between whites and blacks in that region. Diop concludes by saying: "This cursory review of the evidence of the ancient Graceo-Latin writers on the Egyptians' race shows that the extent of agreement between them is impressive" (ibid., p. 39).

Besides the textual evidence, there is also linguistic evidence. On that point, Diop states: "Wolof, a Senegalese language spoken in the extreme West of Africa on the Atlantic Ocean, is perhaps as close to ancient Egyptian as Coptic" (ibid., 46).

An exhaustive comparative linguistic study between certain languages spoken in present-day West Africa and in Ancient Egypt has been carried out by C.A. Diop, who has asserted a close connection between Wolof and ancient Egyptian. (See C.A. Diop, *Parenté génétique de l'égyptien pharaonique et des langues négro-africaines*, 1977).

On the relationship between Ancient Egypt and Ancient Greece and the heavy influence the former had had on the latter, Peter Worsley writes:

> According to [Cheikh Anta] Diop, the Greeks were little more than competent 'implementors' of Egyptian (African) discoveries and inventions. In the process, they removed the spiritual content; they reduced the unity and richness of African thought and action to a 'dry materialism,' consonant with the harshness of their Eurasiatic life, deriving from an easy, rich, peaceful, and settled social order, and permeated by a 'vitalist' philosophy,

were brought down to the level of earth-bound man.
(1977: 123)

Finally, Eugene Guernier offers another testimony on the African origin of the pharaonic civilization and dynasties, at least during their first sixteen centuries:

Les Dynasties qui régnèrent pendant les 16 premiers siècles étaient incontestablement africains; les autres, pour la plupart étaient d'importation asiatique ou méditerranéenne.

La civilisation égyptienne malgré la situation de l'Egypte au confluent des trois continents: Afrique - Asie - Europe a donc pris racine en Afrique. C'est ce que confirme l'étude de son art, de sa science et de sa métaphysique. Le miracle égyptien est bien, dans son origine, africain. Plus tard l'apport asiatique sera patent. La convergence des deux apports constituera l'amorce du miracle grec, c'est-à-dire la base même de la civilisation occidentale. (Guernier 1952: 86-87)

The reason why a historian like C. A. Diop put so much emphasis on the African and Black origins of Ancient Egypt is illustrated by Basil Davidson in the following manner: "Whenever any historical site or achievement in old Africa was found to be large and impressive, it was at once put down to the work or influence of people who had come from somewhere else" (1994: 264).

143 The toponym Nobara is not in the Old Testament.

143-167 The names Xaabil and Haabib are not in the Old Testament. However, Haabib is an Arabic name and many men in Senegal bear it. The master of the word has certainly gotten these two names Xaabil and Haabib (l. 147) from the Qur'an: "The two sons of Adam were Habil (in the English Bible, Abel) and

Qabil (in English, Cain)" (*The Holy Qur'an, Text, Translation, and Commentary* by Y. Ali 1983: 250). In the Wolof tale, Xaabil is Qabil, thus Cain, and Haabib is Habil, representing Abel. However, in the Wolof tale the singer links Cain and Abel to Ham's lineage, whereas in the Qur'an, they are Adam's sons.

150-151 In the Wolof text, the singer pronounces "Sordan" because the sound "J" as pronounced in Jordan does not exist in the Wolof language. On the pronunciation of Arabic names in African languages, V. Monteil comments:

> La *prononciation* de l'arabe est profondémént altérée. Les Noirs rencontrent de grandes difficultés à prononcer certains sons, notamment les interdentales, qui deviennent des spirantes: les sons qui correspondent, en arabe, aux deux th de l'anglais ('dur' et 'doux') deviennent, respectivement, s et z. Quant au phonème caractéristique de l'arabe, le *dâd*, il passe, généralement, à l'*l*: le 'cadi' (juge musulman) devient alkali (comme en espagnol: *alcalde*). Parfois, la transformation phonétique d'un mot arabe est telle que son identification devient malaisée: le haoussa *gaskiya* ne ressemble plus guère à l'arabe *hadîqa* (vérité). (Monteil 1963: 16)

The Wolof borrowed massively from the Arabic and French languages. In most cases, the borrowed word or expression is so diluted in Wolof that it is hard to recognize its Arabic or French origin. For instance, the word *alxuraan* stands for the Qur'an; *barke* (i. e., blessing) is originally from Arabic as well as *malaaka* (i. e., angel). (For more detail, see A. Samb, "Réflexions sur les croyances Wolof à travers les expressions linguistiques," *Notes Africaines*, 43 (1974): 77-80 and Pierre Dumont, "Les dictionnaires wolof-français et les mots d' origine française," *Notes Africaines* , 43 (1974): 80-4).

That the singer is referring to the present-day area in the Middle East that bears the name Jordan is uncertain, although that is the most likely identification.

We could attempt an identification by appealing once again to the Old Testament (Genesis 15:19) where reference is made to Sodom. But the most plausible clue as to the origin of Jordan in the Wolof memory-text may be provided by the Qur'an; moreover, that clue has a very strong historical consideration. Thus:

> Dynasties XV to XVII [Egyptian] were concerned with the Hyksos (or shepherd) kings. They were foreigners from Asia, but it is not quite clear exactly what race they belonged to....It has been conjectured that they [the foreigners] were Phoenicians, or Amalekites, or Hittites. In any case they were Semites. They founded a city called Zoam (Tanis) on one of the eastern branches of the Deltaic Nile. (*The Holy Qur'an, Text, Translation, and Commentary* by Y. Ali 1983: 405)

The name "Zoam" is similar to Sordan and is situated on the African continent, namely in Egypt. However, changes of names of regions and of towns occur constantly in oral tradition.

In the last analysis, one can assert that the Semitic contribution to Ancient Egypt started only after the Pharaonic civilization had been in existence for sixteen centuries (Guernier, 1952).

153 In Genesis 6 /20 the names of the whole clan of Ham are mentioned, but without these ethnonyms. However, a concordance between the names in the

Wolof tale and those in Genesis may be established: "Nayaasin" may be "An'amin," Egypt's (or Mizra) son and Ham's grandson. Sanaaf has the vowel configuration and medial n̲ of Canaan, Ham's son. Saxéwil may have been suggested by Hav'ilah.

155 The Empire of Ghana (sixth century to thirteenth A.D.) is the first empire to be created in West Africa. Thus, according to H. Gravrand:

> Du 8ème au 11ème siècles, il n'existe guère que l'Empire du Ghana, fondé justement par les Mandé du nord, les Soninké. Ils furent détruits en tant que puissance par les Almoravides à la fin du 11ème siècle et cette destruction entraîna au 12ème siècle un bouleversement politique considérable et des migrations de peuples. (1980: 49)

The empire of Ghana covered a large area going from the eastern part of Senegal to the mid-area of the River Niger, covering roughly what used to be the French Sudan (parts of present-day countries Senegal, Mali, Guinea, northern Ivory Coast, northern Ghana, and Niger). Actually, this empire was a centralized state and the capital was Aoudaghost. Ghana was ruled by the Saraxolé [also referred to as Soninke] who moved further west to the region of the Senegal River after the destruction of the Ghana Empire by the Almoravids. Monteil cites an Arab author named Az-Zohrî who gave 1076 as the date of the destruction of Ghana; Monteil also mentions that, according to Ibn Khaldûn, writing at the end of the sixteenth century, "les Almoravides ont attaqué Ghana, l'ont pillé et ont amené beaucoup de Noirs à embrasser l'Islam" (Monteil 1966: 26). The Almoravids, like the Berbers, the Kabyls, and the Tuaregs, were among the most ancient indigenous peoples who lived in North Africa, in the oases of the Sahara Desert and all the way to its southern fringes. R. Oliver and J. Fage give an explanation as to the origins of the Almoravid movement in their work entitled *A Short History of Africa*:

> The traditional story related by Ibn Khaldun and other Muslim authorities starts with the pilgrimage of a desert Sanhaja chieftain to Mecca. This led him to appreciate the debasement of his people's Islam, and when he came home he brought a Muslim divine from near Sijilmasa, one Ibn Yasin, to undertake a reforming mission. The Sanhaja Tuareg at first did not take well to Ibn Yasin's puritan principles. But after initial difficulties, he was able to train a religious and military élite capable of enforcing his disciplines throughout the confederacy. This was the beginning of the Almoravids. Once the Almoravid doctrine had been established among the Sanhaja tribesmen, they swept out from the desert to conquer both north and south. (Oliver and Fage 1975: 82-83)

In a footnote, Oliver and Fage add that the word Almoravid originally came from the Arabic *al-murabitun* (meaning something like 'the body of men committed to the fight of establishing true Islam').

162   Ababakar Sadèx is a deformation of Abu Bakr. In the Wolof name, the second part "Sadex" was added. He was the prophet Muhammad's father-in-law and companion. They fought in the Battle of Uhud where Muhammad was wounded. At the death of the prophet in 632, Abu Bakr replaced him and became the first Caliph, or leader of Islam. He belonged to the tribe of the Quraysh: "His early name was Abdullah and Abu Bakar was his surname. Though born in an age of misbelief, superstitions, corruptions and other vices of the Arab life, Abu Bakar was well known for his purity, simplicity,

incorruptibility, sincerity, truthfulness" (A. Rahim 1981: 58). It is interesting to note that Muhammad was Abu Bakr's son-in-law for the prophet married Abu Bakr's daughter, Aicha Bin Abi Bakr. Actually, it was from Ali's descendants that came the contact between the Berbers of North Africa and Islam. Ibn Haucal writes: "Un petit-fils d'Ali échappe à la fureur de ses ennemis [in Arabia] et arrive jusqu'en Afrique. Accueilli avec empressement par les Berbers, qui habitaient la partie occidentale de ce pays, il y fonde la dynastie Edrîsite" (1842: 155).

164 Omar Ibn Xatab was the second caliph of Islam (634-44 A.D.)

168 Bubakar Umar like Ababakar Sadex, is a deformation of Abu Bakr ben 'Omar. (See the note to line 162).

In their account on the genesis of the Almoravid movement, Oliver and Fage recall that the Almoravid movement split. One wing went north to conquer Morocco and Spain and the other wing "under Abu Bakr, struck south against the Negro empire of Ghana" (Fage and Oliver 1975: 83). The Abu Bakr mentioned in the Wolof epic tale is probably a conflation of the seventh century and the twelfth century figures of the same name, since he is both a figure of high antiquity and a leader who came to West Africa. Another Abu Bakr played a role in West African history five centuries later, Abì Bakr al-wàrglànì. Tadeusz Lewicki remarks that Abù zakarìyà (or Abì Bakr al-wàrglànì) "était natif de Wàrglàn (Ouargla), comme son ethnique indique, et qu'il vivait dans la deuxième moitié du Ve = XIe s. et au commencement du VIe = XIIe siècle. Il était encore en vie en 504 = 1110/1111" (Lewicki 1960: 2, citing *Kitàb as Sìra wahbàr al-a'imma*).

There are examples of conflations and appropriations of historical names in the European medieval vernacular epic. In the Romance epic *Chanson d'Antioche,* "Graindor [a jongleur] conflates Robert II, count of Flanders, with his father Robert 'the Frisian' who was not present on the expedition but had journeyed to the Holy Land in 1087" (J. Duggan 1986: 298).

Bubakar Umar is also mentioned under the name Abubacar (P. Diagne 1967: 150). The Almoravid Abu Bakr's companion was Abdallah Ibn Yasin. However, in the Wolof tale, Abubakar's companion is Ibn Xabab. If we tally the two statements, we can conclude that Ibn Yasin and Ibn Xatab are actually the same person.

In the translation (from Arabic), of Siré-Abbâs-Soh's *Chroniques du Foûta sénégalais,* M. Delafosse cites a monograph written by a colonial administration called Colombani; the latter monograph recounts the meeting between Abu Bakr and El-Adrami. However, contrary to the Wolof griot, Colombani is elaborating on the Arabic folk epic known as the *Hilaliya.* In this instance, Abu Bakr and El-Adrami are fighting a Jewish King in Atar (present-day Mauritania). Ghana is not mentioned; the region of Fuuta is mentioned. It is worth quoting Colombani at length:

> A la fin du onzième ou au commencement du douzième, un grand nombre de tribus berbères, chassées du Maghreb par l'invasion hilalienne, descendirent vers le sud, conduites par un personnage nommé sîdi Boubakar ben Amar [Bubakar Umar or Abu Bakr]. Elles s'avancèrent justque dans l'oued Noun, où régnait un roi juif. Ce dernier fut tué au cours d'un combat. Un autre roi juif, qui avait le roi de l'Oued Noun sous sa dépendance, habitait dans l'Adrar, dans la région d'Atar. Sa ville était gardée par des chiens qui en défendaient l'accès à tous ceux gui l'approchaient avec de mauvais desseins. Lorsque Sîdi Boubakar ben Amar apprit cette particularité, il fut indécis sur ce qu'il ferait.

Retournerait-il sur ses pas ou marcherait-il contre les gens aux chiens? Il réunit donc les chefs de ses soldats et leur demanda conseil. Or un saint homme aimé de dieu, nommé El-Imâm El-Adrami, se leva et lui dit: "O prince, marche vers eux, je suffirai seul à tenir les chiens en respect." - "Pourrais-tu vraiment le faire?" Leur demanda Sîdi Boubakar. - "Oui," répondit El-Adrami. La colonne se mit donc en route et, lorsqu'elle approcha d'Atar, la ville aux chiens, El-Adrami se porta en avant des troupes.

Les chiens se précipitèrent sur celles-ci; mais, quand ils virent El-Adrami, ils s'arrêtèrent auprès de lui et l'entourèrent sans lui faire aucun mal. Ce que voyant, les juifs d'Atar comprirent que c'en était fait de leur puissance et, après un combat livré en dehors de la ville, ils y rentrèrent et s'y fortifièrent. Ils ne purent résister longtemps à l'attaque de leurs ennemis.

Atar ouvrit ses portes à l'armée de Boubakar. Mais la victoire coûta cher aux vainqueurs, car El-Imâm El-Adrami fut tué, le jour même où les troupes assaillantes entrèrent dans la ville, par un Juif, qui, quoique aveugle, tirait de l'arc.

L'expédition de Boubakar ben Amar se dirigea ensuite sur le Tagant, dont les habitants étaient des foulanes (Peuls ou toucouleurs). Ceux-ci rejetèrent les troupes de Boubakar vers le Blâd-et-Tekrour (pays des Toucouleurs). Ce pays toucouleur n'était autre que le Hodh, où régnait un roi foulane nommé Aïl. (Colombani [December 1912]; cited by M. Delafosse in *Chroniques du Foûta sénégalais*, 1913, pp. 133-34)

Another interesting case of conflation in the West African area is found in the Bambara epic of Mali (*La prise de Dionkoloni*) sung by Sissoko Kabinè, recorded and transcribed by L. Kesteloot, G. Dumestre, and J. B. Traoré. In that epic, the Bambara hero Silamakan of Segou defeats Dionkoloni. Then, the griots lengthen the eqic by adding a new episode. The latter episode concerns a totally different place, ethnic group, and hero and is about Ardo Silamaka

Diko the Peul hero of Macina who rebelled against the Bambara King of Segou DaMonzon. Ardo Silamaka was killed during that rebellion. It is important to note that Silamak*an* the Bambara hero and Ardo Silmak*a* the Peul hero lived at the same time and this fact can explain their conflation:

> Les griots ont donc joint les deux histoires, et confondu l'Ardo Silamaka et Silamakan Koumba pour le plus grand bien de la littérature. L'art des griots a rendu la couture invisible et doublé l'envergure du texte épique. Coupant par-ci, modifiant par là, ils ont intensifié la cohésion psychologique des personnages et agrandi la dimension des conflits. (Kesteloot, Dumestre, Traoré 1975: 15)

Things get a little bit complicated with the following statement:

> Vers 1061, les guerriers almoravides d'Abou Bark [Abu Bakr]
> et *de son frère Yaya Ibn Omar* se heurtèrent à l'empire animiste du Ghana, qui brillait depuis le IVe siècle de notre ère, dans le Soudan occidental, entre l'Atlantique et le fleuve Niger.
> (Daniel A. Cissé 1988: 20; [emphasis added])

In the above account, Abu Bakr's companion is named Yaya Ibn Omar, not Al-Hadrami. Additionally, Yaya is Abu Bakr's brother. We can infer that Yaya is the equivalent of Al-Hadrami and Mbaarik Bô. There are variations according to the various versions coming from different areas of West Africa.

I. Lapidus writes concerning the Muslim influence in the Sudan as well as on the Almoravids:

> The Muslims provided the ruler with interpreters and officials. These local influences, reinforced by Almoravid, economic, diplomatic, and cultural penetration, and by the proselytizing

activities of the Almoravid leader, Abu Bakr (d. 1087), and by his colleague Imam al-Hadrami (d. 1096), prompted the acceptance of Islam. (1988: 491)

The Arabic word Imam means a "guide", a "leader"; thus, in Lapidus's description, Abubakar's companion is called Al-Hadrami, whereas in the Wolof tale it is Mbaarik Bô. Is Mbaarik Bô a Wolof local adaptation of an Arab or Almoravid figure such as al-Hadrami? That is possible. In the Wolof tale, upon the death of Abu Bakr, Mbaarik Bô, his companion, marries his wife Fatumata Abraham Sal (l. 448).

On the question of *jihad*, Y. Ali's definition can serve as a background:

It [*jihad*] may require fighting in God's cause, as a form of self-sacrifice. But its essence consists in (1) a true and sincere faith, which so fixes its gaze on God, that all selfish or worldly motives seem paltry and fade away, and (2) an earnest and ceaseless activity, involving the sacrifice (if need be) of life, person, or property, in the service of God. Mere brutal fighting is opposed to the whole spirit of Jihad, while the sincere scholar's pen or preacher's voice or wealthy man's contributions may be the most valuable forms of jihad. (*The Holy Qur'an, Text, Translation, and Commentary* by Y. Ali 1983: 444)

The very concept of *jihad* originated in Arabia at the time of Muhammad. However, we witness an evolution of that concept. In the nineteenth century in West Africa, the accent of *jihad* was put mostly on physical coercion, on war rather than on the scholar's pen, the preacher's voice, or a man's wealth as said in the Qur'an. Since the Almoravid and other Arab conquerors were Muslim, they waged *jihads* against the local Black populations, often with the aid of local black allies. Thus, they found allies among black leaders such as Osman Dan Fodio (or Uthman dan Fodio 1754 - 1817) in northern Nigeria, and Al-Hajj Umar Taal in northeastern Senegal, among others; the latter fought and converted their own people to Islam. Among these events were the activities of Umar Taal.

(On the history of Hausaland and Northern Nigeria; the establishment of Islam in Hausaland; the Islamic Reform Movement; education and intellectual life among the Muslim Fulaani of Northern Nigeria; Sufism in West Africa; Dan Fodio's mystical experiences; Fodio's personal contribution to the Holy War, see the comprehensive study of Mervyn Hiskett, *The Sword of Truth - The Life and Times of the Shehu Usuman Dan Fodio*, 1973. On Al-Hajj Umar and his clash with the French, his conquest of the Khassonké country (Kaarta), his siege of Médine in 1857, and Umar's return to Fuuta Toro in 1858-1859, see Yves-Jean Saint-Martin, *Le Sénégal sous le second empire*, pp. 353-369).

In order to better grasp the nature of the relationship between the various local populations of the valley of the River Senegal as well as the influence of Islam, it is important to dwell for a while on the relation between the Almoravids and the local populations. Moreover, in the Wolof tale, there is a close association between the local populations and the Almoravids.

In *L'Islam et l'histoire du Sénégal* (p.4), A. Samb observes that the Almoravid movement was very strong in the valley area in the period 1040 - 1147.

In the same order of things, Nehemia Levtzion writes:

> When the Sanhaja nomads reached the southern fringes of the Sahara, this region was by no means empty. Archeological and traditional evidence confirm that the sedentary negro

152

> population had previously extended farther north from its present habitation, covering the Hodth, Tagant, and Adrar. The gradual dessication of the Sahara, caused by climatic changes, initiated the retreat of the sedentary population, and this retreat was accelerated by the invading nomads, who pushed the Sudanese southwards....
>
> Some time between the second and the fifth centuries, the northern among the Sudanese peoples -- Wolof-Serer, Soninke, and Songhay -- came into direct contact with the newcomers from across the Sahara. This contact, accompanied by the well-known pressure of nomads on sedentary people, stimulated development of political organization among the Sudanese. (Levetzion 1976: 121)

Note that the Western Sudan is also simply called the Sudan or French Sudan. The latter expression was coined during the era of French colonization; the French Sudan was made up of the eastern part of present-day Senegal, northern present-day Guinea, and most regions of present-day Mali. French Sudan is distinct from the country called Sudan in East Africa.

One of the most important figures of *Jihad* is Al-Haj Umar from Fuuta. He lived in the nineteenth century and fought the French as well as converting the local population to Islam. However, the spread of *Jihad* as well as the formation of the Muslim state of Fuuta are much earlier than the reign of Al-Hajj Umar. Moreover, there was a close cooperation between the Almoravids and the leaders of Fuuta. This cooperation started in the eleventh century:

Le Tékrour [or Takruur], dont l'aristocratie est acquise à l'Islam, abrite au XIe siècle le mouvement Almoravide. L'appui militaire que le lam Toro accorde au prédicateur A. Ibn Yasin et à son allié, le chef Lemtonna Abubacar, conféra à l'épopée Almoravide toute sa force. Aoudaghost [capital of the Ghana Empire] est détruit par les Tékrouriens et leurs alliés berbères en 1054. Ghana, qui était à partir du IVe siècle l'état le plus important de l'Afrique Occidentale, est définitivement ruiné en 1075. (P. Diagne 1967: 150)

The concept of *jihad* was taught (or brought) to the people of Fuuta by the Almoravids. On the strength and influence of the Almoravids, Diagne adds that "l'épopée almoravide témoigne certes des possibilités que la nouvelle religion [Islam] possédait dès ses débuts pour se frayer une voie au bout du sabre des croyants" (Diagne, ibid., 153).

A source on the *jihad* in Fuuta as well as on al Hajj Umar is the work of D. Robinson. This author combines elements he has gotten from frequent fieldwork in that region of Senegal with written sources on the same topic. D. Robinson enlisted local people in the various stages of his project: collection, translation, transcription, and critical study (Cf. *The Islamic Regime of Fuuta Tooro*, 1984).

The question of *Jihad* in West Africa should be appreciated within the wider context of the tensions, conflicts, battles, crusades between the medieval Christian Western Europe and the Muslim Orient. In his discussion of Raymond Lulle's apologetics (more precisely, the latter's defense of Christianity in the 13th century), Ramón Sugranyes de Franch points ou that "la chrétienté a cru à un certain moment que le monde musulman pourrait être attiré dans le giron de l'église" (1983: 376). However, in his writings, Lulle opposed any use of force in the conversion of people to christianity. Sugranyes de French adds that "Lulle s'oppose à l'usage de la force pour conquérir les âmes et fait l'apologie des armes spirituelles - celles qui ne s'émoussent ni se rompent, celles qui, plus on les utilise plus elles deviennent aigües et efficaces -, les armes du Christ et des Apôtres" (Sugranyes de Franch, Ibidem).

171-182 Bubakar Umar and Mbaarik Bô travel together from Jordan to Ghana. Actually, Ghana is just a temporary stop, for as we will see later in the tale, the two companions will go farther west.

Monteil mentions the destruction of Ghana by the Almoravid chief, Abu Bakr ben 'Omar (p. 26). Concerning Mbaarik Bô, Monteil observes:

> Les chroniqueurs ne s'accordent pas sur l'origine de ce Mbârik. Les uns prétendent qu'il fut confié, tout jeune, à Ibn 'Omar [or Bubakar Umar], au cours de ses voyages au Soudan. Les autres, plus nombreux, soutiennent qu'il [Mbarik Bô] avait été acheté (*dyend-on* ["bought" in Wolof]) par le chef almoravide. (1966: 27)

In Ñan's epic tale, Mbaarik Bô has his nose pierced and wears a ring (ll. 175-181). This is an indication that Mbaarik was of local indigenous stock for the Arabs and Almoravids who were converted to Islam (at least the men) did not have the custom of piercing their nose, forbidden by Islam; men are not supposed to wear jewelry and this prohibition is dictated by the fact that among the principles and tenets of Islam, humility and simplicity in appearance are very important. Additionally, Mbaarik was converted into Islam by Bubakar (l. 257).

Another feature of this passage is the doubling or pairing of the two heroes: Bubakar Umar and Mbaarik Bô. Doubling is a characteristic of many epic tales which typically feature a pair of heroes. Other notable instances of doubling are Roland and Oliver in *Song of Roland,* Gilgamesh and Enkidu in *Gilgamesh,* and Achilles and Patroclus in the *Iliad.*

A. Lord draws a parallel between the *Iliad* and *Gilgamesh* by comparing Achilles to Gilgamesh when considering which member of the respective pairs will perish: Enkidu dies, not Gilgamesh, and Patroclus, not Achilles (Lord 1960: 197). One must note that both in *Gilgamesh* and in the *Iliad*, the gods intervene whereas in the Wolof tale there is no direct divine help. Interestingly enough, and conversely to *Gilgamesh* and the *Iliad*, Bubakar Umar is the one who dies in the Wolof tale, not his aide (l. 355).

174 The identification of Masaasi is problematic.

187-189 There is a chronological reversal in this instance. The formation of the state of Ghana occurred around the 4th century A. D. (Diagne 1967: 150), whereas Gana Kamara came to power in the 11th century. The phonetic similarity between 'Ghana' and 'Gana' has led the master of the word to posit the second as the origin of the first. However, despite this chronological discordance, the fact remains that the state of Ghana was created by the Saraxolé.

The Saraxolé country is called Guidimaka. The Saraxolé also have a legend concerning the origins of the name Guidimaka. The latter is linked to Gana Kamara. Once again, Colombani's monograph describes Kamara's battles against Sunjaata Keïta, emperor of Mali as well as the former's migration to the South and the subsequent foundation of the country of the Saraxolé:

Ganné Kamara, chef guerrier qui s'était acquis une grande réputation de bravoure dans les innombrables combats qu'il avait livrés aux ennemis de son chef Soundiata Keïta, roi du pays mandé, se sépara de ce dernier à la suite d'un dissentiment et, avec un grand nombre d'hommes (la légende dit 999), se dirigea vers le Ouagadou, où il conquit une quinzaine de villages dont il se proclama chef; que soundiata Keïta, jaloux de la puissance croissante de Ganné, envoya, contre lui une armée; que Ganné mit cette armee en deroute et qu'il se dirigea ensuite vers le sud à la recherche d'un royaume. (Colombani [1912]; cited by M. Delafosse in *Chroniques du Foûta sénégalais*, 1913, pp. 131-32).

In present-day Senegal, there are men who bear the name Gana. V. Monteil attributes the fall of Ghana to the Almoravids. This assertion is based on accounts given first by the Arab author, Az-Zohri, and later on by Ibn Khaldûn who said that the Almoravids attacked and ransacked the Empire of Ghana.

Monteil writes: "Après la destruction de Ghana par le chef des Almoravides Abu Bakr Ben 'Omar, les peuplades noires qui l'habitaient se dispersèrent vers l' ouest" (1966: 26).

Most traditionalists of Senegal do mention the founding and fall of Ghana in their performances (Ñan, for instance), but what the Ghana episode highlights is the continual westward movement of the black populations that created and inhabited the Empire of Ghana (Levtzion, 1976). Thus, after the fall of Ghana, the Saraxolé moved farther west to the valley of the Senegal River and occupied Fuuta Tooro. (On the fall of Ghana, see B. Davidson 1965: 43-44).

The Arab author Ibn Hawqal (also known as Abū 'l-Qāsim Muhammad al-Nusaybi) gave a detailed description of the trade routes between North Africa and Africa South of the Sahara and the Sudan in general (see J.F.P. Hopkins, N.

Levtzion, *Corpus of early Arabic sources for West African history*, pp. 43-44).

222   The theme of the dream as a way of foreseeing future events is an important component of the epic world. Bubakar Umar will be killed by the Sereer chief, Hamar-the Scolder-of-Old-People. Bubakar does not foresee his death in the dream, but he sees his encounter with Hamar. Premonitory dreams are common in epic traditions. In the *Song of Roland*, Charles has many dreams, for instance about the battles he is going to wage, about bears and snakes who want to devour his men, about a lion (J. Bédier, ed., pp. 211-13). Then, Charles has another dream about thirty bears the largest of whom is attacked by his dog (pp. 213-15). Scholars have interpreted these dreams variously; for instance, the thirty bears are said to represent the Saracens and the dog is the champion Thierry who will defend Charles' point of view in a judicial combat. The bears speak just like the men in the epic.

230   The village of Muderi Jaawara is situated in Upper Senegal, a region primarily inhabited by the Saraxolé and whose main town is Bakel, which was developed by Governor Faidherbe in the nineteenth century. Faidherbe built a military fortress in Bakel; the ruins of that fortress can still be seen today on top of a hill overlooking the town. Jaawara is also a Saraxolé family name.

In fact there are two separate villages bearing the same name Muderi Jawara and seven kilometers distant from each other (information provided to me by a personal friend called Ibrahima Bâ on June 19, 1993 in Dakar, Senegal. Mr Bâ is originally from that area and belongs to the Saraxolé ethnic group).

231   There is a discrepancy in the story of Abraham Sal for when Bubakar

Umar and Mbaarik Bô arrive at Muderi Jaawara, the man they find there bears the Semitic name Abraham. The Biblical Abraham is, of course, a founding figure in the three great Western and Middle Eastern religious traditions, Judaism, Christianity, and Islam. His name is found in the Old Testament as well as in the Qur'an. In lines 268-269, we learn that Abraham Sal was converted to Islam by Bubakar Umar and his companion. While 'Abraham' is a name coming ultimately from the Jewish tradition, Sal is a typical Tukulor name of northern Senegal. Then, we are told twice (ll. 232, 270) that Abraham thought Bubakar was Bilal, the companion of the prophet Muhammad (l. 271). If Abraham were aware of the existence of Bilal, he must have had a fairly detailed knowledge of Islam before B. Umar's arrival. This strains one's sense of verisimilitude, as non-Muslim Africans are extremely unlikely to have had a thorough knowledge of Islam and of its history in the Middle Ages. Conversely, the master of the word may be implying that Abraham Sal was just superficially converted to Islam. This was very common in Africa. I. Lapidus notes that "while Islam became an imperial cult and the religion of state elites and trading peoples, the agricultural populations maintained their traditional beliefs" (1988: 491). In the same vein, P. Diagne declares that: "L'Islam très tôt se concilie les détenteurs du pouvoir politique tandis que les masses restent réticentes ou tout au moins réservées" (1967: 154).

The early presence of Islam in African courts has been well documented:

La religion musulmane s'est implantée en tant que religion de cour. Propagée par des lettrés étrangers admis dans l'entourage des rois autochtones en qualité de conseillers, elle s'est trouvée longtemps confinée aux milieux aristocratiques. (G. Nicolas 1978: 366)

In the tale, it is said that Abraham Sal was the ancestor of all the people bearing the name "Sal," among the Lamtooro, the Tukulor people (l. 274-276). The Lamtooro constitute an aristocratic feudal ruling class among the Tukulor: Thus, Abraham Sal is represented as a chief and a mythical or actual founder of a clan and a village just like Njaajaan Njaay.

The relations between Islam and the African chiefs is summed up by J. O. Hunwick, who writes that the advantages to a ruler of adopting Islam seem to be rather less than obvious. If a ruler were directly involved in trade, the adoption of Islam might enable him to get better terms, or perhaps to obtain 'strategic' commodities -- swords, chain-mail, and horses for example. On the other hand, the ruler's non-acceptance of Islam did not exclude his state from fruitful contact with the Islamic trading network or, in several known cases, from at least some of the advantages of Arabic literacy. Hunwick concludes his remarks by giving the example of ancient Ghana as described by the Arab author, Al-Bakri:

> There [in Ghana] the ruler was a non-Muslim, though apparently well disposed towards Muslims. He allowed the Muslim merchants to establish a town of their own near his capital and he employed Muslims in the most important state posts as ministers, including one who was in charge of finances, and as 'interpreters', who presumably handled the diplomatic side of foreign affairs. (J. O. Hunwick 1974: 14-15)

232   Bilal was a companion of the prophet Muhammad, as the poet states in l. 271. He was also the muezzin, calling the faithful to prayer. It is generally said that Bilal was the first Black convert to Islam, an attribute emphasized by Senegalese Muslims. The story of Bilal is linked to that of the historical Abu

Bakr (b. 573 - d. 634). Abu Bakr was a rich tradesman and used to buy slaves and then set them free; one of these slaves was Bilal. A. Dhina remarks:

Il [Abu Bakr] s'employait à secourir les plus malheureux, notamment les eslaves que les païens maltraitaient à cause de leur adhésion à l'Islam. Il les rachetait pour les affranchir, comme il le fit pour le Nègre Bilâl, futur mou'adhim du prophète. (Amar Dhina 1986: 15)

The figure of Bilal is also present in the myths of origins of the Mandinka people of Mali. Actually, Bilal is linked to the ancestry of Mandinka kings, founders and heroes. D. Conrad writes:

Bilāl ibn Rabāh, whom the Manding call Bilali, was a freed black slave who became a companion of the Prophet and the first *mu'adh dĥin* (caller to prayers).

Freed by Abū Bakr, a prominent Muslim who was impressed by the strength of the slave's conviction, Bilāl joined the company of Muhammad. (1985: 37).

Along the same lines, Massa Diabaté recounts how Bilal (the Prophet Muhammad's slave) had two sons; at his turn, the eldest son engendered three children; the latter migrated to West Africa and consequently founded the Mande Country:

Jon Bilal, l'esclave du Prophète, eut deux fils, Mamadu Kanu er Kaba Malike. L'aîné, Mamadu Kanu, engendra trois fils: Kanu Sinbon, Kanu Nyongon Sinbon et Lavali Sinbon.

Les trois Sinbon vinrent au Mande où ils fondérent le village de Kikoroni. (M. M. Diabaté 1970: 12).

Thus, in Arab culture, Bilal is assimilated with slavery. Up to today, the Black person does not have a high regard in that culture. This lack of respect and consideration for the Black person goes back to the days of Bilal. There is, however, a very important distinction to be made to the effect that the Bilal episode was not initially in the Qu'ran. It is much later that the commentators and exegetes of the Holy Book have introduced that episode in the Qu'ran. Along the same lines, Daniel Amara Cissé writes:

> Le nègre <<bilal>> est toujours l'équivalent de l'esclave et du damné dans l'esprit et la culture arabe. (1988: 232)

234 This line is among the most important of the epic tale, positing Njaajaan Njaay as ruler of Waalo as a unified state. Nothing is known about the historical Njaajaan Njaay except for what oral tradition tells about him. Bubakar Umar is Njaajaan's father in the tale as well as in many other accounts (Monteil, Barry). There are two traditions concerning the period during which Njaajaan Njaay lived. R. Cornevin makes the following remark:

> Qui est- ce N'Diadiane N'Diaye? Selon Rousseau (1931) ce serait un chef ouolof et l'action se situerait au XIIe siècle; selon J.L. Monod (1926) il s'agirait d'un descendant d' Abdu Dardai et l'action se situerait au XIVe siècle. (1960: 266)

Rousseau bases his study on the writings left by an educated Senegalese man called Rawane Boy. Rawane lived in Saint-Louis and served in the French colonial administration from 1866 to 1908. He was the interpreter of the French governor Pinet-Laprade. Rawane notes that "N'Diadiane N'Diaye vient, lui aussi, de l'est" (Rousseau 1931: 345). As to the chronology of Njaajaan's reign, there are variations among the various scholars and griots. B. Barry writes:

> Amadou WADE ('Chronique du Walo...') situe le règne de Ndyaadyaan Ndaay entre 1187 et 1202. Boubou Sall propose 1215 comme date initiale du règne; Yoro DYAW qui donne au règne une durée de quarante ans (seize ans selon A. WADE), le place de 1212 à 1256. Enfin, pour LE BRASSEUR, il ne règne que deux ans. (Barry 1985: 46)

According to Ñan, Njaajaan stayed for 16 years in Waalo (l. 949). R. Cornevin (1960, 266) simply says that Njaajaan ruled Waalo in the twelfth century. Still, according to Cornevin, J. L. Arnod (1926) states that Njaajaan ruled Waalo in the fourteenth century.

Njaajaan is said to have taken an active part in the formation of the Wolof kingdom of Jolof (Rousseau, p. 340). C. A. Diop states that Abou Dardaï was Njaajaan's father (1949: 850), the role played in the text by Bubakar Umar.

A. Samb gives yet another version on the origins of Njaajaan: "Abû Dardâ'i, un des compagnons de Mahomet, arrivé sur les rives du Sénégal aurait épousé une Noire appelée Absa dont il aurait eu N'Dyâdyân N'Dyây" (A. Samb 1974: 6; citing Brasseur, "Détails historiques et politiques," 1778).

Henri Gaden gives another version as to the origins of Njaajaan:

> Le fameux Ndyadyane Ndyâye était un marabout toucouleur originaire de Podor. Son père se serait appelé Abdoullâhi et ses descendants rattachent leur origine à ce légendaire Abou-Dardaï,

qui passe pour avoir apporté l'Islam dans le pays et qu'on dit avoir été enterré sous le tumulus situé en face de Mboumba du Lâo. On pourrait alors supposer que, cette famille de l'empereur du Tekroûr - *qui n'a laissé aucune trace dans le pays* - ayant été chassée du Tekroûr, son dernier représentant réussit à se sauver et à se réfugier, au Ouâlo, où il fut au bout de quelque temps élu chef parce que marabout et sage. (H. Gaden; cited by M. Delafosse in *Chroniques du Foûta sénégalais*, p. 184; [author's emphasis])

Later on, H. Gaden mentions a Wolof griot named Bouna (probably his informant) as well as giving his personal opinion on the origin of Njaajaan:

Je m'empresse d'ajouter que ni Bouna ni les griots ouolofs n'ont aucun souvenir de l'Empire de Tekroûr. Bouna dit seulement que Ndyadyane, l'ancêtre fondateur de la dynastie, fit son apparition dans le Ouâlo par le marigot de Menguèye; que c'était un marabout originaire de Podor, Fils d'Abdou llâhi, et descendant d'Abou-Dardaï; qu'il fut nommé chef et que lui et ses premiers descendants furent des hommes religieux et pacifiques et que ce n'est qu'à partir d'un de ses descendants sur lequel je n'ai pas pour le moment, de renseignements, que les *bourba* [Wolof kings] retournèrent au paganisme et devinrent conquérants. L'hypothèse rattachant Ndyadyane aux chefs du Tekroûr est donc personnelle et repose sur peu de preuves. Elle a contre elle d'être complètement ignorée par la famille actuelle des *bourba* et il paraît vraisemblable que, s'ils descendaient de l'empereur du Tekroûr, ils le sauraient. (H. Gaden, op. cit., pp. 184-85; [Author's emphases]).

In the 19th century, Joseph Du Sorbier de la Tourrasse traveled to Wolof country. There, he met a fisherman named Souleyman. The latter took the French writer along for a fishing party. Souleyman told the author about the origins of the Wolof and mentioned that a man named Bay Samsane was the first ancestor of the Wolof (J. S. de La Tourrasse, 1897?: 164-67).

It is important to keep in mind that the Wolof griot mentions that Njaajaan's mother (Fatumata Sal) is of Tukulor stock, not his father.

A detailed study of the history of the Waalo state is Boubacar Barry's *Le Royaume du Waalo. Le Sénégal avant la conquête* (Paris: Éditions Karthala, 1985).

According to Monteil, prior to the advent of Njaajaan, Waalo was dependent on the state of Fuuta, which was ruled by petty Peul chiefs; Waalo was then a small state (Monteil, p. 27); an important feature of most African medieval states was that there was no centralized power before the advent of a unifier like Njaajaan in Waalo or Sunjaata in Mali:

> Sudanic states had their origin in family groups led by patriarchs, councils of elders, or chiefs of villages. The state came into existence when a local elder, an immigrant warrior or perhaps a priestly ruler, established his control over other communities. (Lapidus 1988: 490)

Overall, there were powerful kingships in medieval West Africa. As a closing remark on state and kingdom formation, Basil Davidson remarks that "one needs to see [these] Wolof Kingdoms [Jolof, Kayor, Waalo, Bawol] as part of a process of state formation which arose, primarily, from the *internal* dynamics of the region" (1994: 39, [Author's emphasis]).

Apparently the historical Njaajaan unified the clans and smaller states; prior to him, there were warring factions in Waalo. Abdoulaye-Bara Diop writes:

Le thème constant des différentes versions de la légende de
Njaajaan Njaay est celui d'un sage choisi comme souverain du
pays parce qu'il a réussi à ramener la paix entre les bélligérants
en arbitrant équitablement leurs conflits de propriété. (1981: 135)

235-244   It is a commonplace among researchers that one should be careful
about certain statements coming from the griot. This is not because the griot is
totally unreliable, but because there are different versions of a given story and
they need to be tested against each other. The griot may embellish his
performance according to the size of the presents he expects from members of
the audience. Iba Der Thiam comments:

> Beaucoup de traditions orales donnent une vision que j'appellerai
> mutilante, de l'histoire. C'est le cas, lorsque la tradition orale n'a
> fixé le souvenir que d'une personne, ou d'un groupe dominant
> c'est-à-dire des classes privilégiées, laissant ainsi inexplorées des
> aires sociales autrement plus importantes. (1980: 75)

Thus, Ñan talks about my ancestors, about my father. According to the
griot, our ancestors took part in the founding history of Waalo, but to what
extent?

In his study of the *Sunjaata Epic,* G. Innes (1974: 10-11) cites instances
in which the griot's statements appear to be a public relations ploy. Innes shows
how at a performance a griot would rehearse the praises of certain members of
the audience, and a man who is the object of such attention is obliged to give
the griot an appropriate reward. But if that man cannot afford to give what is
expected from him, he is likely to be publicly humiliated by the griot's reaction
to what he considers inadequate recompense. Conversely, if the person being
sung about or praised steps forward with a substantial present or if the griot

senses that that person is going to be generous, the griot may add to his story elements that never existed. On a more personal level, still in his study of the *Sunjaata Epic*, G. Innes gives the example of a member of the audience named Sidibé, a noble who confided to Innes that:

> listening to the Sunjata epic not only gives a man a feeling of intense pride, but also makes him look at his own life -- what has he achieved, has he acquitted himself in a way befitting a man in his position, has he enhanced the family name, or at any rate not diminished it. (Innes 1974: 10)

Another case study, that of D. Robinson on the *jihad* of Al-Hajj Umar, also highlights the liberty that the griot may take, according to the composition of his audience as well as the goals he is aiming to achieve. There are several versions of that *jihad* and Robinson argues that:

> Ces épisodes [of the *jihad*] sont l'apanage des récits des griots qui, quant à eux, ne s'intéressent guère aux implications théologiques du *jihad*, mais davantage à la possibilité de satisfaire un auditoire aux croyances et pratiques religieuses variées. Les griots jouissaient de la liberté de critiquer leurs protecteurs et de celle de pouvoir éventuellement en changer. (1985: 419)

Robinson adds:

> En conséquence, plusieurs griots prirent quelques libertés avec la tradition d'Umar et le *jihad*. Sans toutefois se montrer hostiles, ils ne se privèrent pas d'augmenter leurs histoires de récits à perspectives multiples. (Ibid.)

Commenting on the political organization of Waalo, J. Robin remarks that it is the clan of the Diaw who kept the state of Waalo together. He writes:

> L'unité et l'équilibre intérieurs du Walo n'ont pu être maintenus que par des compromis perpétuels dont tout le mérite revient aux Diaw.
> Ces Diaw pourraient être les derniers vestiges de la dynastie Peule des Dyajo. (J. Robin 1946: 252)

The clan of the Diop is not mentioned in Robin's passage. However, the clan of the Diop were involved in the polical affairs of Waalo. Elaborating on the ruling families and princes (*kangamm*) of Waalo, H. Azan remarks: "Le *Békio* ou *Béthio* possédait tout le pays compris entre Kham et Mengueye. Il était choisi de préférence dans la famille des Diop" (1864a: 355).

The guiding principle on the question of how much participation a clan or family had in the formation and rule of the kingdom of Waalo is that one must be very cautious. The griot may state certain facts simply to please a certain audience; conversely, he may decide to forego or to delete some other facts for the same reason.

238 *Jogomaay* was a dignitary title. The *jogomaay* was among those who elected the barak (besides the *dyawdin* and the *maalo*). Thus, according to Barry (1985: 73), "le *dyogomaay* était le maître des eaux, président de l'assemblée, et gouverneur du royaume pendant les interrègnes." Then the *jogomaay* was accountable to the barak: "Chaque matin, le *dyogomay* était tenu de se rendre chez le *brak* pour lui rendre compte des faits de la veille et prendre ses instructions pour la journée" (Monteil 1966: 35).

Even though the Wolof poet says that the barak was the chief of the army, it seems that he had all the attributes of a king as well as those of a healer. B. Durand writes: "le *Brak* du Walo semble lui aussi avoir conservé un caractère sacré trés prononcé; chargé d'apporter l'abondance dans le pays, soumis au rituel païen du bain sacré et aux différents sacrifices, significatifs de sa sanctification originelle, le *brak* est supposé par le peuple avoir 'le don de guérir' " (1983: 343).

Thus, the military function of the *Brak* was paramount. As pointed out by V. Monteil, "le Brak, qui avait le commandement suprême du pays, n'était, en fait chargé d'aucune fonction administrative" (1966: 34). Additionally, the barak' s power was counterbalanced by other institutions such as the parliament or the Council of Elders. J. Vansina observes that within the African kingdoms, "a recurrent, but not universal, feature is the existence at the top of the state structure of one or several councils which balance the power wielded by the king" (1962: 328).

Y. J. Saint-Martin discusses in detail the political structure of the Kingdom of Waalo as well as the role that the dignitaries such as the *brak*, the *Kangām*, the *diawdin*, and the *sek ak baor* assembly (*Le Sénégal sous le second Empire*, pp. 65-68).

253 The story of Hawaat is not mentioned in Monteil's text (1966). Perhaps the name was added by the singer.

258 Concerning the name "Gaye", Monteil notes: "Les *sant* [i.e. families] qui quittèrent le Walo pour suivre Ndyadyan dans son exil au Dyolof sont les suivants: Dyaw, Gey, Sek, Yada, Saar, Waad, Bôôy" (1962: 32). In Wolof, variation between the names "Gey" [or Guèye] and "Gaye" is dialectal.

261 The name "Aydara" is mentioned neither in Monteil's version (1966) nor in Barry (1985: 311-328). The most plausible explanation for the insertion of Berber or Arab names is that they add more authority to the narrative. The same motivation may be behind ll. 518-19 where the singer claims that a Moor and a white person look alike in paleness.

In his study of the epic of Mali, Youssouf Cissé writes in a footnote: "En Afrique occidentale, ceux qui se disent descendants du prophète Mahomet se font appeler Haïdara. Ce mot est en réalité la déformation du mot arabe *el-haydar*, <<le lion>>, que l'on donna comme surnom à Ali, gendre de Mahomet, à cause de sa grande bravoure" (1988: 91).

According to V. Monteil, the ancestor of the people bearing the name Aydara was from Morocco and was a descendant of the prophet Muhammad. Thus:

> Les chérifs (*shortâ*), ou descendants du Prophète de l'Islam, sont, bien entendu, ceux dont la *baraka* est la plus active. Il y en a, à Tombouctou, que l'on appelle *haydara*, dont l'ancêtre était un Marocain Rebelle, Ali ben Haydar, Réfugié au Soudan en 1672. (V. Monteil 1980: 157)

The idea of a Berber or Arab mythical founder or invading warrior in Black Africa is emphasized by B. Connelly in a passage on the tradition of the Arab folk epic, the *Hilàliya*; citing H. Norris's *The Adventures of 'Antar* (Warminster: Aris and Phillips, 1980), she observes that: "Epics of Sayf and the Bani Hilàl also, in Norris' view, recount Arab expeditions into Africa and describe the Arab-Muslim founders of African kingdoms as civilizing heroes" (Connelly 1986: 230). On his remarks on the Hausa and on their legend of origin, J. Ayoade notes: "The Hausas also claim that their ancestor came from

the Middle East and married the Queen of Daura north of present Kano City"
(1980: 161).

The Yoruba ethnic group of Nigeria has the same concept of Islam as a
prestige culture. Thus: "The modern Yoruba themselves usually confused the
Near East with Arabia and owing to the prestige of Islam locate their origin in
Mecca. The probable place is Upper Egypt rather than the Yemen." (B.
Davidson 1993: 84; citing S. O. Biobaku's *Lugard Lectures* [Lagos: 1955]).

In his study of the historical aspects of Somali genealogies, I.M. Lewis
tells of descent [among the Somali] being traced outside Somaliland to Arabia;
Lewis goes further by giving the example of a Sheikh named Isaaq (or rather his
descendants) who "have arabicized their genealogy as a means of acquiring
prestige " (Lewis 1962: 46). Most singers in Senegal who are versed in Islam
tend to posit an Arab origin for black African peoples because they identify
Islam as a prestige culture. They also tend to associate Islam with Arabia, their
logic being that a good Muslim should necessarily be from Arab stock and must
speak the Arabic language too; if not, he might gain prestige by retracing his
ancestral roots, at least in part, to a mythical Arab conqueror or a saint waging
war against the pagans in the name of Islam. This problem of retracing or
claiming descent from a holy figure also existed among the Arabs themselves;
thus, after the death of the prophet Muhammad, there were various lineages who
laid claims to the leadership and E. Gellner observes that "those lineages claim
descent from the Prophet" (1973: 197).

Along the same lines, L. Kesteloot treats the frequent mention of Islamic
and Arabic names, expressions, or legends in West African oral narratives. In
her analysis of the Bambara narrative of the empire of Segou sung by a griot
called Taïrou, Kesteloot poses the following question:

Que penser des mentions fréquentes de l'Islam dans ces récits? D'abord elles dépendent du degré d'islamisation des locuteurs et ceci est valable pour tous les griots qui content non seulement Biton [founder of the empire of Segou], mais les autres épisodes de l'épopée bambara.

Certains griots comme Taïrou "baptisent" abondamment cette épopée animiste, surtout au début et à la fin du récit (certains le commencent même par une prière). En réalité ces utilisations de l'Islam sont certainement postérieures aux faits puisque Biton n'était guère musulman. (1980: 594)

Hugo Zemp also remarks a tendency among the Mandinka (Malinké) griots to "islamize" their myths and legends. In his study, Zemp remarks that in the Mandinka version of a cosmogonical myth as sung by a griot,

l'ancêtre des griots porte le même nom que dans les légendes islamisées: Sourakata, nom que nous avons identifié comme dérivé du nom de l'Arabe Suraqa ben Malik, dont l'aventure du triple enlisement en présence de Mahomet a été intégrée dans la légende des griots malinké. (Zemp 1966: 642)

David Conrad stresses the point that "Surakata is traditionally claimed by Manding griots as their collective progenitor" (1985: 35). The same author also notes that "among the Islamic ideals absorbed by Western Sudanic Muslims was the notion that direct ancestral links to the Prophet and his original followers were especially desirable sources of prestige, and genealogies or descent lists were manipulated accordingly" (Ibid., p. 36).

Finally, just like the Wolof and the Mandinka, the Saraxolé also have a myth of origin which is traced back to Mecca and to Arabia. In this case, the Arab mythic ancestor is Mohammadu Hanafi. Adrian Adams writes:

Les Tanjigora [a common last name] sont issus de Ali Buna ba Talibe. Ali Buna ba Talibe a épousé une femme; c'est elle qui a mis au monde tous les Tanjigora. Celui qu'elle a mis au monde s'appelait Mohammadu Hanafi. Mohammadu Hanafi a quitté la terre de la Mecque; il a traversé le Nil, il a continué jusqu'à ce qu'il arrive à Soxolo. Arrivé à Soxolo il a rencontré là-bas une femme qui s'appelait Moni. Elle avait un enfant qui venait d'être sevré; son mari était mort. Mohammadu Hanafi a épousé Moni.

Le premier enfant de Moni s'appelait Manga. Elle a eu un enfant de Tanjigora, qui s'appelait Satanga. Comme le nom de la mère était Moni, on disait: Satanga Moni, Manga Moni. C'est de Manga que sont issus les Baacili [another last Saraxolé name]; c'est de Satanga que sont issus les Tanjigora (1985: 42).

In his study of the pre-colonial state of Baté in Upper Guinea (present-day Republic of Guinea, West Africa), Lansiné Kaba observes:

The taking of Arab genealogy and patronymics is common in West Africa, for it serves to ennoble one's origin and faith. It also testifies to an early incorporation of Islamic myths into the indigenous traditions. However, this is not to disregard such claims as pure fabrication in some cases. (1973: 330)

As we can see, Kaba makes room for possible descent from the union of a black African and an Arab. However, the most plausible hypothesis is that, if such a kinship exists, it would likely be a matter of relationships between the Almoravids or Berbers of North Africa on one hand and the Black populations south of the Sahara desert. The Sahara desert is a fictitious dividing line, and the inhabitants of North Africa and those south of the Sahara have made many contributions to each other's culture.

264-68   It is of some interest to draw a parallel of the story of Abraham Sal in the tale with the story of Abraham in the Qur'an:

> He lived among the Chaldeans, who had great knowledge of the stars and heavenly bodies. But he got beyond that physical world and saw the spiritual world behind. His ancestral idols meant nothing to him. That was the first step. But God took him many degrees higher....This allegory shows the stages of Abraham's spiritual enlightenment. (*The Holy Qur'an, Text, Translation, and Commentary* by Y. Ali 1983: 309)

The choice of Abraham as a name in the Wolof tale as a name is symbolic.   Abraham Sal constitutes a disruption of the traditional African setting, which has strong connections with Nature.   There is a strong analogy here between Abraham Sal, who was probably pagan and converted to Islam, and Abraham in the Qur'an, who left his idol-worshipping Chaldean people and joined the realm of revealed religions.   There is an osmosis between the pre-Islamic, pre-Judaic, and pre-Christian worlds on the one hand and the three revealed religions on the other.

276   Even though the text concerns mostly the Wolof and the state of Waalo, the singer here mentions another ethnic group, the Tukulor. Most of the authors who have studied the Waalo state agreed on the fact that it is of Wolof origin, even though we may problematize this assertion by remarking that there are speculations about the origin of Njaajaan, the founder of that state; he may have been of Almoravid, Tukulor, Peul, or Sereer background.   However, it is important to point out that the three sub-Saharan ethnic groups -- Wolof, Sereer, and Tukulor -- are closely related to each other and that all three had

participated in the formation of the state of Waalo.

Charles A. Seligman gives a general account about the various ethnic groups living in Western Africa and speaking languages all belonging to the Sudanic family. He then adds a rather funny [and racist] remark about the Wolof:

> The Wolof, besides occupying the seaboard between St. Louis and Cape Verde (including Dakar) and the south bank of the [River] Senegal, extend inland for a considerable distance. They are said to be the blackest and most garrulous of African peoples. (Seligman 1930: 59)

Seligman's last remark on the Wolof should be appreciated within the frame of European colonial anthropology and "civilizing" mission. In the European colonial enterprise and discourse, the African (who was also the Other) was only a voiceless passive object. As remarked by P. D. Curtin: "Anthropology was [then] concerned to study people as 'primitive' and untouched by 'civilzation' as possible....Anthropologists have been among the principal authors of racist interpretations of African history" (1964: 8-9).

Baumann and Westermann give a short summary of the political institutions of the ancient Wolof states:

> Dans l'ancien Royaume des Wolof qui comprenait le Cayor, le Oualo et le Djolof, le roi s'appelait le *bur*. Il commandait au *damel* du Cayor et au *teigne* du Baol qui étaient de grands chefs titulaires. (1957: 369)

The inter-mixing of certain ethnic groups of Senegal is an established fact. Even though today the Wolof constitute the predominant group of Senegal, they had in the past a very close relationship with the Tukulor and the Sereer. C. A. Diop comments on that aspect:

> Quoi qu'il soit, nous voyons que les Valafs [or Wolof] sont issus d'un long métissage qui se poursuit encore à l'heure actuelle sous nos yeux. On devient Valaf chaque jour. (1949: 852)

The inter-mixing of various ethnic groups is also a reality in other parts of the African continent. J. Vansina makes the following remark about the Bakuba of present-day Zaïre, Central Africa:

> The [Ba]Kuba culture has thus been built up by a core of culturally related tribes from the Kwango area, but their culture has been influenced by infiltrations of Mongo, Lulua, Luba, and even Pende cultures, through the channel of isolated family immigrations, since the eighteenth century at least. (1960b: 261)

In the Wolof case, indications point to very ancient relations between the various groups, at least as early as the twelth century, which coincides with the earliest hypothesis about the reign of Njaajaan Njaay. West Africa is largely open savannah space which facilitates trade and migrations, whereas population movements and the processes of ethnic mixing were much more restricted in Central Africa.

279-282 Fatumata is obviously coming out of a patrilocal marriage meaning that her mother has joined the father's clan; thus, the child bears the father's name (Sal in this case); moreover, she has the father's first name as a middle name. This is a clear mark of distinction referring to the father's clan. This kind of filiation is very unusual in Wolof society; however, it gives us a clue to the extent of Islamic influence in Wolof society, in which the matrilineal filiation prevails over the patrilineal one. On the origin of Negro matriarchy, C.A. Diop writes:

> What is the origin of Negro matriarchy? We do not know for certain at the present time; however, current opinion holds that the matriarchal system is related to farming. If agriculture was discovered by women, as is sometimes thought, if it be true that they were the first to think of selecting nourishing herbs, by the very fact that they remained at home while the men engaged in more dangerous activities (hunting, warfare, etc.), this, along with matriarchy, would explain an important but almost unnoticed aspect of African life. (1974: 144-45)

The patrilineal system is a main feature in Islam. Among the Wolof, the maternal uncle has a lot of influence on his sister's children, most of all in their education. He gives a sense of authority as well to the male children. It is a Wolof custom to affix the mother's name to the child's first name. This kind of filiation is referred to as absolute matrilineality. Citing F. Nadel ("Filiation bilatérale dans les Monts Nuba," in *Systèmes familiaux et matrimoniaux en Afrique*), C. A. Diop comments on Nadel's observations of the Nuba Tullushi's system of filiation:

> Chez les Nuba Tullushi qui pratiquent apparemment le partriarcat, l'identification de l'individu se fait néanmoins par le clan de la mère; l'enfant est appelé par le nom de sa mère plutôt que par son nom personnel. (C.A. Diop 1973: 782)

There is also a system of filiation referred to as a bilateral filiation; it is the intermediary link between the system of absolute matrilineality and the patrilineal system (Diop, op. cit., 779).

Generally speaking, the matrilineal filiation is found among peoples with a settled way of life as opposed to the nomadic system in which patrilineal structures tend to dominate.

On the same argument, W. Glinga writes:

> Cheikh Anta Diop, der das matrilineare Verwards-chaftssystem für genuin afrikanisch und das patrilineare für indoeuropaïsch hält, hebt hervor, doß zwischen beiden Abstammungs-linien Meen und Geño eine grundstätzliche Asymmetrie herrsche. In den Geño-Verwandten realisiert sich Gesellschaft. Der patrilineare Halbbrunder (also von einer anderen Mutter, aber vom selben vater) ist "un rival social, on doit le dépasser ou, tout au moins, l'égaler en toutes choses." In den Meen-Verwandten realisiert sich hingegen Individualität, "sans hyprocrisie sociale." (W. Glinga 1990: 182-83)

The story of Fatumata Abraham Sal in the Wolof tale resembles very much that of Fatima, the prophet Muhammad's daughter. The name Fatumata is derived from Fatima; Fatima was also called Az Zuhra (meaning "the Beautiful One", "the Glittery One" in Arabic). Fatima was given in marriage to Muhammad's cousin Ali. This is how A. Dhina comments on Fatima's story:

> Selon Ibn Sa'ad, dans ses *Tabaqat*, lorsque le Prophète fit connaître à sa fille la promesse qu'il avait faite à Ali, sans la consulter selon toute vraisemblance, elle garda le silence; son silence fut interprété comme un consentement tacite. D'après d'autres sources, Fatima protesta contre ce marriage, et son père

dut la calmer en lui faisant apparaître les qualités de noblesse, de courage, de science de Ali, sans oublier qu'il fut le premier à embrasser l'Islam. (Dhina 1986: 261)

In the Wolof tale, we are not told whether Fatumata gave her consent when she was being married to Bubakar Umar. Like Fatima in some traditions, Fatumata refuses to marry the various pretenders after Bubakar Umar's death (ll. 385-89).

284-85 The singer means Godo but he said Dogo, metathesizing the consonant sounds. He corrects himself. The village in question is Gédé, in the Bakel area. Njaajaan later spends two years in the River Senegal in Gédé (see l. 508).

289   Among the few studies on the Sereer are: Aujas, " Les Sérères du Sénégal" (1931); Bourgeau, "Notes sur les coutumes Sérères du Sine Saloum" (1933); and F. Lafont, "Le Gandoul et les Niominkas" (1938). Article-length studies that focus on linguistic aspects as well as on political institutions are: P. Diagne (1965; see also Diagne's detailed analysis of political institutions in Sereer society, in *Pouvoir politique traditionnel en Afrique occidentale*, 1967, pp. 56-94), C. A. Diop (1949), L. Homburger (1957), H. Gravrand (1961, 1980), D. P. Gamble (1957), and M. Dupire (1979), just to name the most important. Concerning the oral literature, religion, and customs of the Sereer, there are works and articles written by M.C. N'Doye (1947,1948), Raphaël N'Diaye (1986), and Léon Sobel Diagne (1989).

The Sereer are among the few ethnic groups of Senegal to have kept their traditional customs, religion, and beliefs with little or no influence from Islam. Conversely, they were among the first to be exposed to and converted to

Catholicism by the French missionaries. P. Diagne (1965) retraces the migration path of the Sereer from the north-west of Senegal (Waalo, Fuuta, Cayor, Bawal) to the center-west along the Atlantic Ocean. Baumann and Westermann argue that "nous voyons dans les Sérères le peuple typique de ce cercle Atlantique de l'Ouest" (1957: 369).

Other authors such as C.A. Diop (1949) emphasize the inter-mixing between the Sereer and the other ethnic groups such as the Wolof, the Peul, and the Sose (or Mandinka). In the fourteenth century, the Sereer experienced the advent of new princes called *gelwaar*. H. Gravrand points out that with the arrival of those princes, "les Sérèer avaient élaboré, à partir de leurs multiples apports, une civilisation homogène" (1980: 50).

Like the Wolof, the Sereer also have a legend of origin:

Après la destruction de l'empire de Ghana par les Almoravides, les Serer, les Sose et les Peuls, refusant de se laisser islamiser, auraient émigré sous la conduite des Peuls et gagné l'Ouest du Territoire de l'actuelle Mauritanie, où ils se seraient installés à proximité de l'Océan. Un beau jour, Serer et Sose remarquèrent des traces de chameaux dans les environs de leur village et comprirent par là que les Almoravides les poursuivaient et avaient repéré leur situation. Les fétiches furent consultés et une nouvelle émigration fut décidée. Un oiseau fut capturé, déplumé et attaché par un fil à la patte à l'arbre central du village; à une branche du même arbre fut suspendu un "kalamba", petite calebasse qui est utilisée comme unité de mesure: les traces des chameaux furent recouvertes avec des calebasses, et Serer et Sose s'en allèrent, laissant aux Peuls, qui étaient absents à ce moment-là, le soin de comprendre la raison de leur départ. Les Peuls comprirent effectivement dès leur retour, après avoir examiné les traces de chameaux qui avaient été conservées intactes grâce aux calebasses qui les recouvraient, le motif de l'exode: le kalamba et l'oiseau déplumé étaient le symbole des

tributs à payer et de la taille des habitants. Ils suivirent Serer et
Sose dans leur exode vers le sud. Peuls, Serer et Sose restent
indissolublement associés dans les légendes qui se rapportent aux
sites d' anciens villages. (J. Robin: 1946)

It seems that the black populations were exiled from the Sahara by the
Berbers and under the thrust of conquering Arabs around the eighth century.
After the eighth century, the embryonic structures of the first Wolof state of
Dyolof (or Waalo) came into existence in northern present-day Sénégal. C.A.
Diop comments that the Sereer, Wolof, and Tukulor probably have a common
origin; they split later on to create independent linguistic and collective
groupings. The earliest Wolof states around the fifteenth century were occupied
by the Sereer. Diop writes:

A l'origine, l'histoire du Cayor-Baol était essentiellement sérère.
Pourtant c'est la même histoire qui continue jusqu'au dernier
Damel Lat Dior Diop, et jusqu'à nous en se métamorphosant petit
à petit en une histoire des Valafs, sans une invasion massive
d'une race Valaf, sans rupture. Quand on parle aujourd'hui de
l'histoire des Valafs, c'est au fond de cette histoire qui
n'appartient plus aux uns qu' aux autres, dont il s'agit. (1949:
852)

Along the same lines Donald Wright remarks that "in spite of the ethnic
and linguistic diversity in the region [Senegambia], culturally and socially many
of the people living there shared much in common. The basis of the economies
of most of the area was agriculture. Millet formed the staple crop for Mandinka,
Serer, and Wolof, though each grew different varieties in different ways. Along
the Gambia [River], Mandinka women supplemented the diet with rice; Serer
and Wolof grew cotton and some maize as well. Cattle to all three groups were

of secondary importance...

Holding together Mandinka, Serer, Wolof, and Fulbe society and lending unity to the wider Senegambian social and cultural region were a tripartite social structure and strong kinship relations" (D. R. Wright 1979: 18).

291   The   presence   in   the   epic   tale   of   a   character   such   as Hamar-the-Scolder-of-Old-People was unavoidable. The latter is also mentioned by V. Monteil (1966: 26) under the name of Amar Gödömat. However, the latter spelling does not give a clue to the reader of what the meaning of that name is in Wolof. Ñan adds on line 292 tautologically that Hamar used to scold old people. This attribute is very similar to blasphemy for, in traditional African society, the respect of the elders by younger people is very important. One can draw a parallel between Hamar-the-Scolder-of-Old-People and Soumaoro in *The Sunjaata Epic*:

> Soumaoro était un génie du mal; sa puissance n'avait servi qu'à verser le sang; devant lui rien n'était tabou: son plus grand plaisir était de fouetter publiquement des vieillards respectables; il avait souillé toutes les familles; dans son vaste empire, il y avait partout des villages peuplés des filles qu'il avait enlevées de force à leur famille, sans marriage. (D.T. Niane 1960: 79-80)

Hamar is an anti-hero like Soumaoro in *Sunjaata* and the antithesis of Njaajaan. The anti-hero thrives on transgression as well as evolving within the spheres of the asocial. Moreover, Hamar is guilty of a crime and deserves to be punished by Njaajaan (see l. 384).

293 Mbaarik Bô's function corresponds to that of the helper in Propp's analysis

of the dramatis personae of the Russian fairy tale. That function may be fitted into Propp's third category (1990: 79):

> 3. The sphere of action of the helper. Constituents: the spatial transference of the hero (G); liquidation of misfortune or lack (K); rescue from pursuit (Rs); the solution of difficult tasks (N); transfiguration of the hero (T).

Although the hero in the Wolof tale is Njaajaan, he comes into action only in line 380, even though he is mentioned for the first time in the poem in l. 215. Bubakar, his father, is the hero of the epic tale up until his death (l. 355). Mbaarik Bô is the helper, accompanying Bubakar and fighting alongside him against the pagans.

335 Bubakar Umar, the departing husband, gives prescriptions to his wife as to who she should be married after his death. This is an Islamic custom for, in Wolof society, when the husband dies, his widow is remarried by the family. Actually, the widow is remarried to one of the brothers of the deceased. This latter custom is dictated by the need to keep the wealth and children within the deceased husband's family.

345-347 According to Monteil's version (1966), Njaajaan was given Amadou Boubakar Ibn 'Omar as a name at birth. In the account of the myth of Njaajaan as recited by a griot called Assane Marokaya Samb, Njaajaan is known as Mouhamadou Ben Oumar (cited by L. Kesteloot and B. Dieng 1989: 184-85). Amadou is a deformation of Muhammadu, a form of Muhammad. Njaajaan is thus named for the Prophet, yet another instance of the tracing of roots back to

Islamic and Arab origins.

Why is it so important for the Wolof singer to insist on the names of the mythical founder? He deals with the hero's last name (Aydara) in lines 940-41. V. Mudimbe asserts that "proper names both colonize the past and organize the geography of current customs and traditions. They signify a dynamic political structure: the believable, the memorable, and the primitive" (1991: 90). To some extent, Njaajaan's name plays a dual function: *Njaajaan* is the reflection of the indigenous African past whereas the hero's other name *Muhammadu Aydara*, is the evidence of outside influence, namely Berber, Arabic, and Islamic influences within the Wolof traditions.

355-357   Monteil, who makes use of an oral account by a Senegalese oral historian Amadou Wade, collected in 1941, mentions the death of Bubakar Umar:

> Après la destruction de Ghana par le chef des Almoravides, Abû-Bakr ben 'Omar, les peuplades noires qui l'habitaient se dispersèrent vers l'ouest. A leur arrivée à Kêlöw, près du lac Cayor (Khôômak), le Sérère (sêêrêr) Amar Gödömat (un des fuyards) se retourna soudain, et, faisant face à Abû-Bakr, de son arc le blessa grièvement.   Ce dernier abandonna la poursuite, rentra à Chiguitti (Siingöti), où il mourut plus tard, des suites de cette blessure. (Monteil 1966: 26)

Monteil cites an Arab author Ibn Abî-Zar (*Ramd al-Qurtas*, 1326) who dates the death of Abu Bakr to 1087. There is a discrepancy among the various dates as well as a chronological gap. Monteil gives 1186-1202 as the dates of Njaajaan's reign. That date would be the closest one to Bubakar's death. There is nonetheless a gap of ninety-nine years between the death of Bubakar and the beginning of the reign of his supposed son, Njaajaan, with whom Fatumata is pregnant in the Wolof epic tale. Singiti is located in the present-day Islamic Republic of Mauritania.

362 Ablutions are prescribed in Islam. They consist in washing specific parts of the body (face, mouth, ears, hands, head, nose, feet) before each of the five daily prayers.

380-84 The fight described in this passage is the only physical combat in the tale.

385 This is the first action in the epic tale in which a woman is the center of the narrative attention. Fatumata is a Muslim woman and this is an exception for in the kingdom of Waalo the majority of the population was non-Muslim. In the nineteenth century, a French priest, David Boilat, who travelled to the northern part of Senegal and Waalo, gave an account of the role played by women in kingship:

> Ce royaume (Waalo) est ordinairement gouverné par un roi qui prend le titre de *brak* . Je dis ordinairement, parce que la couronne peut échoir aux hommes et aux femmes, suivant leur droit. Dans le cas où une femme règne, elle prend le titre de *bour* qui signifie roi ou reine et son mari prend le titre de *marroso.* Alors on donne le nom de *brak* au prince qui approche le plus de la famille régnante. (1984: 284)

Thus, both men and women ruled in the Wolof kingdom of Waalo even though men have a prevailing position in the tale. Fatumata is given a passive role, and accepts the will of her late husband, Bubakar, just as she submitted to her father's will earlier in the tale.

Concerning a very different tradition from the Wolof one, in her comparative study of the Chinese Heroic Poems and European Epic, Marie Chan (1974) emphasizes the fact that the feminine figure plays an important role in Chinese war poems; this was during the Warring States period in China (around 221 B.C.); moreover, Chan suggests that the Chinese poet is trying to achieve a particular effect through the accentuation of woman and therefore highlights the dominant mood of grief and loss (p.158). However, a monumental difference between the Chinese poem on the one hand and the European and African (Wolof in this case) is that the basic framework in which the Chinese poems are built as well as the focus in these poems is upon the pathetic victims rather than upon enviable victors (Chan, p. 157). The situation is the converse in the Wolof epic tale. The conclusion of Chan's argument is that in China, the elegy is the dominant form and the epic an extremely weak strain (Chan, p. 167).

439 The word door-keeper is the translation of the Wolof word *bëkke nèk*. This word literally means "the guardian of the door that leads to the room." In this case, the guardian is Mbaarik Bô keeping watch on his master's door. This tradition still exists in present-day Senegal where most Muslim religious leaders have a door-keeper, but not quite in Mbaarik Bô's style. The role of these contemporary intermediaries is to introduce visitors and appointees to the chief or leader. These intermediaries also play the role of go-betweens, of confidants, and of peacemakers.

Among the Akan people of Ghana is a man who has functions that are

186

similar to those of the Wolof *bëkke nèk;* he is called *okyeame*   or royal

spokesman. This is how Akosua Anyidoho describes the *okyeame*:

> The duty of an okyeame in the Akan royal house is to receive
> messages meant for the chief and to rephrase them in proverbial,
> figurative language suitable for presentation to the chief. The
> okyeame also relates instructions and information from the chief
> to his subjects. In the Akan chiefship system, no one talks
> directly to the chief, except through his intermediary, the
> okyeame. This may explain why the position of the okyeame is
> reserved for people with complete mastery   of the history,
> customs, oral traditions, and language of the Akan people. (1991:
> 81)

The Wolof *bëkke nèk* is different from the griot in that the *bëkke nèk*

can belong to the caste of the griot or may not belong to that caste at all. The

main requirements are that the *bëkke nèk*   should have oratorical skills and

should have an expanded knowledge of the traditions and history of his area as

well as of the inhabitants. He should also have an extraordinary mastery of the

Wolof language and be able to convey wisdom from the chief to the people; the

ability to speak figuratively as well as directly, and the ability to make analogies

and to cite proverbs constitute an extra advantage for the *bëkke nèk*. Thus, a

griot who happens to be a learned man (more specifically a griot who is

knowledgeable about the Qur'an) can be a *bëkke nèk.*

463 Waalo-Waalo is a compound word meaning a person who inhabits the

Waalo region. More specifically, Waalo-Waalo means a Wolof who inhabits

Waalo. There is an analogous expression, Jolof-Jolof, which means a person

who inhabits the region of Jolof.

467 Njaajaan's anger as well as his departure are triggered by personal reasons rather than by political ones. In some ways, he rejects his mother's marrying Mbaarik; as it is, she is getting married again. In this episode, the singer puts a lot of emphasis on the aural mode rather than on the oral one, in that Njaajaan hears and listens to other people but in return does not utter a word. Concerning the hero's childhood, L. Kesteloot emphasizes "la tendance de beaucoup de mythes à présenter un héros dont l'enfance est atteinte d' un manque social" (1980: 581). Njaajaan seems to be in an awkward predicament.

474 This anachronism is an element that is part of the Wolof poet's armada, and can be considered a form of poetic flexibility. The enumeration of the gun at the end of the list of weapons is a spontaneous act on the singer's part. Njaajaan was in such a rage that he just grabbed whatever was within reach. Anachronisms are common in oral poetry. J. Opland remarks:

> Homer composed the *Iliad* at a time when chariots were no longer used in battle, but since he had inherited through the tradition a set of poetic phrases referring to chariots, he found occasion to use these in his poems because they were traditional, even though he seems not to have conceived of any function for chariots other than transport to and from battle. (1980: 16-17)

In Homer's case it is a question of his positing use of a form of warfare no longer in use, so the anachronism is properly speaking an archaism.

475 This line signals Njaajaan's withdrawal from human society. Njaajaan is a victim-hero for he plunged into the river and started his journey because his playmates were laughing at him. He was not searching for anything, as heroes

often do in their journeys away from society. He was swimming down river, occasionally stopping to rest and eat. Austin J. Shelton uses the phrase "descending deeper than a diver" to describe Njaajaan's plunge in the river. Actually, Shelton is making reference to L. Senghor's poem entitled *Le Totem*. Shelton writes:

> *Descending deeper than a diver*: This suggests Ndyadyane Ndyaya, mythical head of all Wolof peoples, who mysteriously rose from the depths of a lake to bring peace, then returned to the waters. (1968a: 73)

The hero's passage through water in general and a river in particular is found in many mythical tales. We have the example of the mythical Yoruba god Ogun (Nigeria) who came to a river, on which he saw a man called Olodo punting a boat; the latter refused to take Ogun across the river:

> Ogun vanished, only to reappear across the deep river on the other bank in absolute disregard of Olodo, who subsequently spread about the news of Ogun's feat and of the special chanted utterance which had preceded it. (S.A. Babalola 1966: 7)

Heroes and mythical founders often disappear into water in what may be an act of purification.

477 The River Senegal.

478-81 This suicide attempt by Njaajaan is also mentioned in Monteil's version (1966: 28):

Dès qu' Amadou Boubakar [Njaajaan] apprit la conclusion de ce mariage [between his mother Fatumata and Mbaarik Bô], il en fut si indigné qu'il courut se jeter dans le fleuve. Amadou Boubakar, arrivé au fond de l'eau, et sentant les premiers effets de l'asphyxie, s'était empressé, en bon nageur qu'il était, de revenir à la surface.

There is a saying in Wolof that was probably inspired by Njaajaan's suicide attempt in the river: *ku mun fèèy, du xaru ci déx* which means literally: "Never would a good swimmer drown in water by way of suicide."

501-02 These lines may reflect the syncretism of Ñan's approach to the myth: God gave Njaajaan Njaay the power (Islamic point of view) but nature also gave it to him (animist point of view). There is a strong association between nature and the hero of the tale, to the extent that it appears as if the two constitute one unit.

518-28 Concerning the physical appearance of Njaajaan, there are apparently contradictory implications about his ethnic origins. Is he black? Is he Arab? Is he a Berber?

Citing J. L. Monod's *Histoire de l'Afrique occidentale* (1926), Robert Cornevin states that Njaajaan might be a descendant of an Almoravid chief called Abou Dardaï who lived in the fourteenth century (Cornevin 1960: 266). Cornevin also cites Rousseau' s *Le Sénégal d'autrefois* (1931), who states that Njaajaan was probably a Wolof chief (Cornevin, ibid.).

In his book entitled *Literatur in Senegal*, the German Scholar Werner Glinga adheres to J. L. Monod's hypothesis affirming Njaajaan's Berber and Almoravid origin:

Njajan Njay ist einerseits Sohn des Führers der islamischen Bewegung der Almoraviden, des Berber Abu Bakr, der Krieg gegen Ghana führte und den schwarzen Völker den Islam gebracht haben soll. Ebenso aber ist er der Gründer des ersten Wolofstaates, der anderen oralen Überlieferungen zufolge animistisch war. (W. Glinga op.cit., p. 58)

Just like the Wolof griot Ñan, Glinga mentions Njaajaan's father Abu Bakr, who fought the Black people in Ghana and converted them to Islam. The author also emphasizes the fact that the Wolof states were animistic prior to the advent of Islam.

The question of origin is very complex; however, I will attempt to untie the knots that surround it. G. Nicolas insists on the mixing between the Wolof and the other ethnic groups of Senegal and specifically in the northern part of the country. He writes:

Cette ethnie [Wolof] s'est constituée par association progressive de populations côtières autochtones et de groupes immigrants d'origine diverse: Toucouleur, Peul, Bérbères, Maures, Serer, Haratin du Sahara ou Soninké. (1978: 363)

However, as I pointed out earlier, the question of origin and of migrations is by no means simple for there are intermarriages within the various ethnic groups; moreover, some groups borrow customs, language, and beliefs from others. J. Vansina elaborates on the complexity of the problem in Africa:

Le processus des origines n'est jamais simple. En effet, toutes les cultures sont mélangées, c'est-à-dire ont emprunté certains éléments à d'autres cultures et en ont inventé ou développé d'autres *in situ* ; les populations elles aussi sont mélangées en ce sens qu'il semble y avoir un mouvement incessant et quasi péristaltique de mariages et de migrations individuelles ou familiales de façon à ce que dans maints cas des réseaux de classes s'étendent sur différentes tribus; et même la langue qui est l'élément le moins mélangé d'une culture, change par emprunts et accroissement interne. (1976: 17)

C.A. Diop develops a hypothesis which runs counter to W. Glinga and Monod's assumption that Njaajaan is of Berber stock; however, Diop's argument is closer to Rousseau's. According to Diop, Njaajaan could not be from Berber or Arab stock because of his last name Njaay, which is a Wolof totemic name. He makes the following point about Njaajaan's ancestry:

Revenons sur les noms de Diop et de N'Diaye qui passent pour les seuls typiquement valafs. Essayons de pénétrer leurs origines. L'histoire nous enseigne que le roi N'Diadiane N'Diaye, le premier roi des Valafs est issu d'une mère Toucouleur et d'un père arabe. Mais il y a ici une contradiction évidente. Le fils d'un arabe ne peut guère porter le nom totémique N'Diaye. Et on sait que le nom comme le prénom de ce roi viennent du cri de stupéfaction "ça c'est N'Diadiane N'Diaye" (expression voulant dire calamité) que le fétichiste sérère prononça quand pour la première fois, on lui présenta N'Diadiane dont l'apparition était un miracle aux yeux des Djoloff-Djoloffs. (C.A. Diop 1949: 850)

The origin of the name Njaajaan as explained by Diop is also recounted by the Wolof singer (line 811). Njaajaan means 'puzzle', 'stupefaction' in Sereer. The Sereer chief Maysa Waali Jon pronounces it when the messengers sent by the rulers of the Waalo kingdom tell him about the man who came out of the river, and the word becomes his name.

In a separate article devoted to a linguistic comparative study between various sub-Saharan African languages (including Wolof) on one hand and northern African languages such as Coptic or Berber on the other, Diop made the point that there was no genealogical kinship between Wolof and Berber (1973: 774). Monteil labels Njaajaan as being "le fils du guerrier almoravide [Bubakar Umar] et de la femme torôdo [Fatumata]" (1966: 28).

Finally, Njaajaan's description in the Wolof tale as having hair all over his body is also found in Monteil's version. The episode in which this occurs is the encounter with the fishermen of the village of Mengeny (or Mbégèñ, one of the villages where Njaajaan stops during his journey). The fishermen thought that Njaajaan came out of the river whereas he came out of his hiding place. Thus, when the fishermen saw Njaajaan "ils eurent peur, à cause de sa longue chevelure, des poils qu'il avait sur presque tout le corps" (Monteil 1966: 29). What does this hairy quality signify? Does Njaajaan have an animal-like quality about him?

We find the same physical characteristics in Enkidu in *Gilgamesh*. Epic heroes are often not entirely human and are at times endowed with characteristics or peculiar marks that make them stand out. Apparently, the Wolof tradition is giving Njaajaan these extraordinary qualities in order to portray the hero as different from the normal human being. We find the same situation in the founding myth of the Luba people of Central Africa as described by V. Mudimbe, the story of Nkongolo, the mythical founder and ancestor of the Luba. Citing H. Womersley (*Legends and History of the Luba*, 1984), Mudimbe observes that Nkongolo's original name is Mwamba and he is the son of Bondo wa Baleya:

> There is a legend about his father being a hyena and he is consequently referred to as *Muntu utyila wadi wa malwa* , that is to say, 'A red or clear skinned man who was a monstrosity.' He

MAPATE DIOP
(the father of the author of this book, Samba Diop)

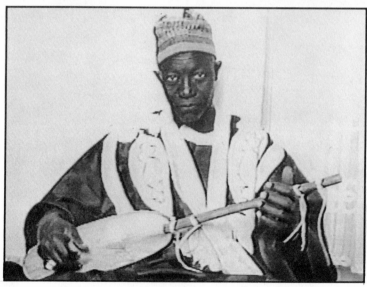

SEQ NAN
(two positions in performance)

ANCUMBU CAAM

From left to right:
ANCUMBU CAAM, MAPATE DIOP, MAGATE CAAM (Ancumbu's son)

was supposed to be so ugly that no one resembled him before or since. (Mudimbe 1991: 90)

The exceptional physical and spiritual characteristics are also found in the Igbo (Nigeria) epic of *Ameke Okoyè*. This romantic epic was performed over a period of five nights by Osita Ajaana, a non-professional but specialist amateur artist, who lives and works as a yam-farmer in Illah in Bendel state. The hero of this romantic epic narrative,

> Ameke Okoyè is conceived in extraordinary circumstances after a long period of barrenness on the part of his mother, Mbaago. His birth also takes place in extraordinary circumstances after an extraordinarily long pregnancy of thirty-nine years! (C. Azuonye 1984: 4)

Like Njaajaan's story, Nkongolo's and Okeyè's constitute myths of foundation as well as of finality for these mythical founders of African kingdoms are unique. No one looked like them before and nobody will look like them either in the future.

539-78 All these settlements and villages, Lamnaajo, Gédé, Mbégèñ, Dagana, Kawas, Mbilor, Xéwéw Gaal, Mbégèñ Booy are extant places. My father was born in Mbilor in 1917. A feature common to all these villages is that they are ancient settlements situated on the left bank of the river. Njaajaan's journey follows a linear progression downstream that is parallel to the geographical disposition of these villages. Only Mengeny (Mbégèñ) is mentioned in Monteil's version (1966: 29-32). Monteil (or his informant) has summarized and thereby shortened the story of Njaajaan. In Ñan' s version, Mbégèñ Booy is mentioned in addition to Mbégèñ (l. 578). In Ñan's tale, Mbégèñ is the first and original settlement and is situated upriver whereas Mbégèñ Booy is situated downstream, near Saint-Louis, and was probably created by a clan that bore the name Booy (or Boye).

From Upper-Senegal (Bakel area) to the lower part (Saint-Louis and the mouth of the river), the river bends from east-southeast to west-northwest. About Wolof settlements, Robinson says that "they are strong in the region, and they become stronger as one moves towards the west and the southwest" (1984: 4).

541 The number seven in this line is also used on lines 573 and 580. Its usage, no doubt symbolic, is not restricted to the Wolof tradition but is also characteristic of other traditions both Qur'anic and indigenous.

582-94 There are two other versions on this episode of the quarrel, reported respectively by Monteil and Gamble. For the Wolof poet Ñan, it is a quarrel among children. In Monteil's version, it is simply a quarrel among the fisherfolk of Mengeny:

> Mais un jour que les pêcheurs de Mengeny, revenus de la pêche, ne pouvaient s'entendre, comme cela leur arrivait souvent, sur le partage du produit de leur pêche, et allaient en venir aux mains, Amadou Boubakar Ibn 'Omar (Njaajaan) sortit précipitamment de sa cachette et se dirigea vers eux. (Monteil 1966: 29)

D. Gamble's writings on the traditional origin of Wolof rule based on previous authors such as René Geoffroy de Villeneuve (1814), Boilat (1853), Bérenger-Féraud (1879), and Shoberl (early nineteenth century), recounts that "one day a quarrel arose between neighbouring villages in Walo over wood which was being gathered on the banks of a lake. Bloodshed was threatened when suddenly a man arose from the waters, divided the wood among the parties, and returned to the lake without uttering a word" (D.P. Gamble 1957: 16).

In both Ñan's version and in the one reported by Monteil, the body of water referred to is the River Senegal whereas in Gamble's (citing H. Gaden, 1912, p. 129), it is a lake called Ndyassèou (or Ndyalakhar). In Gamble's and Monteil's, the antagonists are adults whereas in Ñan's tale, they are children. The casual and trivial situation of the children is actualized on the more serious level of the adult fishermen and farmers in the versions reported earlier. Within Ñan's tale there is a shift from the apparently insignificant quarrel between the children to the more serious devising of a plan to catch Njaajaan (ll. 646-47).

618 The oral aspect of this poem is reinforced by the Wolof singer's statement that he received the epic tale from his father. (See also ll. 676, 693, 697, 968, and 974 as well as Appendix I, interview with ancumbu Caam and his son Magate)

655-57 The sentiment found in these lines corresponds to a social convention in Wolof society. There are values associated with the concept of nobility: honor, dignity, bravery, sense of responsibility and of duty, and awareness of a noble's role within society and vis-à-vis lower classes.

680 Epic heroes are often half-gods. If not, they get their strength and physical endurance from a divine source. Drawing a parallel between Gilgamesh and Achilles, A. Lord writes:

> Gilgamesh, like Achilles, is part divine, two thirds of him is god, one third of him is human. (1960: 197)

However, in the Wolof tale, the singer mentions only that Njaajaan had supernatural powers; there is no reference to the hero's divine nature. See also ll. 501-02 where the Wolof poet alternately says that God gave power to Njaajaan and that nature also gave him power. Thus, we have a combination of spiritual and physical dimensions as well as Islamic and animistic dimensions. The power God gave to Njaajaan is not mentioned in the other versions.

681 The capture of Njaajaan has a symbolic meaning but also a political and ideological bearing. It is an individual versus the group. Njaajaan's capturing is the prelude to the birth of a state, or at least, it is the re-organisation of a dismembered political unit.

In the Wolof epic tale we have a political conflict. B. Dieng argues that:

> Le conflit politique que représente le récit épique peut se traduire en termes de crise d'harmonisation du groupe. Dans une société tendant vers une idéologie communautaire, chaque fois qu'un individu confesse un besoin d'éloignement et de déstructuration, il est récupéré ou neutralisé complètement. (1980: 885)

At this stage of the tale, one could not foresee that the stranger that has just been caught is going to be the ruler of the kingdom of Waalo. The reasons why Njaajaan is caught is that he is a foreigner, and then the villagers think that he is coming out of the river whereas he is coming out of the reeds that grow on the banks of the river, which constitute his hiding place.

686   The theme of the silent or dumb hero is found in many traditions.   For other examples, see Stith Thompson, *Motif-index of Folk-literature: A Classification of Narrative Elements in Folktales, Ballads, Myths, Fables, Mediaeval Romances, Exempla, Fabliaux, Jestbooks, and Local Legends* (revised and enlarged edition; Bloomington: Indiana University Press, 1989), L 124.2, "The Silent Hero."

691   The Wolof singer mentions Bata Booy as a man whereas in Monteil's version, Bata Booy is a woman. Njaajaan married her and they had a son called Waaré Ndyadyan Ndyay (1966: 32).   However, this son is not listed among Njaajaan's children in the Wolof tale (lines 902-906).   According to Rawane Boy, "ce furent les gens de Menguèye qui s'emparèrent de N'Diadiane N'Diaye, le portèrent à Boyou-Gare, village commandé par l'aîné des fils de Yamnone, Abdou Boy... Sa fille [Yamnone's] Fatoumata Boy, qui réussit à faire parler N'Diadiane, en devint la première femme" (cited in Rousseau 1931: 340).

The Wolof singer insists that his father told him that it was Maramu Gaaya who made Njaajaan come out of his silence. Did the father have any reason to favor Gaaya over Booy? Perhaps he favored Maramu for the latter was a Peul whereas Booy was a Sereer. Geographically speaking, the Peul are closer to the Wolof in the Waalo region; the former are cattle-herders whereas the latter are farmers and they exchanged agricultural products against dairy products. However, culturally speaking, the Sereer are closer to the Wolof for their languages are related.

694   Maramu Gaye is not mentioned in the other versions. The name Gaaya (as used by the griot in some instances) is the equivalent of Gaye. According to C.A. Diop, the people who bear the name Gaye originally come from the eastern part of Africa or from the Nile valley area like many other people living in present-day West Africa. He argues that "les Gaya (Gaye, Sénégal) vivent sur les bords du lac Victoria" (1973: 786).

699   The name Sirabawar is also spelled *Seb-ak-Bawar* or *Seb-ag-Baor* or *Seb-ak-baor*. However, they all mean the same thing. In Wolof, *bawar* means an assembly. J. Robin states that "il s'agit de l'assemblée plénière des trois premières familles nobles du pays" (1946: 253). B. Barry is of a similar opinion in writing that the assembly of the *seb ak baor* was made up of the electors of the country; those electors were the people who had the titles of *dyogomaay*, *dyawdin*, and *maalo* (Barry 1985: 73). According to Monteil:

> Le *Seb-ag-Baor* était une assemblée formée de trois membres: le Diogomaye, le Diawdine et le Malo.   Elle avait pour mission d'assister le Brak dans son administration et pouvait le destituer ou le maintenir au pouvoir, suivant sa bonne ou mauvaise foi. (1966: 43)

Thus, the assembly of the Sirabawar was devised to balance out the power of the barak. Njaajaan is going to be the first barak of Waalo.

The Jawdin was also a prime minister, or at least was given those functions as stressed by A. Mapaté Diagne in his article entitled "Un pays de pilleurs d'épaves - Le Gandiole," p. 146.

701-9   Maramu devises a trick in order to make Njaajaan talk by tantalizing him with food. In D. Gamble's version, no trick is involved but after Njaajaan is caught, he is forcibly detained and refuses to eat. Thus: "All the women and girls of the neighbourhood were brought to see if any of them could induce him to eat and to stay. He was seen to be moved by the sight of one beautiful girl, she was given to him in marriage and he consented to stay, gradually becoming more human" (Gamble 1957: 160).

In Monteil's version (p. 30), a woman named Bat Bôôy (Bata Booy in the epic tale) decided that she would succeed in making Njaajaan talk. She married him. Later on, the woman is going to use the trick of the stone and the cauldron (as in Ñan's tale) after having failed to make Njaajaan talk, as Maramu Gaye does in Ñan's tale. Once again, we have differing details within the same story coming from different informants.

Besides the trick, the motif of the game (draughts or checkers) is found in many epics in medieval Europe as well as in Medieval West Africa and among the Peul in particular. The latter have a great devotion to the concepts of personal freedom and independence and this is due to their nomandic way of life. Concerning the Peul epic, C. Seydou remarks:

> Loin de mettre le feu aux poudres comme dans l'épopée médiévale française, le jeu sert au contraire ici [in the Peul epic] d'alibi pour susciter un a affrontement certes mais aussi pour empêcher la situation critique ainsi créée de se dénouer dans le sang (1992: 71).

Another important function of the motif of the game is that it helps in the decision as to who is the best of two heroes, the latter two being of equal valor and prowess in physical combat (Seydou, op. cit., 88).

733   This line highlights the multilingual situation of Senegal, more precisely the situation among Wolof, Tukulor, and Sereer. From the conversation I had in Senegal with oral historians and with my father, Njaajaan is said to have grown up in an environment where Hal pulaar (or Tukulor) was spoken.

The Tukulor are related to the Peul; the latter are cattle herders and are found from Senegal to Cameroon. Thus, the Peul language is spoken on that strip of land called the Sahel and going from the Atlantic ocean in Senegal to Cameroon and Nigeria further east.

The following three ethnic groups belong to the big family of the Peul [or Fulaani elsewhere]: Tukulor, Peul, and Hal pulaarén. On the sense of the word Tukulor, L. Homburger remarks:

"Toucouleur," nom assez répandu en France, viendrait du nom *Tokolor* employé par les Wolofs pour désigner toute personne qui parle la langue des Peuls....Des textes arabes du moyen âge parlent du *Tkrr* au delà du Ghana et du Mali. (1957: 56)

The word Tukulor refers to the language as well as to the ethnic group and is used in Senegal. According to this account, the Wolof did not make any distinction between the Tukulor and the Peul people and language. At this moment in Senegal, Hal pulaar is the language spoken by that group and alludes to the language as well as to the ethnic group; it is also used only within the geographical spaces of Senegal and Mauritania. In present-day Senegal, the Tukulor people prefer the word Hal pularén to that of Tukulor when referring to the ethnic group or Hal pulaar when referring to the language.

The word Fulaani is widely used in countries such as Mali, Niger, Nigeria, Tchad, and Cameroon and refers both to the language and the ethnic group.

The kingdom of Tekrur where the Tukulor lived was among the first states created in the westernmost part of Africa after the decline of the large empires such as Ghana and Mali. The founder of Tekrur was War Djabi (d. 1040-1), the first Muslim king of Tekrur. From a small kingdom, Tekrur grew in size and power:

> Ce royaume de Tekrur, devenu Fouta Toro vers 1512 avec Koli Tenguela Ba, fondateur de la dynastie des Deniankobe, était peuplé vers le dixième siècle de diverses ethnies: Berbère, Maure, Peul, Malinké, Manding, Soninké, Wolof, Seereer, Toucouleur, etc...Aucune des grandes ethnies du Sénégal actuel ne manque à l'appel.. (A. Samb 1974: 4)

In the Wolof tale, we learn that Njaajaan was going to be the first ruler of the Wolof states of Waalo and Jolof. However, he is represented as originally speaking a language that was distinct from Wolof.

On my father's side, my maternal grandmother Bôy Kane was a Tukulor. Kane is a typical name of the Tukulor and the Kane clan founded a village in Fuuta called Kanène, up the River Senegal, east of Waalo.

790 In Senegal, it is believed that Njaay and Diop are the typical Wolof names. It seems that there were other names anterior to Diop and Njaay, including Kane, Sy, Ly, Ka; they are typical of the Tukulor and the Peul. Their origin is situated in the Nile valley and in the Sudan by C.A. Diop (1960: 65-66). Still according to C.A. Diop, the Diop come from the Njaay, not the other way

around. He observes:

> Diop et N'Diaye sont des tribus soeurs ce qui exige leur
> contemporanéité. Mieux que cela, nous savons que tous les Diop
> sont descendants de Guet, fils aîné de N'Diadiane N'Diaye. Par
> suite d'un incident au sein de la famille royale, Guet avait, en
> effet, renié le nom de son père pour adopter celui de Diop.
> (1949: 851)

This change of name that is said to have resulted from a quarrel between

Njaajaan and his son is recounted in the Wolof tale (ll.934-7). Concluding on

the origin and relationship of the two names of Diop and Njaay,   C.A.Diop

writes:

> Nous ne saisissons guère que des origines étrangères artificielles
> quand à ces deux noms qui seuls passent pour typiquement
> Valafs.   Ils sont nés tardivement, au hasard des circonstances
> historiques et se sont répandus grâce à l'importance du rang
> social des personnes qui les ont portés au cours du temps. (1949:
> 851)

The late appearance of these two names constitutes more evidence

concerning the intermixing of the different ethnic groups of Senegal as well as

the fact that Wolof as a language and an ethnic group is the result of that

intermixing between the Tukulor and the Sereer.

797-99 In the poem, Maysa Waali is presented as the king of the Sereer. The

prefix Maysa is a title meaning king or leader and probably comes from the

Mandinka word Mansa meaning the same thing. If we consider that the Sereer

and the Mandinka are mixed, that origin for the word Maysa is very plausible.

Baumann and Westermann qualify the Sereer as being "le peuple typique de ce cercle Atlantique de l'Ouest" (1957: 369). They add:

> Les Wolofs s'en sont fortement éloignés [from the Sereer] par suite de l'islamisation et aussi de la pénétration des Maures et des Peuls qui a influé sur leur civilisation et sur leurs caractères physiques. (loc. cit.)

On the origin of the Sereer, there are indications that they migrated from east to west like many other ethnic groups and nations of West Africa. According to C.A. Diop:

> The Serer probably came to Senegal from the Nile basin; their route was said to be marked by the upright stones found at the same latitude, from almost as far as Ethiopia to Sine-Saloum. This hypothesis can be supported by a series of facts taken from the analysis of an article by Dr. Joseph Maes ("Pierres levées de Tundi-Daro", 1924) on the upright stones in the "French" Sudan village known as Tundi-Daro. (1974: 192-93)

Citing Dr. Verneau (1895), R. Cornevin states that the Sereer come from an intermixing between the Mandinka (or Sose) and the Wolof (Cornevin 1960: 266).

J. Robin insists that the Sereer and Peul are closely linked in spite of their different ways of life; the former are farmers and sedentary whereas the latter are shepherds and nomads (1946: 252). Actually, there is a joking relationship between the Peul and the Sereer. Both ethnic groups are conscious of their close kinship resulting from intermixing. The Sereer claim that the Peul are their slaves and the Peul say the same thing about the Sereer. However, this joking relationship is a friendly one which does not lead to open hostility.

Besides the joking relationship between ethnic groups, there are also jokes within each ethnic group. Marguerite Dupire recounts the obscene jokes in Sereer society. She reflects that:

> Les Serer Sinsin et les Lébou [fishermen living on a 30 miles stretch on the coast from Dakar to Bargny] ont la réputation auprès de leurs concitoyens sénégalais, de jurer à tout propos, probablement parce qu'ils sont peu islamisés et les grossièretés qui ont la préférence des Serer se rapportent à l'anus du père. (1979: 83)

It is important to differentiate between what is commonly called a 'joking relationship' and a 'cathartic relationship.' M. Griaule's article entitled "L'alliance cathartique" between the Bozo and Dogon of Mali sheds some light on the cathartic relationship:

> The name 'joking relationship' has been applied to a number of institutions displaying the common characteristic of permitting exchange of insults. The present article discusses the relationship between the Bozo and the Dogon of the French Sudan [present-day Mali], which has been imitated in a number of other less important relationships. In daily life the most common manifestations of this relationship or pact are mutual purifications, exchanges of insults, and reconciliations. The pact is based on the supposition that once upon a time a part of the vital force of each party then acts on that part of himself which is in the other and which forms a sort of foundation, in the person of the other, on which he can work. A partner in this relationship is the most suitable agent for integrating and sharing the spiritual powers of the other. This stabilizing function is similar to that exercised by the notion of twinship among certain African peoples. Twinship is indeed at the root of these exchanges, whether on the material or the spiritual plane, which are one element in social equilibrium. (M. Griaule 1948: 258)

Joking relationships and obscenities are found in other cultures. D. F. Thompson's article on the aborigenes of Australia is about the joking relationship in their societies. He writes: "Among the native tribes of Cape York Peninsula, North Queensland, the use of swearing and obscenity is of frequent occurrence and plays an important part in social life" (1935: 460). Thompson adds that "this organized obscenity is well known in African and Melanesian societies" (loc. cit.).

In his study on insulting and obscene words in Senegal, I. Sow highlights the social functions of obscenity among the Wolof and the Pulaar (Tukulor). He writes:

> The insulting word, though it generally refers to sexual images and phantasms, creating both a concrete, symbolic denuded and allusive style, it appears to be the main and original way to denote and reveal the power of man's speech. Even though it is strictly repressed and controlled, it remains very effective in the different classes of the society whose representations, anxiousness, preoccupations and fears, it contributes to reveal. (1986-1987: 344)

806 Note that the messengers call the king Jon although the singer has just said (ll. 802-03) that his name at that time was not Jon but Jaxaté.

812 This is an instance of folk etymology. Njaajaan means 'strange' in Sereer; it also means 'extraordinary', 'unusual'. The name Njaajaan Njaay has become identified with the history of the Wolof. Citing Père Zanno (1960), Monteil maintains that *Ndyadyan* means a "misfortune" (1966: 31).

817-19 This is a gerontocratic system in which the main criterion is age. One can draw a parallel with another Wolof kingdom, the kingdom of Kayor. As pointed out by B. Dieng (1980: 878-79), in that kind of society, an older person has more rights and claims than a younger person. The latter should show respect to an older person as well as taking orders from him; the younger person should also keep in the background in all social activities. An older person is considered as having more wisdom and knowledge than the younger one. However, in the Wolof epic tale, that social order is upside down. A young man, Njaajaan Njaay is the one who plays a primary role on the political scene, not an elder. Even though we do not know his exact age, we can infer that he must be young because of his prowess and physical achievements.

In the tale, the elders of Waalo have sent messengers to the Sereer king Maysa Waali Jon, who is known to possess oracles as well as being versed in fetishism. Generally speaking, the Sereer are considered as the people who safeguard the traditional indigenous beliefs that are not greatly tainted by either Christianity or Islam. As highlighted by L. Monnier, magic and religion play an important role in the conception of power among the peoples of the savannah (1966: 29).

822-24 According to the version available to Monteil, Mbarak Barka is Njaajaan's half-brother and is the son of Mbaarik Bô, Fatumata Sal's second husband. That must also be the case here. In a separate account on Mbarak Barka, J. Robin states that Barka Bo is a bastard child born from the union between a Peul slave and a Tukulor princess called Fatimata Sall" (1946: 254).

858-62 This is a case of name change due to pronunciation. In Monteil's version Mbarak is given various names: Barka Mbaarik, Barka Faatimata Sal, Barka Bô, Barka Mbody (1966: 33). The last name, Mbody, would correspond to Mboj in the tale. This name is still in usage in present-day Senegal. According to J. Robin, the name M'Bodj is derived from Ba or Bo (1946: 254). Ba (or Bâ) is a typical Peul name.

Name changes or the adaptation of a name from one area to another within the Senegambian area are indeed very common. For instance, in Senegal we have the name Samb; in Gambia, people tend to say Samba instead of Samb. Conversely, Samba is a first name in Senegal. In Senegal, we have the name Diop which is actually a French transcription whereas in Gambia, it is Jobe. The latter form better renders that name from its original Wolof pronunciation. Certain variations and differences between Senegal and Gambia have more to do with the legacy of European colonization and partition than anything else. In fact, there are more commonalities than differences between the two entities. Senegal was colonized by the French and Gambia by the British. Therefore, there are influences of the French and English languages in both countries when it comes to the transcription and pronunciation of names and expressions that come originally from the national languages such as Wolof or Mandika. (For a more detailed analysis of that topic, see Sulayman S. Nyang, "Ten Years of Gambia's Independence: A Political Analysis," *Présence Africaine*, 104 (1977): 28-45).

Within Senegal, we also have Jaw (Diaw), Jaak (Diack) and Ja (Dia), Ba and Baal, Sék (Seck) and Sok, Ñan (Niang) and Ñaan (Niane), Jaw and Caw (Thiaw), Bari (Barry) and Barro, etc.

882-85 There is a problem of chronology here. In the tale, we learn that Barka

Bô replaced Njaajaan as the ruler of Waalo. In a separate account (Appendix II), Ñan asserts that Mbañ Wadde was part of a collegial team of nine rulers that were kin. By the same token, Monteil also observes that Barka Bô, Njaajaan's half-brother, was third in the leadership of Waalo, the first being Njaajaan and the second Mbay Wad (or Mbañ Wadde). Still, according to Monteil, it is when Njaajaan went to Jolof that the elders chose Mbañ Wadde to succeed him. When Wadde died, he was then replaced by Barka Bô (p.33). In the chronological list of B. Barry (1985: 311-13), we have two separate and different accounts:

-In Amadou Wade's chronicle (translated by Bassirou Cissé, annotated and published by V. Monteil in 1943), Mbany Waad and his sisters come after Njaajaan; we find again the collegial team as in Ñan's list as well as the affirmation that Waad and his sisters ruled for nine years.

-In Samba Ndienne Bara Gaye's account (collected by Boubou Sall in 1944 and published by Félix Brigaud), Barka Bô comes after Njaajaan; thus he is the second ruler of Waalo.

Samba Ndienne Bara Baye and Sèq Ñan thus agree that Barka was the second ruler. They also agree that Barka stayed in power for 24 years.

886-87 The Wolof poet repeats that Njaajaan's last name was Aydara, not Njaay. Earlier on, in line 261, Ñan remarked that Njaajaan's father Bubakar had Aydara as a family name. (See also the note to l. 253.)

888-90 Once again, it is of the utmost importance to be cautious about the griot's statement. There is always a possibility of partisanship on the griot's part, since he is the griot of my family and the context within which he is performing is a determining factor. The performance took place in my father's compound; my father and I were present. However, this piece of advice relating to a cautionary attitude as to the griot's statement does not undermine in any fashion the latter's importance and social role within Wolof society or the longstanding and solid relationship that have existed between the griot's ancestors and my family and more specifically between Ñan and my father.

894 The singer refers to the advent of European traders in late sixteenth century.

895-99 Was Waalo a state, an empire, or a kingdom? There are subtle nuances among these terms. J. Vansina's following observation can be of some help in distinguishing between these concepts:

> It is possible to distinguish between the two terms [kingdom and state]. A state would then be a political organization where kinship ties are not used as a basic principle of organization in the pattern of delegation of authority. A kingdom would be any political organization which has a single hereditary head from which all authority stems. Used in those senses not all states have to be kingdoms, nor would all kingdoms be states. But in Africa all kingdoms seem in fact to be states, including even the celebrated Shilluk [Sudan, East Africa] .
> This is based to such an extent on inheritance of chieftainship in local dominant lineages that it can be seen as a case of segmentary lineage structure. But it is equally possible to stress the fact that whoever resides in an administrative unit, whatever his kin-connexions, accepts the authority of the local chieftain. Even this case can be considered to be a state. (1962: 324)

Actually, in the case of Waalo, we have all the indications that the terms "state" and "kingdom" would equally apply to it. The inheritance of power is not strictly confined to a hereditary lineage.

897 The Wolof equivalent of democracy is *nguur guñu sédélé ba mu mat.* It literally means "a power [political] that is equally shared till it is well rounded." This a very explicit statement which gives a sense of equality, of sharing; moreover, it is an attempt to find a kind of balance between various spheres of power within the kingdom of Waalo, namely between the barak (executive) and the sirabawar (parliament). We do not have enough information on the judiciary; but it seems (through the tale) that the people of Waalo were more concerned with the strengthening of the executive; to that end, there was a branch of vassal chieftaincies that were accountable to the centralized administration; the chieftains were known as *kangaam.* The latter were sent to the adjoining territories of the Waalo kingdom such as Jolof in order to fulfill administrative duties. In turn, the barak's power was counterbalanced and kept under control by the Sirabawar assembly.

At another level, in many Wolof states and kingdoms such as Waalo, we have a gradual transformation from the clanic structure to the monarchic structure with the specification of colleges of power and with the division of labour and the strengthening of the caste system (C.A. Diop 1973: 783). In an article devoted to traditional African political institutions and systems, P. Diagne makes the general statement that "la tradition politique africaine préislamique, préchrétienne et précoloniale, aussi longtemps qu'elle concerne des sociétés rurales, peu urbanisées, repose sur une forme de démocratie, c'est-à-dire sur des formes populaires de pouvoir, qui opèrent à travers des régimes et des systèmes légalistes, légitimistes, conservateurs et inégalitaristes" (1976: 26). More specifically on the Wolof, the author adds that "la démocratie directe est exercice d'un pouvoir villageois et de quartier. L'assemblée du village ou du quartier (*'Ndaje waa dékk'* ou *'Ndaje waa gox'* en wolof) bat le rappel de tous les éléments qui vivent ensemble quel que soit leur statut ou fonction sociale, à propos d'un problème local: répartition des tâches économiques de portée collective, élection des autorités locales, etc" (Diagne p. 29).

In the political organization of the kingdom of Waalo, the various spheres of power reflect the will to create checks and balances, therefore to try to create a system based on equality.

900. Monteil observes:

> Ndyadyan Ndyay (premier Brak), sous le règne duquel le Wâlo prit son indépendance et s'organisa, ne resta à la tête de ce pays que pendant une période de seize années (1186-1202). (1966:32)

902-06 This is an enumeration that is rapidly uttered by the singer. For the griot, aesthetic considerations may be more important in this instance than strict accuracy.

V. Monteil in "Le Dyolof et Al-Bouri Ndiaye" (1966: 606) reports that on December 20, 1965, at a public performance at the recreational and cultural center of Bopp in Dakar, a griot called Leyti Gisê, who was originally from Jolof recited a genealogy of Njaajaan Njaay. That performance was recorded by Mustapha Lô. Gisê lists the earliest rulers of Waalo as:

1. Ndyadyan Ndyay (ruled 44 years);
2. Sarê Ndyadyan (his son);
3. Ndiklan Sarê;

212

4. Tyukuli Ndiklan.

Ñan and Gisê agree that Njaajaan was the first ruler, but Ñan mentions Gèt Njaajaan as his succesor whereas Gisê does not. They both mention Sarê Ndyadyan. Dombur Njaajaan and Nafaye Njaajaan are not in Gisê's list, nor is Fukili Njaajaan.

It is important to realize that Gisê is from Jolof; he may give preference or primacy to the history of Jolof and thus focus more on the genealogy of Njaajaan in Jolof whereas Ñan would give the edge to Waalo. Thus, even within the same country, within a fairly small geographical space shared by the same ethnic group, the Wolof, we have different versions of the same history.

In his study of the epic narratives of the Wolof kingdom of Kayor, B. Dieng (1980: 862) observes that his griot sings the praises of the Jolof kingdom by saying that it was in command of Kayor, Bawol, Siin, Saalum, and other countries. However, the griot does not mention Waalo.

The second observation is that we must be cautious about the transcription of Wolof and Senegalese names by French authors such as V. Monteil. Throughout the history of French colonization of Senegal, we have numerous examples of Senegalese names being transcribed in a different way in French; or, a French writer or author would just write down a name by omitting a sound that exists in Wolof but does not in French. The transcription of the name Njaay is a case in point. That name has been transcribed in French as N'Diaye (N-Di-a-ye); we have four syllables here whereas in Wolof, the whole word (in its original Wolof meaning) is only one syllable. The same applies to Joobe (Diop in French) and these are just two examples.

902 Interestingly, Njaajaan's death is not mentioned by the Wolof singer.

In his study of the tribal life of the Gikuyu people of Kenya, East Africa, J. Kenyatta propounds the mythical legend of the foundation of the Gikuyu nation by a man and a woman: Gikuyu and Moombi:

> Gikuyu and Moombi had many grand-- and great-grandchildren. When Gikuyu and Moombi died, their daughters inherited their movable and immovable property which they shared equally among them. (1965: 7)

Gikuyu and Moobi (like Njaajaan) have a line of descent but in the Wolof legend there is no rupture in that line (death); on the contrary, the accent is put on life and on continuity.

Another relevant example is that of the Bambara empire of Ségou (present-day republic of Mali). Biton Koulibaly is the mythical founder of that empire. L. Kesteloot writes:

> Le mythe ne parle jamais de la mort de Biton, et le mystère reste épais, même en interrogeant l'histoire. Tétanos ou assassinat? même le lieu exact de sa tombe reste caché, comme c'est du reste la tradition pour tout grand roi manding. Pudeur ou prudence? (1980: 606)

Biton's successors are mentioned and the griot carries on his narrative (p. 608).

909 Saalum is a region inhabited primarily by the Wolof and is situated in the center of Senegal; but since Saalum is next to Siin which is inhabited by the Sereer, one could expect similar demographic inter-mixing between the two

regions. When Senegal became an independent state in 1960, Saalum became a governorship with a governor at its head to be chosen by the Minister of the Interior. The regional capital is Kaolack. However, with subsequent administrative re-organizations, that whole region is now known as "Région de Kaolack."

910 Tundu Gèt literally means "Gèt's hill." The hill was named after Gèt and is situated between Waalo and Jolof.

912-914 Warxox literally means in Wolof "to be exhausted on horseback" (*war* means "to mount" and *xox* "to be tired"). V. Monteil notes that "Warkhokh was the capital of Dyolof" (1966: 60).

In his recounting of the famous *Bataille de Guîlé* (Battle of Guîlé, which opposed the Wolof Kingdoms of Jolof and Kayor on June 6, 1886), Amadou Duguay-Clédor mentions Warxox as well as the Njaay, descendants of Njaajaan:

Du côté du Djoloff, il y avait les N'Diaye, tous fils de rois, de princes ou de grands notables du Djoloff, les gens de Thieng ue et de Ouarkhokhe [Warxox]. (Duguay-Clédor 1931, Rpt. 1985: 46).

917 Yang-yang is an extant place. V. Monteil qualifies it as a traditional administrative district (1966: 599-600). The full name of the village is Yang-yang Gèèböl.

921 The region of Jolof is mostly inhabited by the Peul who herd their cattle on the vast grasslands extending from the Atlantic Ocean to the semi-desert region of Ferlo in the East.

In Monteil's version, we learn that Njaajaan came to Jolof and married a Peul woman called Ufö, who corresponds to Këyfa in the Wolof epic tale. Where Monteil's version agrees with that of Ñan is that Njaajaan spent only one night with the woman, but after that point the two versions differ again. According to Monteil's version, a son was born from that union and was named Lêlê-Fulu Fak, whereas in the Wolof epic tale no name is given; the text simply goes on to mention the name of Saajo Njaay (l. 930) as a descendant of Njaajaan. Njaajaan came to Jolof as a conqueror for he was sent by the elders of Waalo. As far as the people of Jolof were concerned, he was a foreigner.

L. Monnier tells us about a mythical narrative in the Lower-Congo (Central Africa), recounted by G. Balandier (*La vie quotidienne au Royaume de Kongo du XVIe au XVIIIe siècle*, 1965), whose hero is the prince Ntinu from the kingdom of Vungu. After having conquered a region, Ntinu's authority was not recognized because his ancestors were not buried in that land. As far as the conquered people were concerned, Ntinu was a stranger, and thus he could not control the fertility of the land (Monnier 1966: 25).

Njaajaan overcame his "foreignness" by having a child with a local woman. Although Njaajaan is from a noble and aristocratic lineage, he is marrying a commoner in a morganatic marriage.

In another West African mythical narrative ("The Legend of Queen Pokou" of the Akan people of present-day Ghana and Ivory Coast), there is another instance of a morganatic marriage between prince Dakon and a female slave named Talouamah (Gérard Lezou 1979: 44).

930 The Wolof singer casually mentions the name Saajo Njaay. We do not know if Saajo was alive at the time of performance, which seems to be implied

by the use of the present tense, or if he was an ancestor who lived in the time of Njaajaan. However, in this instance, the audience is the most important factor for the singer addresses an audience that is composed only of Wolof-speaking people. Therefore, he takes it for granted that all those present know about Saajo, which is why he does not elaborate on Saajo.

931 Xuma is an extant place; it is an old settlement in Waalo.

932 Richard-Toll is also an extant place, in Waalo by the River Senegal.

937 The singer's assertion as to the change of name is accepted by C.A. Diop who observes that "all the people bearing the name Diop are descendents of Guét, Njaajaan's eldest son" (1949: 851).

941 On the name Aydara, see above, note to ll. 345-47

947 This 400-year period may be an exaggeration on the singer's part. However, there were petty kingdoms during that period that had no real political link between them; with the advent of Njaajaan, the concept of a centralization of power was brought to Waalo. Njaajaan can be perceived as a unifier. There are three stages in the representation of history in the epic tale:

-The past is marked by some kind of social order. However, that order was unstable for there were wars among the petty kingdoms.
-Then, there is the present that is marked by the coming of Njaajaan. The latter came in a time of crisis and brought some kind of order; however, the main

feature of the present is crisis.

-Finally, we have the future which heralds a definite social order as well as some kind of stability.

PAST	_____	PRESENT	_____	FUTURE

Waalo existed for 400 years   Njaajaan (time of crisis)   Stability

950-51 The coming of Njaajaan to Jolof constitutes a case of internal colonization.

959-60 According to various written sources as well as to Wolof traditions, the Sereer and the Peul were forced south of the River Senegal (Robin 1946: 251). Thus, Jolof is south of the river as well as south of Waalo.

In his article entitled "Royaumes Seréres. Les institutions traditionnelles du Sine Saloum," P. Diagne explains in detail the political and social structures of the Sereer kingdoms. The Sereer have been traditionally confined to the areas of Siin and Saalum which are situated in the center of Senegal. However, according to oral historical accounts, the Sereer used to live farther north of Siin and Saalum, namely in Waalo, Fuuta, Jolof, and Kayor. In those areas, there are remnants of Sereer cultural elements (Diagne 1965: 143).

C.A. Diop argues that in the beginning, Kayor and Bawal were essentially Sereer (1949: 852).

However, one must add that the most visible of those remnants is the linguistic one. For instance, there are many similarities between the Wolof language and the Sereer, which point to the fact that the two belong to the same family of languages, the West Atlantic branch of the Niger-Kordofanian languages (Pulleybank 1990: 962-63).   C.A. Diop (1949: 852) adds that Wolof is an offshoot of Sereer.

The *lamanes* were 'masters of the lands', people who had cleared the land and thus had the right to cultivate it (Diagne 1965: 148).

In his study of land-holding in the rural areas inhabited by the Wolof, Abdoulaye B. Diop defines the *lamanate* system as being "le mode de tenure foncière le plus ancien que nous connaissions. Il existait à l'époque où la région était habitée par les *Sereer,* bien avant l'institution des monarchies du Kayor et du Baol, au milieu du XVIe siècle" (1968: 48).

965   Ganaar is the Wolof name for Mauritania. It actually designates a geographical, cultural, and linguistic space inhabited by the light skin Arabo-Berber or Moors, also called *Naar* in Wolof.

On the origins of the Moors, C.A. Diop (1974: 52) argues that the Moors descend directly from post-Islamic invaders who, starting from Yemen, conquered Egypt, North Africa, and Spain between the seventh and fifteenth centuries. From Spain they fell back on Africa. Thus, the Moors are basically Arab Muslims whose installation in Africa is quite recent.

A distinction has to be made here for present-day Mauritania has not always been inhabited by the Arabo-Berbers. For instance the adjoining territory that is situated on the right bank of the River Senegal has always been inhabited by the Black populations who made a living from farming and cattle herding. However, 10 miles north of the river, one enters a desert region. The Berbers have a different lifestyle: they herd livestock consisting of sheep, camels, and goats. They do not farm; they are engaged in trade. They live in tents called *xayma*. The largest part of present-day Mauritania is desert and the Black populations and the Wolof in particular refer to that desert region when they evoke the name *Ganaar*.

CHAPTER IV: THE WOLOF

Part Two: Study

The history and geography of the Wolof are marked by the development and growth of the geographical space inhabited by the Wolof as well as their demographic expansion from a small area to a much larger region.   That region covers most of the northern, central, and the coastal parts of Senegal.

A - *Geography and Language*

In the middle of the nineteenth century, scholarly studies on the Wolof started to appear.   For instance, H. Azan gives a very detailed description of Oualo (or Waalo) (1863a: 395-404), which includes its hydrology, land use, and meteorology.

Around the year 1884, D. Boilat traveled to most of the regions of Senegal writing that "les royaumes habités par les Wolofs sont: le Cayor, le Walo, le Dhiolof [or Jolof], une grande partie du Baol intérieur et la république [léboue] de Dakar"   (1984:278).   The most important landform of the geographical space inhabited by the Wolof is the valley of the River Senegal.

The geographic distribution of the space inhabited by the Wolof has not changed much since the earliest European accounts.   One notable aspect is the migratory movement within and outside Senegal.   The Wolof moved farther south to Casamance where they cleared lands for cultivation, and also migrated (mostly at the beginning of the twentieth century) to various regions of Africa (Ivory Coast, Gabon, Congo) and to France. The migration of the Wolof outside of Senegal can be explained by the fact that they tended to be more educated and were skilled in trades such as carpentry, masonry, construction, blacksmithing, and commerce. The Wolof were also drafted in great numbers into the French colonial army (also known as *la coloniale*) where they were known as the *tirailleurs sénégalais*. Overall, the main factors that explain the head start of the Wolof in the areas of education, work, and military skills were their early contact with the French and exposure to European traders. Dr Lasnet wrote: "Les Ouolofs sont de moeurs douces, habitués aux Européens depuis des siècles et n'ayant point le fanatisme farouche qui éloigne de nous les Maures et souvent les Toucouleurs" (1900: 122).

Thus, Senegal was the beachhead of French penetration in West Africa. The first educational and military institutions, as well as trading posts, were established in the Saint-Louis area which was primarily inhabited by the Wolof. During the nineteenth century and first half of the twentieth, nationals of the other French colonies such as the French Sudan (present-day Mali), Upper Volta (present-day Burkina Faso), Dahomey (present-day Benin), Ivory Coast, and Cameroon were sent to Senegal for military training or to attend schools such as the Ecole William Ponty of Gorée, the Lycée Faidherbe of Saint-Louis, or the Lycée Van Vollenhoven of Dakar.

Thus, Peter Worsley remarks that "French official policy, indeed, had encouraged sons of rulers and other upper-class individuals to acquire Western education from as early as 1856, when the quaintly-named Ecoles des Otages were set up" (1977: 141).

There is a relationship between the advent of Njaajaan as the founder of the Wolof nation and the Wolof language itself. The personage of Njaajaan and the language are inseparable. This connection is well illustrated in the following passage:

> Le processus de création, de diffusion et d'adoption de la langue Wolof est indissociablement lié au rôle moteur d'un étranger [Njaajaan] dépositaire d'un pouvoir à la fois technologique, arbitral et religieux, fondement de sa légitimité. (Yoro Fall 1989: 119)

The Wolof language is the most widely spoken language of Senegal and its "lingua franca." L. Homburger remarked that "au sud du fleuve [Sénégal], sur la côte et à l'intérieur, on parle Wolof, dans le Diolof, le Walo, le Cayor et le Baol et jusque dans la Gambie" (1957: 54-5). Dr Lasnet added that "la langue ouolofe est distincte des autres dialectes africains, c'est la langue usuelle du commerce dans toute la Sénégambie; à ce titre elle a une grande importance et est comprise partout où sont des traitants et se font des échanges" (1900: 112). It is important to stress the fact that in Africa, many languages overlap ethnic and tribal boundaries. Mazrui writes:

> African languages have been adopted as a lingua franca beyond the ethnic boundaries of that language, for example, Wolof in Senegal and Hausa in the north of Nigeria and in parts of the neighboring states. (A. Mazrui 1986: 258)

B - *Customs and Beliefs of the Wolof, and a Brief Historical Outline*

D. Gamble observes that "the earliest mention of the name Wolof appears in the writings of Cada Mosto" (1455-57) (1957: 16). Citing Joire (1955) on the origins of the Wolof, Gamble adds that the tumuli excavated near Rao might have been constructed in the fourteenth century, prior to the emergence of the Wolof as a recognizable entity.

Most traditional historians of Senegal stress the fact that the region that lies around the River Senegal and is now occupied by the Wolof was originally inhabited by the Sereer; the latter were driven farther south by the Wolof. This point of view is also held by Ñan, the singer of the Wolof epic tale.

H. Azan argues that "les Oualofs appartiennent au rameau éthiopien de la race nègre" (opt. cit., p. 413). However, there is no such thing as a Wolof of pure race as emphasized by Azan (loc. cit.). (See my note to 1. 276 of the epic tale, on the inter-mixing of the Wolof, Sereer, and Tukulor.)

Concerning the relationship between the various Wolof Kingdoms, R. Cornevin observes:

> Le Djolof n'acquiert son indépendance qu'avec N'Diadiane N'Diaye qui réussit à débarrasser le pays de l'influence toucouleur du Fouta. (1960: 265)

Cornevin's statement seems to corroborate Ñan's argument as to the primacy of Waalo over Jolof for the singer says that Njaajaan was sent to Jolof (in the middle of the Waalo empire) in order to organize that territory (ll. 890-91).

Bérenger-Féraud does not make any differenciation between these kingdoms. He simply writes:

> Au temps jadis, le Cayor, le Oualo, le Djiolof, le Baol, le Sine et le Saloum formaient une sorte de république sans chef suprême, et dans laquelle chaque village était absolument indépendant des voisins. Il y avait souvent, on le comprend, des altercations et des batailles de villages à village, de sorte que la tranquillité du

pays était perpétuellement troublée. (1885: 191).

J. Vansina defines the African kingdoms as "sovereign political groups, headed by a single leader who delegates authority to representatives in charge of the territorial units into which the country is divided" (1962: 325). However, in the case of Waalo as depicted by Ñan, it was the Council of the Elders that decided to send Njaajaan to Jolof, in the middle of the empire.

On the relationship between Waalo and Jolof, it seems that Jolof was anterior to Waalo, at least in G. Nicolas's account:

> Les trois états du Waalo, du Cayor et du Baol se sont émancipés de l'autorité de la vieille dynastie du Dyolof et de la tutelle peul et ont refoulé les Serer vers le Sud. (1978:364)

Traditionally speaking, the Wolof were animists. Even though most of the Wolof people are Muslims today, there are still remnants of their traditional religion and considerable syncretism exists among them. H. Azan remarked that:

> Le mahométisme [Islam] est la seule religion connue dans le pays parmi les Oualofs, soit du Oualo, soit du Cayor, soit du Djolof; les uns se déclarent musulmans et suivent d'une manière très confuse les différents préceptes du Coran sous la direction de prêtres fanatiques et ignorants nommés sérignes; les autres affectent le plus superbe dédain pour toute pratique religieuse, et n'ont foi qu'en leur gris-gris [i.e., charms, amulets] *(Têrê)* . (1863a: 414)

The Wolof still believe in spirits and witches associated with their traditional religion.[1]

Wolof society is organized into a caste system. Citing B. Barry ("Le Royaume du Walo"), P. Curtin writes: "The Wolof in the seventeenth century distinguished five separate occupations as the basis for endogamous social groups -- fishermen (*cubaalo*), weavers (*rabb-ser*), woodworkers (*lawbe*), smiths (*tegg*), and minstrels [or griots] (*gewel*). This would be a minimal list of occupations, even though some societies counted two or even three different kinds of minstrels. Approximately the same complexity of caste division still survives in the middle and lower Senegal valley" (Curtin 1975:32).

The oldest writings on the Wolof were published by European (mostly French) authors. However, there are more recent studies by Senegalese as well as other historians, linguists, and sociologists.[2]

As a closing remark on Wolof contemporary society, I quote an observation by D. Gamble:

> It is not a simple matter to generalize about the Wolof. Their culture now spans an enormous range, from small rural villages where the old ways predominate, to modern cities like Dakar, from illiteracy [in French] to college training; from lineage and village headship to political parties and ministerial government; from traditional entertainments to radios and football. Even within the rural Wolof society there is considerable variation, the values of those of aristocratic origin differing from those descended from former slaves. The variability in Wolof culture means that almost every statement about them needs to be accompanied by a label as to time and place. (D. Gamble 1967: vii; cited in Michael Coolen, "Wolof Xalam Tradition," 1983, p. 482.)

This variability requires great caution on the part of scholars attempting to account for the various literary manifestations of Wolof society.

Notes to Chapter Four

1.   See David Ames, "Belief in 'Witches' among the rural Wolof of the Gambia," *Africa*, 29 (1959): 263-73.

2. See C. A. Diop (1949, 1973), D. Gamble (1957), O. Silla (1966), P. Diagne (1967, 1976), Abdoulaye B. Diop (1968, 1981), A. Samb (1974a, 1974b), V. Bomba (1977), J. Irvine (1978), A. Sylla (1978), B. Wright (1989).

CHAPTER V

Performance, Audience, and Music.
Social Functions of the Tale.
The Griot in Wolof Society

In this study, performance is the core element, as is the case with all oral traditions. The Wolof have an orally-based culture and civilization. In Wolof society, the spoken word is paramount. The performance during which the epic tale that constitutes the basis of this study was sung is the subject of this chapter. Equally important is the interplay between the verbal performance and the music, namely the lute that the performer is playing at the same time as he sings. The role of the audience is of central importance to the performer. An audience is a prerequisite; if there is no audience, there is no oral tradition either. Lastly, the role of the griot in the African past as well as in contemporary Wolof society will be analyzed. Performance has a multi-dimensional aspect.

A - Performance, Audience and Music.

In the introduction to this study, I recounted the circumstances that led to the performance of *The Epic Tale of the Waalo kingdom* by Sèq Ñan. The performance was arranged by my father in his house in Rosso-Sénégal. An arranged performance is slightly different from a spontaneous one. However, in contemporary Wolof society, most performances are arranged for set occasions such as festivities, pilgrims returning from the holy pilgrimage to Mecca, naming ceremonies, or weddings. The major difference between the two kinds of performances is that a festivity gives a mark of distinctiveness to the performance; for instance people wear their most elegant clothing whereas they do not necessarily do so at a spontaneous performance. Concerning the substance of the performance, there are not major variations between the two types. As we will see later, the element that influences the singer most is the audience.

When the singer performs the same song or poem at different times, the story line and plot remain basically the same, but he may embellish the poem in one instance but not in the other. Thus no two performances are exactly the same in form and content. Each performance must be studied and appreciated separately. This phenomenon was well described by A. Lord who wrote that "in a sense each performance is 'an' original, if not 'the' original" (1960:101).

In S. Ñan's oral narrative performance, an important element is that he is very well acquainted with the patron, in this instance my father. The singer is highly conscious of the relationship between the patron and himself. Beside the gift-exchange relationship, there is a relationship based on friendship and loyalty that goes way back to their ancestors, the awareness of which deserves to be underscored. If the singer were confronted with a patron he did not know very well, that would certainly have a major effect on the performance for he would create a story or a genealogy to please the new patron as well as to fit the occasion.

In Rosso-Sénégal, the atmosphere of the performance was very casual.

The singer performed indoors, in a large living room with oriental rugs on the floor. The design and decoration of the living-room reflected the influence that Islamic and North African culture have in that part of Senegal, as well as the proximity of the Maghreb. The singer as well as the audience were seated on the carpets. Women and children do attend such performances, but on this particular occasion the children and women were outside doing whatever they would do on a normal day: The children were playing and the women were conversing and once in a while would run an errand or would prepare a meal or take a nap. The performance proper did not have much immediate impact on the lives of the members of the household. They were acquainted with the singer and had heard him perform before, so he was no novelty to them. Singing and music are parts of the daily lives of these people. The members of the household were not surprised when Ñan started plucking his lute and started singing; they would not be surprised either if the singer spent a whole day in the house without singing or playing music at all; he came to the house just like any ordinary visitor, as he did on countless occasions.

Thus the impact an audience would usually have upon a performer was lessened here by the familiar and casual relationship that Ñan enjoyed with his listeners. Another important aspect was that even though most of the time four people and the singer were present, neighbors would come in to visit once in a while but never stayed too long. For them too, the performance that was taking place was an ordinary event; there was no reason for them to stay longer than they ordinarily deemed necessary. These visits on the part of the neighbors constituted an honor and a show of respect for the family because my father belonged to one of the royal houses of Waalo; he was also a leading citizen and a person of distinction in Rosso.

On the relationship between the performer and the audience, R. Finnegan remarks that "the performer/composer is aware of the need to speak in accordance with the demands of his audience rather than some authenticated but remote prototype" (1973:125). This is generally true for most performances. In this case, however, because of the nature of the relationship between the performer and his patron, the situation was intensified because the patron was as knowledgeable about the history of Waalo as the singer, if not more so. Therefore, the singer was doing his best not to distort the historical accounts, most of all the genealogical account. There is a verbal bond between the performer and the audience, which shows its appreciation of the performance by uttering in Wolof stock expressions such as "dëgge la" (that is true), "xamon nañka" (we knew it), "laa ilaa ila laah" (an Islamic expression that is uttered to express amazement and surprise), "cëy !", "ëskëy!"[1] In turn, the performer relies on three components in his interaction with the audience: "captivation of audience, retention of audience, and the transfer of cognitive experience to the audience" (Ropo Sekoni 1990: 140, citing Modupe Broderick's "Social Significance of Binary Oppositions and Narrative Patterns in Three West African Oral Narratives," 1981). Ñan himself uses conflict-producing images and conflict-resolving images as dialectical devices that are sure to provoke audible reactions from the audience. One instance in the Wolof epic tale occurs when Njaajaan fights Hamar-the-Scolder-of-Old-People (lines 381-84). While the singer was recounting that struggle, the members of the audience were captivated; they uttered exclamations and their facial expressions showed support for the would-be hero against the villain.

Conversely, when Maramu Gaye finally succeeds in making Njaajaan come out of his silence (ll. 702-86), members of the audience reacted to the resolution of the conflict by exclaiming: "We knew that it was going to be that way." It was not the first time that they had heard these epic accounts; however, their reactions to the performance were genuine, as if it was the first time that this tale was being narrated to them.

There is a three-way relationship among the performer, the audience, and the normative function of the tale that rests on what I. Basgöz labels extra-constructional elements (1975: 147). Ñan draws elements from the Qur'an, for instance the story of the Flood and the conversions to Islam. The Wolof singer opposes good and evil and, as is to be expected, good wins out. Also in lines 930-33, he uses the present tense to tell the audience that a man called Saajo Njaay descends from a woman called Këyfa who had a child with Njaajaan. According to I. Basgöz, "the teller finds a vehicle in these extra-constructional elements to advise his audience of acceptable behavior, of good conduct, of the moves cherished by society; to teach them history, geography, literature, and to strengthen their religious beliefs" (loc. cit.). The performer, his story, and the audience constitute aspects of a single process. D. Ben-Amos remarks in this vein that "the narrator, his story, and his audience are all related to each other as components of a single continuum, which is the communicative event" (1971: 10).

The place of music in African oral traditions is wonderfully highlighted by the griot Mamadou Kouyaté who sang the *Sunjaata Epic.* Kouyaté was recounting the deeds of another griot, Balla Fasséké, the griot who accompanied Sunjaata. Entering a palace without the king's knowledge, Fasséké saw a xylophone and could not resist the temptation to play it; however, he had come there primarily to spy. Concerning Fasséké's attitude toward the musical instrument, Kouyaté remarks that "le griot a toujours un faible pour la musique, car la musique est l'âme du griot" (D.T. Niane 1960: 75). Similarly, in his analysis of the poetry of the Ewe of present-day Ghana, S.A. Amegbleame remarks that "en ewe, la poésie est fille de la musique et l'une ne peut être conçue sans l'autre" (1981: 91). Amegbleame's remark can be extended to Wolof society and to most African societies. Music, whether drumming or the playing of other instruments such as the *xalam*, is a component of everyday life. A *xalam* is a lute, played by plucking. Most Senegalese entertainers (whether traditional or non-traditional) use some kind of musical instrument in their performance.

As a general observation, it is important to note that the epic on the one hand, music and singing on the other are inseparable. Alioune O. Diop notes that "l'épopée à la fois dite et chantée [est] très courante dans la société traditionnelle sénégalaise" (1990: 9).

The most fascinating feature in Ñan's art is the balance he achieves between singing or reciting the epic tale and playing the *xalam* at the same time. The Wolof performer relays many times what his father told him (lines 618, 676, 693, 697, 974), and also says that the tale was handed down to him by his ancestors (l. 968). Likewise, the Wolof singer learned to play the *xalam* from his father. Just like the oral message, the musical message is transmitted from one generation to the other. M.S. Eno Belinga writes:

> Les griots sont caractéristiques de la musique soudanaise où ils forment, en marge de la société, une caste spéciale où la profession musicale est héréditaire. Chaque griot excelle dans sa spécialité: certains sont spécialistes du luth, d'autres de la harpe, d'autres du haut-bois, d'autres du xylophone, certains sont trompettistes, d'autres timbaliers. (1971: 194).

Sèq Ñan plays the *xalam*.[2] There are four kinds of Wolof *xalam* (Coolen, op. cit., p. 484). The Wolof, however, generally acknowledge only two kinds: The *bopp xalam* and the *nderr xalam*. Ñan plays the *nderr xalam*, which has five strings. While reciting the poem, he plays a specific sequence of notes relating to a specific event, deed, or person; the sequence of notes is known as *buum* in Wolof. When the audience hears a *buum*, its members instantly recognize that *buum* as being dedicated to the relevant event or character.

One major difference between the instrumental accompaniment and the recitation of texts is that in the first instance there is almost no variation. Most of the songs and sequences of notes played on the *xalam* were created or composed in former times, usually after a battle or an act of bravery on the part of a hero. Therefore, the musical part of the performance remains more or less the same whereas there are variations in the recitation itself even though the epic tale was first composed a long time ago.

As Calvin S. Brown observes: "The more general literary impact on music, as shown in programmatic aims and practices, the loosening up or breaking down of fixed forms, and other such purely musical considerations, is usually considered the province of the musicologist rather than the literary scholar" (1970:104-05). One of the poet's essential tasks is to try to combine the text and the music into an organic whole. Further, there is the task of translating a literary text into musical terms. Brown adds that in that process, "the musical translation is not substituted for the original, but added to it."

In the case of the Wolof singer, the task consists in locating the musical set *(buum)* that corresponds to a specific event or deed as he narrates it. As I am not trained in ethnomusicology, I will not elaborate further on this aspect of the performance.

B - *Social Functions of the Tale.*

During the European Middle Ages, the epic was a multi-functional genre and the jongleurs, scribes, and authors all participated in its functions (Duggan 1986b: 730). Among the most important functions were "entertainment, information, sanction of conduct, preserving awareness of the past, and providing models for imitation" (loc. cit.). These five functions can be applied to the epic tale, and it is the griot who carries them out primarily in contemporary Senegalese society. The economic function is also very important. A distinction must be made between the group of professional griots on one hand and the group formed by griots who perform other work in order to support their families. In the interview I had with Ancumbu Caam (see appendix I), Caam emphasizes the fact that he used to be a farmer besides being a performer; later on, he stopped farming and lived solely on performing. The group of professional griots is a force to be reckoned with in contemporary Senegalese society. Professional griots are very powerful and very wealthy. In urban areas such as Dakar, there are nobles who complain that the griots who come to praise them are richer than the nobles themselves; moreover, some of those griots would be driving high-powered cars imported from Germany (Mercedes-Benz, BMW) or France (Renault 25, Peugeot 505) when paying a visit to a noble. Ironically, the noble himself might not own a car; however, he has an obligation to give gifts or money to the griot even if he has to borrow the money or strip his clothes off.[3]

Among other peoples of Central Africa, the epic also plays very important roles. In his analysis of the Mwindo epic of the Nyanga, K. Mateene remarks:

Pour les Nyanga, l'épopée n'est pas seulement un récit

divertissant: document sur leur histoire et leur identité, leurs croyances, coutumes, valeurs et activités, elle constitue un témoignage de leur vision du monde et une réflexion philosophique sur les comportements des hommes et leurs sentiments. (1984: 61)

Besides the *Weltanschauung* that is reflected in the epic, another function of epic is "de maintenir la cohésion du groupe, de ceux qui se réclament d'une origine commune" (G. Lezou 1979:47).

A misleading conception in the study of African traditional societies is to place an over-emphasis on the predominance of the group over the individual. A. Irele corrects that misconception when he stresses the importance of individual responsibility within the group in the traditional setting: "For the Yoruba, the balance of human life, the very sense of human existence, consists in the dynamic correlation of *individual responsibility* and the pressure of external events and forces. In the oral literature, the understanding that human fate is as much a matter of chance as of conscious moral choice is what determines its social function -- their [the Yoruba] illustration of the moral and spiritual attributes needed by *the individual* to wrest a human meaning out of his life (1990: 181 [emphases added])." A balance existed between the individual and the group; however, in most scholarship devoted to traditional African societies, the community (as a nebulous ensemble) is presented as the element that regulates all social life; hardly any stress is put on that balance and its intricacies.

The Wolof epic tale reflects values, beliefs, and a way of life that are specific to the Wolof. The medium in which it is sung is Wolof, and the audience is composed of Wolof people. Thus, on both sides, one is aware of belonging to the same ethnic group with its basic shared cultural values reflected in the value terms of the Wolof language. Wolof is thus the conveying medium that makes that communal consciousness possible, and concrete. When the Wolof listen to the performance of the *Epic Tale of the Waalo Kingdom*, they individually and immediately recognize themselves as implicated in that tale, for it tells them about a hero, Njaajaan Njaay, who founded the Wolof kingdom of Waalo. The same observation can, of course, be made about Mandinka society when the *jéli* (bard) is singing the *Sunjaata Epic*, and so on.

The most important function is the preservation of knowledge of the past and the communal interpretation of history, labelled *mémoire collective* by H.R. Jauss. According to Jauss, a social function played by the epic is the one in which it is:

> a primary form of historical transmission for the nonreader, in which the national history of an ideal past (*le passé tel qu'il eût dû être*) is transposed and elevated into an epic-mythic system of world-explanation. (1982: 87)

When we analyze specific passages of the Wolof epic tale, we can see that most of them are closer to myth and legend than they are to history and to actual events. An example is when the singer says that Mbaarik Bô wore a large ring in his nose and that when it was very hot, the ring used to expand like rubber and fall off (ll. 175-82). In his analysis of the *Sunjaata Epic* , A. Shelton recounts that the griot, Kouyaté, claims that certain events are true whereas they are just legends; moreover, the griot's duty is to preserve and retell a legend. According to Shelton, there are non-historical elements in that epic (1968b: 152).

In the List of the Rulers of Waalo (see Appendix II), on the other hand, the Wolof singer mentions Faidherbe and adds that he ended the rule of traditional chiefs and kings in Waalo in 1854. This is an account of an actual event that happened in the past (See H. Azan [1863a, 1864b], V. Monteil [1966], and B. Barry [1985]). Thus, in the Wolof epic tale, there is an interaction between real historical events and fictitious or mythic elements.

Since sentiments of belonging to a particular ethnicity still prevail in contemporary Senegalese society, the members of the various ethnic groups use the epic tales, genealogies, stories, and riddles performed in their various languages as points of relevance, as guiding cultural referents to which they can relate. Each ethnic group of Senegal has its own oral traditions; those traditions are alive and are currently performed by bards for the Wolof, the Tukulor, the Sereer, the Diola, the Saraxolé, and so on. The scholar has to go beyond the epic tale and explore the realm of oral traditions in general. As A. Dundes observes, "one of the functions of myth is to provide a sacred precedent for present action" (1964: 256). Beyond the concept of myth itself, the customs, events and history of the Waalo kingdom must be taken into account when one considers contemporary Wolof society. The fact that the Wolof singer ends his tale by insisting on how these events and customs were handed down to him by his father and other ancestors is a proof of the dynamic impulses of oral traditions and the role they play in contemporary Wolof society. After diachronically relating events that span more than 1200 years (from the Flood myth as found in the Qur'an to the colonization of Waalo in 1854 by the French), the singer is the living symbol that embodies that historical and mythical consciousness in his words, gestures, clothing and expressions.

One of the functions of the oral poet among the Wolof is to tell the truth; the bard[4] or griot has the freedom to speak his mind without any censorship. Nobles are very careful not to humiliate the griot for he later can publicly retaliate with his skilful use of words. The Wolof singer tells the Wolof not only about their past, but about the present; that is the topic of the next chapter, in which I will consider the role the griot played in pre-colonial traditional Wolof society as well as the role he plays in contemporary Senegalese society. The Wolof poet also tells his audience about the distant past of the Wolof.

In an article devoted to *Beowulf*, R.P. Creed points out that "the Anglo-Saxon singer, who with his Danish singer establishes the remote beginning of the song of Beowulf, and Homer, who through Demodocus links himself with a singer contemporary with Odysseus, are telling us what really happened in those distant days" (1962: 52). Creed adds that "the Anglo-Saxon singer of *Beowulf* seems to be saying through this image that *he* has *heard tell* of Beowulf from a singer and so on back to that Danish singer contemporary with Beowulf himself" (loc. cit. [author's emphases]). This statement identifies one of the driving forces behind oral traditions. As we have seen, the Wolof bard repeats many times what he was told by his father; at the end of the epic tale, he humbly says that the story of Njaajaan Njaay was handed down to him by his ancestors.

An analogous example is found in Niane's *Sunjaata Epic* as told to him by Mamadou Kouyaté, in which Kouyaté recalls the contemporary griot who accompanied Sunjaata Keïta, the founder of the Mali empire. Even though Kouyaté is recounting West African events contemporary with the European Middle Ages, he makes a link with a distant griot who witnessed the events that he is currently narrating. Thus, in oral traditions, there is always that unbroken link that the present singer attempts to establish with a distant singer who witnessed the events and composed the song, story, or poem that is being performed in the present.

C - *Social Functions of the Griot; Performer and Author*

The griot belongs to the lower level of social stratification.[5] He also claims to belong to a caste. The term *caste* itself is an adaptation of the Spanish and Portuguese *casta*, meaning race, lineage, or breed. In its modern sense, it was originally applied by the Portuguese to India around the middle of the sixteenth century (B. Wright 1989: 54). Other terms such as political order and social or socio-professional class are also used in order to explain the stratification of African societies; it seems that the term *caste* is more relevant to India than to Africa.

C. A. Diop writes: "la caste des griots est un héritage direct de l'Égypte des Fari (société pharaonique)" (1981: 213).

Bérenger-Féraud remarks that the griots are the "précurseurs de la civilisation, ils ont en cela servi à l' accroissement du domaine intellectuel des peuples de l'Afrique, et quelque minime que soit le progrès qu'on leur doive, on ne saurait leur refuser leur mérite de l'avoir importé dans plus d'un endroit" (1882: 274).

As far back as 1829, Baron Roger made the following remark:

> On appelle *ghéwal*, en ouolof, et *griots*, en français, des espèces de baladins faisant le métier de chanter et d'égayer les autres. Ils sont très recherchés, et forment la société habituelle des chefs, dont ils amusent le désœuvrement. (1829: 140)

In 1594, a Portuguese captain named André Alvares d'Almada visited the country of the Wolof (he refers to the latter as *Jalofos*). In his *Tratado breve dos Rios de Guiné*, he describes a group of people he calls *Judeus*; the author adds that "Quand ils meurent, on ne les enterre pas comme les autres, mais on

les ensevelit dans des troncs d'arbre, ou on les pend aux branches, car les autres
noirs croient, bien à tort, que, s'ils les mettent en terre, il ne pleuvra pas et que
l'année sera sèche. On les tient pour une race maudite" (Cited by V. Monteil
1968: 777). On March 15, 1955, the Institut Fondamental d'Afrique Noire
(I.F.A.N.) in Dakar was notified of the discovery of a *baobab* tree (also known
as "*Bok*") that contained human skeletal remains. On the nineteenth day of the
same month, the Anthropology section of I.F.A.N. sent a team to the location
of the tree. The human remains were removed and then sent to the laboratory
for analysis. The results of the analysis were compared with information
obtained from the people who lived in the vicinity: that tree was the place where
the griots were buried; actually, at their death, the bodies of the griots (adults
and children alike) were just placed on the base inside the tree. R. Mauny who
was working at I.F.A.N. at the time of the discovery writes:

> Le sens de cette découverte ne fait aucun doute: nous avons
> affaire à un Baobab ayant servi de sépulture à des griots dans un
> passé récent: le Baobab de Bok est d'ailleurs connu également
> dans le voisinage sous le nom de "goui guevel" (Baobab à griots).
> (1955: 73)

R. Mauny adds:

> L'enterrement des griots dans les arbres creux est d'ailleurs
> signalé de longue date au Sénégal. Il est toujours pratiqué en
> pays sérère: cette coutume ne semble pas avoir été connue hors
> du territoire et semble complètement abandonnée, par exemple en
> pays wolof où elle dut être autrefois pratiquée. (R. Mauny, ibid.,
> p. 74)

Along the same lines, Alioune Oumy Diop notes that "dans certaines localités du Sénégal, le griot, après sa mort, était déposé au creux d'un baobab, au lieu d'être enterré comme les autres" (1990: 8).

The reason why the griots were buried inside the *Baobab* trees was because people believed that it would not rain if they were given a proper burial as pointed out earlier by Monteil (citing André A. d'Almada). However, because of fate, the remains of those griots were better preserved than those of the nobles for the simple reason that the temperatures inside the trees helped to conserve the remains whereas the remains of the nobles who were buried in conventional cemeteries were reduced to dust because of the high level of humidity of the sand (R. Mauny: 1955: 75).

Throughout the history of the Wolof, the griot has played an important role. In the royal courts, the griot was an emissary and a confidant of the kings and chiefs. In pre-colonial Africa, the griots even had their own villages. These villages were actual centers of learning to which young people came in order to learn by heart the history of their people. In the present-day republic of Mali, there is such a village called Kéyla. According to D.T. Niane, "Kéyla est le village des griots dépositaires des traditions orales de la famille impériale des Keïta. C'est le clan Jabaté [or Diabaté, i.e. griots] de Kéyla qui organise, tous les sept ans la cérémonie de réfection de la toiture de la case murée ou Kamablon de Kangaba" (1985: 151). The Wolof griots also had their own centers of learning of oral lore. In Waalo, Guidakhar was such a center. According to H. Azan:

> Les gens de ce village appartiennent presque tous à une famille particulière, celle des Gantenns, qui forme dans la population du pays une classe à part offrant quelques traits de ressemblance

avec celle des griots. (1863b: 613)

Guidakhar still exists. I cannot ascertain whether it does exist with this function. An important role played by the griots was their participation in battle. I refer here to Appendix I, where there is a translation of the interview I had with Ancumbu Caam and his son Magate Caam. Ancumbu emphasized the participation of his ancestors in battles alongside the chiefs, kings, and warriors of Waalo. C.A. Diop writes:

> Au sein de cette armée [in traditional settings] où régnait une mentalité seigneuriale, aristocratique, le rôle du griot apparaît dans toute sa signification sociologique. Par ses chants, qui sont un récit vivant de l'histoire du pays en général et des familles aux membres desquelles il s'adresse, il aide, il force même le combattant indécis, peureux, à se conduire en brave, et le brave à se conduire en héros, à faire des miracles. Sa contribution à la victoire est très importante: il est d'une bravoure, souvent d'une témérité incontestable, car il est aussi exposé que les combattants dont il chante les louanges; même au plus fort de la mêlée, ceux-ci doivent entendre ses exhortations qui leur remontent le moral. Les griots n'étaient donc pas des êtres superflus; leur utilité était évidente: ils avaient une fonction sociale, 'homérique' à remplir. (1960: 91)

Along the same lines, the person of a griot was sacred. No one was supposed to do him harm. G. Innes writes that "griots were commonly used as intermediaries between warring kings; they could pass freely through enemy territory, for the person of a griot was inviolable. To kill or even ill treat a griot was regarded as a particularly heinous crime."

S. Anozie points out that myth, folklore, and oral tradition in general may be among the most fundamental of cultural codes. The codes are manifest in the way the griot "writes" history. Anozie adds: "When the minstrel intones the deeds of a legendary hero, he is writing the history of his people with his tongue, restoring to them the divine profundity of the myth" (1981: 90; citing L. Senghor's "The Spirit of Civilization, of the Laws of African Negro Culture," 1956: 57).

In peacetime, the griot devotes himself to entertainment and to the safekeeping of the collective memory. J. Clifford (1988: 9) raised the topic of writing about culture from a standpoint of participant observation as well as from that of the "native informants." Ñan is more than an informant; he is, as an individual, the equivalent of an author. There is a prevailing theory in oral literature scholarship which posits that oral accounts, poems, stories, and genealogies are usually anonymous. Perhaps this stems from the fact that so much of this scholarship deals with traditions that are no longer living. In this project, there is an author in the person of Ñan and there are also data available on his life.

C. Achebe observes that "one of the most critical consequences [in Africa] of the transition from oral traditions to written forms of literature is the emergence of individual authorship" (1989: 47). The emergence of African fiction and most of all the novel written in European languages has imposed individual authorship as a new paradigm. In African oral societies such as that of the Wolof, however, authorship has always existed. The only difference from the modern period is that in the past there was no writing.[6] Another aspect of African traditional societies on which most authors insist is communalism, which is usually considered as the polar opposite of individualism. This exclusionary opposition is misleading. I insist on the fact that individual author-performers existed in traditional Wolof society and they were known by name. Ñan is very aware of the fact that there were previous performers (his ancestors) who handed his knowledge down to him. He knows his genealogical line of descent as well as the names of his ancestors. Towa remarks that in Africa, "il y a des contes et des mythes qui ont des auteurs connus" (1979: 96). However, once a collector (such as I) writes down one version of Ñan's performance, the singer becomes the author of that version. Besides undertaking a detailed study of the performance, the collector must also provide biographical data and other pertinent and relevant information on the singer.

Thus, even before performances were recorded and written down, authorship existed in pre-colonial African societies. R. Finnegan writes that "stress on achievement, individualism, and secularization can occur in non-industrial as well as industrial cultures" (1988: 142). Moreover, the bard, griot, or singer was a celebrity. L. White describes the source of poetic reputation in Southern Africa:

> In Southern Africa, it is not the *poet* who is licensed by literary convention; it is the *poem*. If certain poets have achieved a special reputation, it is only because of the poems they have created and not because of any special privilege vested in their office. It is not the performer that is licensed but the performance " (L. White 1989: 36 [author's emphases].)

In West African societies where there is a griot, however, genealogical descent is paramount. A griot learns from his father or ancestors. Thus, the person of a griot has more importance than the performance itself. Although he is recreating a poem that was first composed perhaps eight or ten generations ago, Ñan puts his own personal stamp on the version he is performing. Thus, the Wolof situation is opposite to the situation in Southern Africa as described by L. White. As a general rule, J. Vansina remarks: "Authorship of a tradition does not exist for most genres. Each performer of genres which are not memorized word by word is an author. We know only those whose performances were recorded" (1985: 55).

In the case of Senegalese oral traditions, it has happened that a very popular song or poem was recorded from a singer; from then on, that recorded version became one fixed form and one single version. However, the listeners may be aware of the fact that it was the first time that that song or poem was recorded, or else that that poem or song was orally composed but not recorded for the first time by such a given griot or singer (dead or alive). Thus, to my general knowledge and contrary to Vansina's assertion, a performer of a work which is memorized word by word can still be an author for, as I pointed out earlier, the first composer of a song may be different from the singer who records that song, yet both are known by name to the Wolof or Senegalese audience and public. There are even instances (very few, though) in which the members of an audience refer by name to a composer (who is not alive) of a battle poem or song that was composed in honor of a brave warrior or king. However, that song or poem was orally transmitted for many generations until it was recorded. Vansina observes that it is useful to inquire from whom the authors learned their traditions, even if, in most cases, nothing very definite emerges. He adds that, "it is useful because one does find out that many learned their traditions primarily from other people, still living, to whom one can turn for other versions" (loc. cit.). It is true that Wolof griots and poets learn the traditions and acquire their skills from older people such as their fathers or older renowned poets or griots. However, in order to obtain or record other versions of the same song or poem, one can also turn to other griots and singers who belong to the same age set; moreover, there are cases in which two griots learned the traditions from the same master. When two singers have learned a tradition from the same master, generally the only differences between the two of them are aesthetic; the core and backbone of the poem or story remain the same. This is equally true for many griots who learned a poem from different masters and who do not necessarily belong to the same age set; they may recount the same deeds and events in a similar way but will differ in the way they embellish the poem or song and therefore put a personal stamp on that song or poem.

My stance on the question of an authentic African literature is that only African writers writing in African languages such as Wolof can claim the heritage or office of the traditional griot or bard but not the modern African writer writing in European languages.

Notes to Chapter Five

1. The last two exclamations are Wolof expressions that show admiration, sympathy, or appreciation of a heroic act. The members of the audience tend also to clack their fingers by hitting the thumb against the forefinger, thus producing a noise to accompany the rhythm and beat of the music.

2. Michael T. Coolen has devoted a comprehensive written article to the *xalam* that includes the instrument's historical development, a technical description of the *xalam*, and an account of playing techniques, and musical style. Coolen also provides the musical transcription and analysis of a song (*Alfa Yaya* from the Republic of Guinea). (See Michael T. Coolen, "The Wolof of Xalam Tradition of the Senegambia," *Ethnomusicology*, 27 (1983): 477-98).

Other articles bearing on traditional African music, on the caste system, and on oral traditions in general are the following: Gilbert Rouget, "A propos de la forme dans les musiques de tradition orale," in *Les Colloques de Wégimont*, (1956): 132-143; Walter Salmen, "Zur sozialen Schichtung des Berutsmusikertums in Mittelalterlichen Eurasien und in Afrika," in *Les Colloques de Wégimont*, (1960): 23-32. André Schaeffner, "Situation des musiciens dans trois sociétés" in *Les Colloques de Wégimont*, (1960): 33-49; Klaus Wachsmann, "Problems of Musical Stratigraphy in Africa," in *Les Colloques de Wégimont*, (1964): 19-22.

3. E. Makward (1990) makes an interesting analysis of the economic status of two griots; the first griot is more traditional whereas the second one is more modern (see Appendix II).

4. The following authors have written on the function and status of the West African griot: H. Azan (1864a), Bérenger-Féraud (1882), H. Gaden (1931), D. Gamble (1957), H. Zemp (1964), O. Silla (1966), A.J. Shelton (1968), S. M. Eno Belinga (1971), G. Innes (1974), I. J. Zempleni-Rabain (1974), S. Camara (1976), I. Leymarie-Ortiz (1979), E. Magel (1981), Assane M. Samb (1981), D. Boilat (1984), (D. Robinson (1985), D.T. Niane (1985), Lamine Konte (1986), B. Wright (1989), E. Makward (1990), T. Hale (1990), J. Barou (1990), V. Zanetti (1990), Moussa M. Diabaté (No date).

5. Sory Camara has devoted a study to the social function and role and the condition of the griots in Malinke society. See S. Camara *(Gens de la parole. Essai sur la condition et le rôle des griots dans la société Malinké,* [1976]). On the role and function of the *gesere* (griot) in Saraxolé (also referred to as Soninke) society, see A. Bathily *(Les Portes de l' or* [1989]) and P. F. de Moraes Farias, "Praise as Intrusion and as Foreign Language: A Sunjata Paradigm Seen from the *Gesere* Diaspora in Béninois Borgu [present-day Republic of Benin]," unpublished (1992): 1-40.

See also the discussion of Mamadou Diawara on the *geseru* and the *laxaranto*, <<les gens de la bouche>> (<<people of the word>>) in Saraxolé society (cf. M. Diawara. *La graine de la parole. Dimension sociale et politique des traditions orales du royaume de jaara (Mali) du XV ème au milieu du XIX ème siècle,* 1990, pp. 40-44).

6. A most refreshing and recent study on authorship and on African literatures and criticism in general is that of Oyekan Owomoyela *(Visions and Revisions. Essays on African Literatures and Criticism.* [New York and San Francisco: Peter Lang, 1991]). On the claim of the modern African writer as the heir to the traditional bard, Owomoyela argues that "that claim is illegitimate because there are ties that bind African writers and their European patrons and inasmuch as literacy or non-literacy was the criterion which Europeans used to define civilization and, by extension, humanism, it stands to reason that for them the [African] literary elite exemplifies the best results of colonialism. By their profound assimilation of the essentials of Europeanism, African writers give the lie to any suggestion that the colonizers have reason to be ashamed of their African exploits. Most of the writers received their Eurocentric nurturing at the hands of such Europeans as Ulli Beier, Gerald Moore, John Reed, Clive Wake, and Molly Mahood [I would add Lilyan Kesteloot to this list], all of whom taught in Africa during the colonial period and either retired home at independence or became impresarios, conducting a steady stream of African writers through European universities and lecture circuits to satiate the great thirst for African materials that began in the 1960s and still continues to some extent today. European literary circles also place great value on the African writers for easing their penetration of the African mind by writing about Africa in the languages of the Europeans rather than in African languages." (1991: 24-25)

I would extend the discussion on authorship in oral literature to the important remarks on proverb authorship among the Akan of Ghana by K. Yankah. As a general statement, the author observes that:

> The problem of proverb authorship, even though occasionally explored by scholars, is compounded largely by the imposition of ethnocentric paradigms: the tendency to ignore indigenous modes of interpretation in preference for the scholar's own analytical scheme. Related to this is the scholar's aversion to change: his nostalgic affinity to well established modes of thinking in the face of empirical evidence to the contrary.
> (Yankah 1989: 183-84)

The author also outlines the three ways in which proverb authors have been known to be acknowledged in Africa: "a) the general ascription of proverbs to ancestry and elderhood by the speaker; b) instances of Wellerism whereby proverb authorship or utterance is attributed to an animal, plant, or an imaginary human entity; c) a third type of authorship acknowledgement is where specific individuals are named as authors" (K. Yankak, op. cit., p. 186).

CHAPTER VI

Morphology and Structure of the Tale.
Literary Genre
Myths and Origins

In this section, I will sketch the features collectively comprised in the form and structure of the Wolof epic tale. However, as a preliminary remark, one can state that in most West African oral poems, the singer or poet is not so much concerned with versification as, for example, an English poet of the Romantic period would have been. Actually, a feature that is common to most West African oral poetry is that "the metric line is built on the basis of 'breath-groups' or 'rhythm-segments'; what this entails is that the singer endeavors to get in as many words as he can in a single breath, so long as this is done within individual segments of the rhythmic accompaniment from the background music" (I. Okpewho 1977: 176). In the Wolof tradition, music is as important as the poem itself, as we have seen. Once again, contrary to the practice of a Wordsworth, a Browning or a Coleridge, that musical element is present when the griot is composing his poetry. I do not mean to equate the English and Wolof poets; they deal with separate matters and their backgrounds are very different. The Wolof singer, however, plays music while orally composing the *Epic Tale of the Waalo Kingdom*.

In what follows, I will be dealing only with the poem, not with the music which was touched on the previous chapter.

A - *Morphology and Structural Analysis of the Epic Tale.*

The tale has no titles or sub-headings to indicate the various episodes of the narrative; it is a continuous entity. It can, however, be divided into five sections.

The first episode (ll. 1-170) starts with the narration of the Flood as derived in large part from the Qur'an. It then tells the origin of the Hamitic peoples, the establishment of Jordan (the land of Black people), and the advent of the Prophet Muhammad.

In the second episode (ll. 171-358), the figure of Bubakar Umar dominates. He and Mbaarik Bô undertake a *jihad,* then journey westward to Upper Senegal where Bubakar marries Fatumata, the daughter of Abraham Sal, and is killed by Hamar the Scolder-of-Old-People.

The third episode (ll. 359-448) is dominated by Mbaarik Bô, who fulfills in two passages (ll. 359-378 and ll. 385-448) the conditions Bubakar set for the man whom Fatumata should marry after his death. Between these two passages the birth of Njaajaan is recounted (ll. 379-84).

The fourth episode (ll. 449) is about Njaajaan's childhood, his journey in the river, his capture, and his eventual coronation as the chief of the army of the kingdom of Waalo. The core events of the epic tale are contained in this episode. The beginning of the episode is a build-up that leads to the climax, Njaajaan's coronation as a chief. It could not be otherwise for, after having gone through all the tests and trials that a hero is expected to go through, Njaajaan was successful. From the point of view of the Wolof singer, the ending of the fourth episode is also a catharsis because the audience is relieved;

the hero was not hurt and did not die and the episode has a happy ending. The fourth episode is the backbone of the whole tale. The plot is the ordered unfolding of the narrative, and J. Vansina's tripartite division of the plot into exordium, main action, and conclusion can be of some use when analyzing the fourth episode of the Wolof epic tale (1985: 74).

a. Exordium (ll. 449-65): At the beginning of the episode, we have the presentation of the situation, for while Bubakar is dying, his son Njaajaan is innocently playing with his friends on the bank of the river. Then Njaajaan feels insulted by his friends when the latter allude to his mother marrying his father's door-keeper, namely Mbaarik Bô.

b. The main action (ll. 466-794): Njaajaan becomes angry, grabs several deadly weapons, leaves, and plunges into the river, where he attempts unsuccessfully to drown himself. The attempted drowning is important. It is commonplace that a hero must come very close to death before he reaches the height of his powers.

The main action is the longer part, for it goes from line 483 to line 794. In this section, the poet recounts Njaajaan's journey in the river, the villages near which he stays for a total of seven years and seven days, how he feeds himself, the people he encounters, the sharing out of the fish to the children, his capture, and emergence from silence.

c. The conclusion (ll. 795-819): The elders of Waalo send messengers to the Sereer King Maysa Waali Jon. Maysa Waali sends back the messengers to tell the elders to elect Njaajaan as a ruler. Consequently, Njaajaan is elected as chief of the army and that's where the fourth episode ends.

The fifth and last episode (ll. 820-975) tells about those who succeded Njaajaan and contains historical and geographical information about the Wolof people. In the fifth episode, the Wolof griot informs his audience about their not so distant past. However, the poet skilfully squeezes events that span more than 300 years into that single, final episode. The beginning of the episode concerns Mbarak Barka's visit to his elder brother Njaajaan as the chief of the army (ll. 820-887). The singer then refers briefly to events that happened in the sixteenth century, for instance the arrival of Europeans in Senegal (ll. 894-99). He then lists Njaajaan's first five children, his brief encounter with Këyfa resulting in the creation of the Peul, his entry into Jolof, and his begotting of two children there. Ñan ends with a short reaffirmation of the antiquity and accuracy of his tale.

In the fifth episode, there is the dual presence of the past and the future in a present-day "now." One ought to take into account the fact that the epic tale is not only about the past of the Wolof, it is also about the present and the future. When one considers the traditions proper, the bard always transmits his knowledge to the next generation; however, it may happen that the story or poem is recorded and written down for the first time. Conversely, there may be a generational oral transmission even though the story or poem is recorded or written for the first time and that is the case with Ancumbu Caam and his son. Even though I have recorded Ancumbu, he is still transmitting his knowledge orally to his son Magate; both men are illiterate and do not write. What I am trying to emphasize here is the complexity of possible combinations that exist within the Wolof tradition and others analogous to it. The Wolof singer thus ends the tale by stating how he received it from previous singers and griots; he is not "closing" the tale; it stays "open" for there is still the possibility of an oral transmission. In this regard, C. Uhlig remarks that "texts which have internalized the workings of time are capable of entering into a functional relationship with history, thus gaining the sort of complexity that answers to the contemporary moment" (1985: 299).

An equally important consideration is the setting. The epic tale must be repositioned into its original context, namely the Wolof milieu. Even though the epic tale is about the Wolof foundation myth, or myth of origins, it is not solely confined to the Wolof. Other ethnic groups are included in the tale: Sereer, Peul, Tukulor, Almoravid, Berber; thus, the tale springs from many sources. This leads to another observation which is that the tale incorporates a variety of ethnic, cultural, and linguistic elements; this unifying aspect reinforces the mythic feature of the tale. The Wolof have appropriated Njaajaan Njaay as the founder of their ethnic group and kingdom. However, he is partly Almoravid. Additionally, his mother is Tukulor; therefore, the Tukulor ethnic group can also make a claim on Njaajaan. The same is also true for the Peul since Njaajaan married the Peul woman Këyfa and that woman is the ancestor of all the Peul who bear the name Njaay. Finally, when Njaajaan is made to speak, the language he first utters is Hal Pulaar (l. 733).

It is very important to take into account the influence as well as the impact that these ethnic, cultural, and linguistic aspects have on the structure of the tale which takes on a certain ethnic plasticity; it is very flexible and, metaphorically speaking, the incorporation of different elements which the mythico-epic tale effects can itself be compared to a cauldron. At the end of the process of preparation, the final product is enriched for it has gathered many elements during the process. The tale can serve as a unifying factor for the ethnic groups of this region of West Africa.

Besides this social function, the epic tale has also a poetic function. It has the poetic quality of rhythmic regularity, but instead of the metrical features of conventional written poetry, its structure is built on breath units. Besides the oral aspect of the poem, one has also to consider the idioms and syntax that are specific to the Wolof language and how they influence the poem. According to R. Jakobson, "epic poetry, focused on the third person, strongly involves the referential function of language" (1960: 357). In the Wolof epic tale, the focus is mainly on the third person, the actions of the various characters, primarily Bubakar Umar, Mbaarik Bô, Njaajaan Njaay, Mbarak Barka, Fatumata Sal, and Abraham Sal. The singer gives voice to his characters, having them speak in turn: Bubakar Umar (l. 326), Mbaarik (l. 420), Fatumata (l. 434), Njaajaan (l. 734). However, the singer also intervenes in the tale in the first person, speaking of himself; for instance he emphasizes what his father told him (l. 693) and at the end of the tale he says how his father narrated the story to him (ll. 974-75). According to Jakobson (loc. cit.), when epic poetry is focused on the first person, the result is emotive. Both the referential and the emotive functions play strong roles in the Wolof epic tale.

The structure of the tale has two main components: the themes around which the poet builds the story line and the repetitive devices that have also a mnemonic function and therefore help in constituting the plot, the links between the various themes and units, and the unfolding of the narrative. C. Lévi-Strauss remarks that "on s'est souvent demandé pourquoi les mythes, et plus généralement la littérature orale, font un si fréquent usage de la duplication, triplication ou quadriplication d'une même séquence....La répétition a une fonction propre, qui est de rendre manifeste la structure du mythe....Tout mythe possède donc une structure feuilletée qui transparaît à la surface, si l'on peut dire, dans et par le procédé de répétition" (1958: 254).

M. Ndoye-Mbengue has listed literary devices that create the rhythm of Wolof (Lebu) oral poetry: "Les assonances et allitérations, la répétition, le parallélisme dans la construction, abondance de verbes d'action, les exclamations et onomatopées" (1982: 46). Of these elements, the device that fits best our purpose is repetition. The sequence or pattern that illustrates best the repetitive devices in the epic tale is the one that goes from line 532 to line 581. This sequence tells about Njaajaan leaving a village, swimming down the river, and staying near a succession of villages. Seven repetitions based on the exact same pattern mark this sequence. I will go further than Lévi-Strauss when he says that the repetitive device is inherent to the structure of the myth; I will add that repetition is the strongest feature of an oral performance. When the Wolof singer is repeating the same pattern over and over again, the audience does not get bored. The repetition is orally voiced; as a contrast, in writing, one is tempted to squeeze the repeated patterns from line 532 to 581 into a few lines, for the reader may have a lower tolerance for the repetition; moreover, because of the nature of writing and its relationship to reading, repetition in this context may be a very laborious undertaking on the part of the writer.

Within a set of repetitive patterns there may be variations. In the passage in question, the words and expressions "started swimming," "down the river," "seven days," "seven years," "arrived," "spent," "people," "discover," "presence," are regularly repeated by the Wolof singer. Variation is provided, naturally, by the names of the villages: Lamnaajo, Gédé, Mbéngèñ, Kawas, Xéwéw Gaal, Mbéngèñ Booy. The Wolof audience would certainly pay a lot of attention to these names for the members of the audience know that these villages have historical connotations (be they extant or not); they can be located geographically and there are events associated with some of them. Therefore, while the singer repeats the same words or expressions, he is also introducing new elements and thus producing a new pattern within the repetitive devices. Repetition is not, for the Wolof singer, a monotonously uniform and meaningless device.

Within the larger themes, such as the flood theme, there are sub-themes, such as the theme of voyage, namely Ham's children who set off on a journey looking for their father (ll. 119-141). This journey anticipates a later use of the journey motif, which is paramount in the epic tale, namely Bubakar Umar's and Mbaarik Bô's journey to Ghana. Within that theme, there are the sub-themes of *jihad* or holy war and a double courtship and marriage (Bubakar Umar marries Fatumata Sal; Mbaarik Bô marries Fatumata after Bubakar's death). Later, Njaajaan marries Këyfa. The most memorable voyage, however, is Njaajaan's river voyage. My contention is that just like repetition on the level of words and phrases, repetition of the theme is very important in consolidating the structure of the myth.

In the tale, one episode logically leads to another: the pre-Islamic period (the Flood, Noah and his son) leads to the Islamic era with the advent of Bubakar Umar. The latter, accompanied by Mbaarik Bô fights a *jihad* in the land of the Black people, converting them to the Islamic faith. Bubakar engenders a son, Njaajaan; who goes into exile because he is not happy with his mother marrying his father's door-keeper. Njaajaan's journey ends up with his capture and the stratagem through which he is made to come out of his silence. Then, he is chosen as the chief of the army and sent to Jolof. There, he engenders other children who will consolidate the Wolof kingdom of Jolof.

B - *Literary Genre.*

The literary value of the epic tale should be considered within the scope of African oral literature and African literature written in European languages. Since the 1930's, African intellectuals have been dealing with the definition of African literature (whether in the singular or in the plural). This public discussion still goes on in the 1990's; it is a very painful situation for it shows that, in the post-colonial period, African intellectuals have not yet come to terms with their colonial past; they are still searching for an identity (or identities) as well as for a full recovery of a fragmented personality. This quest is most visible when it comes to defining African literature; is it the literature written and expressed in African languages or the one expressed in European languages? This inquiry can also be seen in the definition of African philosophy. It is necessary to analyze the many facets of this literature and then move on to the question of genres and the equivalents of literary terms (terms as they are defined in European languages and what their equivalents are in the African languages). This background on the definition of African literature is important for it allows us to place in context and assess literary production in Africa. Only after that will it be possible to see how the Wolof tale itself can be situated within West African literary production and then how it fits in the larger field of African literary discourse.

Concerning literary terms, W. Soyinka remarks that "African literature is not consciously formulated around certain frameworks of ideological intent. The problem is partly one of terminology and the associations of literary history, mostly European" (1990: 61). Two quotations from two African writers are revealing of the prevailing malaise in African literary circles. C. Achebe writes:

> Many years ago at a writers' conference in Makerere, Uganda, I attempted (not very successfully) to get my colleagues to defer a definition of African literature which was causing us a lot of

trouble. I suggested that the task might become easier when more of our produce had entered the market. That was ten years ago. I was saying in effect that African literature would define itself in action; so why not leave it alone? I still think it was excellent advice even if it carried a hint of evasiveness or even superstition. (1989: 91)

M. Kunene discusses the concept of an authentic African literature written in African languages:

In the present context, it [authentic literature] is obscured by the glorification and the excessive critical attention accorded to marginal literatures written in foreign languages. Heavily subsidized and promoted by the cultural institutions of the former colonizers, this pseudo-African literature continues to be elevated at the expense of genuine African literatures [in African languages]. (1992: 36)

One major difference between African oral poets and singers on the one hand and African writers in European languages on the other, is that the former express their art through the medium of only one language, the mother tongue, whereas African writers who are expressing themselves in European languages also possess their mother tongues in addition to the European language. Some are even multilingual. The majority of the writers, however, do not write in their native tongues. E. Simpson reflects that "les écrivains africains, tout comme l'élite africaine, n'ont guère effectué leurs études dans leurs propres langues. Ils ne sont pas donc en mesure de créer des oeuvres en langues africaines. Il s'avère en conséquence que la littérature en langues africaines existe presque uniquement au niveau de la tradition orale, littérature que les chercheurs ne commencent qu' à enregistrer et transcrire" (1979: 47).

According to Soyinka, African literature in European languages represents "a social vision but not a literary ideology."

In the field of African literary productions, the epic is only one genre among others such as the tale or the praise poem. I personally asked to both Ñan and Caam how they would qualify or name Njaajaan's birth, his journey on the river, the tests and trials he confronts and then overcomes, his capture, his coronation as chief of the army, his being sent to Jolof in order to establish there a form of government; the answer I got is that Njaajaan's story is called *jaloré* in Wolof; the closest equivalent in English would be *epic* (or *épopée* in French).

The oral aspect (recitation) of *The Epic Tale of the Waalo Kingdom* does not prevent the classification of the poem within the sphere of poetry. When they are told that they are about to hear a *jaloré*, the listeners expect a performance with a lofty style on the singer's part; they also expect to be reminded of their history and of their past. It would be a difficult task to try to classify according to the generic distinctions that most European literatures share among themselves all the literary types in Africa for the simple reason that there might not be a corresponding term in the African language for the genre terms expressed in European languages. Some genres have no names. To that effect, T. Todorov remarks that: "De nombreuses langues (de l'Afrique, par exemple) ne connaissent pas de terme générique pour désigner toutes les productions littéraires" (1978: 13).

When the Wolof audience hears the story of Njaajaan, they know that it is about bravery, tribulations, physical prowess, and combats; moreover, the audience identifies it as *jaloré*. Likewise, when the same audience hears a farming song or a love song, or a praise song dedicated to a wrestler or a hero, that audience knows that this song is not *jaloré*, because it does not fulfill a set of expectations that the term *jaloré* suggests. Within Wolof culture, the people are very aware of the various literary genres that are orally expressed. Each category of poems or songs has a name. For instance, a praise poem dedicated to a wrestler or being sung by a wrestler, is called *bakk*. A praise-poem dedicated to a man or to a woman for his or her generosity is called *tagg*. However, there is a generic term that encompasses all these genres: it is *wëy*. *Wëy* literally means *to sing*. In Wolof culture, poetry and singing are insolubly linked. L. Senghor recounts: "La grande leçon que j'ai retenue de Marôme, la poétesse de mon village, est que la poésie est chant sinon musique ---et ce n'est pas là un cliché littéraire. Le poème est comme une partition de jazz, dont l'exécution est aussi importante que le texte" (1964: 226).

The Wolof epic tale is a verbal act and can be classified within the sphere of *poeticity* (R. Jakobson). Jakobson wonders whether it is possible to limit the range of poetic devices; his answer is negative for "the history of arts attests to their constant mutability" (1987: 369). Elaborating, Jakobson adds that "every verbal act in a sense stylizes and transforms the event it depicts. How it does so is determined by its slant, its emotional content, the audience it is addressed to, the preliminary 'censorship' it undergoes, the supply or ready-made patterns it draws from."

The songs, poems, tales, stories, panegyrics, and genealogical and historical accounts conveyed by African oral traditions have survived throughout the centuries thanks to performance, thanks to the African bard, all across the continent. P. Ngijol has written:

Les oeuvres de la tradition orale sont des productions littéraires

qui doivent non pas leur existence mais leur survie à la fixation
et à la multiplication des textes. (1977: 98)

What Ngijol is stressing here is the act of writing itself. However, most (if not all) African oral productions, including those in Wolof, have existed and survived because there was and still is a caste or a professional group of singers, poets, oral historians who committed themselves to the transmission of the whole cultural heritage from one generation to the next in spite of European colonization and of the imposition of outside languages such as French, English, Portuguese, Arabic, and religions such as Islam and Christianity. These oral traditions are transmitted in the other African languages the way Caam and Ñan do in the Wolof tradition.

C. *Myths and Origins: Historical Relevance*

A basic definition of myth is that it is "a complex set of signs, both verbal and gestural, which aim at accounting for some of the most fundamental problems of life and existence and thus providing man with a sense of security, a vaguely surmised eternal destiny and an explanation of the meaning of his existence in the natural and social milieu in which he lives" (E.A. Ruch 1984: 35).

The myth is often presented as being a "closed" system. C. Lévi-Strauss remarks that we find the same basic features and details within myths in most parts of the world. He then asks: "Si le contenu du mythe est entièrement contingent, comment comprendre que, d'un bout à l'autre de la Terre, les mythes se ressemblent tellement?" (1958: 229).

We will see later on, with a brief analysis of the Wolof epic tale, that the variations and differences among myths resides in what Lévi-Strauss classifies as *mythèmes* or what Jung describes as *archetypes*.

A primary concern here will be the substance of the Wolof myth, but not its style or mode of narration. As remarked by Lévi-Strauss, the substance of myth is intimately linked to language (p. 232). The grid established by V. Propp (1990: 79) can be useful in the assessment of the functions that the various characters such as Njaajaan or Hamar fulfil in the Wolof tale. Propp's first category is:

> The sphere of action of the villain. Constituents: villainy (A); a fight or other forms of struggle with the hero (H); pursuit (Pr).

Njaajaan is the hero (H) and Hamar is the villain (A). Hamar kills Bubakar, Njaajaan's father. The hero avenges his father's death by killing Hamar.

A paramount aspect of the myth is illustrated by the physical combats and the supernatural powers of Njaajaan Njaay. In the Wolof tale, Njaajaan the hero is going to kill Hamar the villain. That preference for the hero is illustrated by Eno Bélinga:

> L'estime va de préférence au héros humain qui se surpasse par sa puissance physique, intellectuelle et morale hors du commun, sans le concours de la magie. (1978: 28)

Besides the encounter between Njaajaan and Hamar, there is also a triangle of elements: Bubakar, Hamar-the-Scolder-of-Old-People, and Njaajaan. Bubakar begot Njaajaan; Hamar kills Bubakar; then Njaajaan kills Hamar. Two men are on one side (Njaajaan and Bubakar) and on the opposite side we have Hamar. When Njaajaan kills Hamar, he reasserts and re-establishes his own lineage, which lineage was threatened with disruption by Hamar. From the perspective of the modern audience, Hamar's killing of Bubakar can be considered as a regicide.

Hamar-the-Scolder-of-Old-People is a name plus epithet. A character that is similar to Hamar is that of Kábúwa-kénda (meaning "The Little-One-Just-Born-he-Walked") of the *Mwindo Epic* as described by Biebuyck and Mateene (1969: 20).

The Wolof singer emphasizes the supernatural powers of Njaajaan. I am going to draw similar examples from two African traditions: *The Sunjaata Epic* and *The Mwindo Epic*.

In the first of these, the hero Sunjaata is endowed with supernatural powers. Also known as Mari-Djata, he is challenged by the blacksmiths to bend an iron bar. He is physically handicapped as a child in his legs and this handicap adds greater dimensions to Sunjaata's prowess and valor:

> Il (Sunjaata) rampa à quatre pattes et s'approcha de la barre de fer. Prenant appui sur ses genoux et sur une main, de l'autre il souleva sans effort la barre de fer et la dressa verticalement. Il tenait la barre de ses deux mains. Dans un grand effort il se détendit et d'un coup il fut sur ses deux jambes, mais la grande barre de fer était tordue et avait pris la forme d'un arc. (D.T. Niane 1960: 45)

Then Niane adds:

Derrière Niani, il y avait un jeune baobab; c'est là que les enfants de la ville venaient cueillir des feuilles pour leur mère. D'un tour de bras, le fils de Sogolon (Sunjaata) arracha l'arbre et le mis sur ses épaules et s'en retourna auprès de sa mère. (Ibid., p. 47)

In the *Mwindo Epic* , the hero Mwindo, is decribed in the following fashion:

He is considered to be a small being, as indicated by the dimunitive prefix *ka* by which he is designated throughout the epic. He is human, although he is not conceived and born as a normal human being (in some versions, he is a product of parthenogenesis; in other versions, he is born from sexual intercourse, but through his mother's medius). He is the son of a chief, rejected in some versions by his father, but ultimately he becomes chief; accepted by his father in other versions, he becomes chief after a partition of the state. He has fabulous gifts (he can move on land, in water, under-ground; he has the gift of premonition); he has powerful human, animal, and supernatural allies (paternal aunt, spiders, bats, lightning); he possesses by birth powerful magic objects (e.g., a *conga* flyswatter made from antelope or buffalo tail) which permit him to escape the worst difficulties. He is the destroyer of evil forces, the savior of people, a generous leader. (Biebuyck and Mateene 1969: 11)

Thus, because of the Islamic factor in West Africa, the myths of Njaajaan and Sunjaata are heavily influenced by Islam. L. Kesteloot and B. Dieng remark that:

Ndiadiane apparaît comme un prince arabe, détenteur de la nouvelle religion. Le mythe privilégie l'aspect religieux qui lui donne intelligence, puissance et clairvoyance...
Ainsi Ndiadiane, descendant des conquérants musulmans, s'identifie à la puissance de la religion islamique qui, en Afrique noire, a élargi les limites du sacré. (1989: 189)

The linkage of the rulers of the Mali empire to Arab ancestors has been emphasized in the *Sunjaata Epic*. As in the legend of Njaajaan, the most distant ancestor of the Mandinka in the *Sunjaata Epic* is said to have been an associate of the prophet Muhammad. That distant ancestor is also linked to Alexander the Great; the latter is referred to as Doul Kar Naïni in the Mandinka language (Niane 1960: 10).

Finally, J. Vansina observes that in the ancient kingoms of Africa, the king is thought of as enjoying special supernatural powers. These supernatural powers are sometimes thought of as inherent in the kingship itself or they are bestowed upon the king by appropriate doctoring. Vansina adds that the kings are of divine origin or at least rule by divine right (1962: 325).

The Wolof myth of origin as expressed in the epic tale is an etiological myth about a personage (Njaajaan Njaay) who creates a new world for the Wolof people. That world is reflected in the present because it is re-enacted by the bard even though it spans a fairly long period of time. However, when we consider the relation between myth and time, we come to the conclusion that chronology and the distribution of events throughout time undergo some serious distortions in this myth. The best example is the conflation of the Abu Bakr that lived in the seventh century and the one that lived in the twelfth century (see the note to 1. 162).

Another example of anachronism is that in the Wolof epic tale we have simultaneously two personages whose historical existence was separated by several hundred years: Abu Bakr, Njaajaan's father, who is said to have lived in the twelfth century and Maysa Waali Jon, the Sereer King who lived in the fourteenth century. Puzzled by the appearance of Njaajaan, the elders of Waalo sent messengers to Maysa Waali. Thus, the myth telescopes three centuries. Kesteloot et al argue that "Ndiadiane n'a évidemment pas pu vivre trois siècles, mais le mythe écrase le temps, s'il respecte assez bien l'espace" (1983: 67). Furthermore, the Wolof myth is not concerned with chronological accuracy; its concern is "le souci d'encadrer Ndiadiane par deux personnages célèbres qui lui serviront de garants pour les générations futures" (id., p. 68).

The importance of the myth is the power it exerts on the collective consciousness of the Wolof, how it is believed by them, and how reality is described and rendered in the myth. Examined from this angle, the myth supersedes history.

In his study of the Yoruba myth of *alasuwada*, A. Akiwowo considers that myth as being also a 'doctrine'. In sociological terms, he classifies the myth under the broad term 'belief system' (1990: 104). Citing B.B. Hess et al (*Sociology*, 1982), A. Akiwowo concludes by saying that *alasuwada* can be confidently described as "'*a vision of the future*' which provides a sense of destiny that unifies all true behaviours and gives meaning to both individual existence and human history " (op. cit., p. 105 [author's emphasis]).

E. Cassirer remarks that "in the relation between myth and history, myth proves to be the primary, history the secondary and derived, factor. It is not by its history that the mythology of a nation is determined but, conversely, its history is determined by its mythology -- or rather, the mythology of a people does not *determine* but *is* its fate, its destiny as decreed from the very beginning " (1975: 5 [author's emphases]). The Wolof singer does not generally question facts. However, sometimes he does not agree with certain aspects as narrated (or recounted by other griots) in other versions of the same epic tale.

When one considers the relation between myth and knowledge, it is natural to inquire as to the singer's attitude. According to E.A. Ruch:

The mythopoet is essentially uncritical. He is less concerned with the facts themselves than with our human response to the facts. He does not "reason why," but accepts the facts as they impress themselves on him, in all their concreteness but also in all their significance. He does not look for alternative solutions: he takes the one that presents itself. (op. cit., p. 47)

Ñan's approach to the myth of Njaajaan does not exhibit this uncritical characteristic. In a broader sense, P. Hountondji states that:

La tradition orale aurait plutôt tendance à favoriser la consolidation du savoir en un système dogmatique et intangible, tandis que la transmission par voie d'archive rendrait davantage possible, d'un individu à l'autre, d'une génération à l'autre, la critique du savoir. (1977: 131)

In this second passage, besides the notion that oral traditions lack critical tools, there is also a concern about the transmission of knowledge from one generation to the next. I think that both these authors make unjustified generalizations in their reflections on the oral poet and his art. What one ought to do is to look closely at specific examples. For instance, in the Wolof epic tale, Ñan does not agree that it was Bata Booy who made Njaajaan come out of his silence; it was rather Maramu Gaaya who did it (ll. 691-96). Why did the Wolof singer did not just accept that it was Bata Booy? He questions that version and then gives his own. The African bard is very skilfull when it comes to criticism, not just historical but in political matters. In the Wolof tradition, there is a famous oral poet or "philosopher" called Kocc Barma (17th Cent?). By way of metaphors, he used to criticize the king.[1]

There are other instances in which the Wolof griot gives his own opinion of a specific matter for he has confidence that he is protected and that harm cannot be done to him. P. Ngijol remarks that "le barde, protégé par son art, exerce son droit naturel de porte-parole du peuple en critiquant ouvertement au cours de veillées certaines décisions de patriarches et certaines pratiques ancestrales jugées désuètes" (op. cit., p. 103). Wisdom and morality, which constitute the basis of the Wolof traditional system of thought, are conveyed orally by the griot; the two concepts are intrinsic components of knowledge in that society.[2]

Many studies have been devoted to the myth or myths across the world. Thus, there is a certain universality in the myth. M. Eliade distinguishes two categories: myths of origins and cosmogonic myths (1963: 33-37). Furthermore, the same author gives a basic definition of the myth that we can apply to the myth of origins of the Wolof:

> Le mythe raconte une histoire sacrée; il relate un événement qui a eu lieu dans le temps primordial, le temps fabuleux des "commencements." Autrement dit, le mythe raconte comment, grâce aux exploits des Etres Surnaturels, une réalité est á l'existence. (M. Eliade, p. 15)

Concerning the heroes of the myths, Eliade remarks that the figures contained in the myths of origins are usually Supernatural Beings; these Beings are known to their community because of their exploits at the "Beginning of Times." Thus, the myths reveal to us the creative activities of these figures while also showing the sacred aspect of (or "sur-naturalité") their works (Eliade, Idem).

The function that the myth of Njaajaan Njaay plays is as important as any other Wolof myth; the myth of Njaajaan is also the oldest of all Wolof myths. Y. Fall delineates a three fold referential function played by Njaajaan:

1) Celle de fondateur de la dynastie des Njaay qui aurait exercé le pouvoir politique suprême dans l'ancien Jolof; celui-ci regroupait le Waalo, le Kajoor, l'actuel Jolof, le Bawol et le Salum, certaines informations y incluant le Siin, voire le Dimar, le Tooro et le Bambuk.

2) Celle d'unificateur d'entités politiques antérieures au Jolof et surtout de gestionnaire pacifique de cette unification.

3) Celle, enfin, de créateur et de transmetteur d'une langue originale, précisément *sui generis*, devenant par ce fait même l'ancêtre de tous les Wolof. (1989: 117)

However, there is no strong evidence as to the actual existence of Njaajaan; consequently we do not know for sure whether Njaajaan was a historical figure. B. Barry labels Njaajaan as "ce personnage mythique de Ndyaadyaan Ndyaay commun à tous ces royaumes [Waalo, Jolof, Kayor]" (1985: 318). Moreover, there are certain anachronisms (he could not have lived three centuries!) and fables (he could not have lived in the river like a fish!). Fables and anachronisms are added to historical truth by the griots or even by the common people. Like the epic in other cultures, however, the tale of Njaajaan Njaay itself makes "a claim to historical truth and the preservation of past acts for enduring memory" (Jauss 1982: 86).

274

1. David Boilat labels Kocc Barma a philosopher. Kocc was originally from a village called Diamathil in the region of Kayor. Kayor is primarily inhabited by the Wolof. Boilat continues: "Le plus remarquable d'entre eux [i.e., Wolof philosophers] est Cothi-Barma. Les traits d'esprit de ce philosophe pourraient parfaitement faire la matière d'un grand ouvrage" (1984: 345-46). Then, Boilat adds: "On attribue à Cothi plus de cinq mille adages ou maximes. D'après la tradition des Wolofs, cet homme d'une rare sagesse n'est pas un être imaginaire, comme on pourrait peut-être le supposer, il a vécu réellement; le village de Dhiamatil est encore gouverné par les prétendus descendants de ce philosophe, qui y sont honorés comme des princes" (pp. 353-54). Boilat mentions another philosopher called Biram-Thiam-Demba: "Cet homme ne s'est occupé que d'énigmes pour amuser les oisifs" (loc. cit.).

B. Dieng also describes Kocc Barma as "le plus grand penseur du monde wolof" (1980: 882). Finally, D. Gamble observes: "Kott-Barma (i.e., Kocc Barma) demeure légendaire par les multiples sentences qu'il a laissées après lui" (1957: 24, citing A. Sadji's novel entitled *Nini*).
Neither of these men that Boilat and Dieng consider to be philosophers wrote down their thoughts; these were orally expressed and were composed of proverbs, sayings, and enigmas. The concept of an oral philosopher must be accorded more importance. Additionally, one cannot exclude oral texts in the practice of philosophy as remarked by M. Towa: "Socrate n'a rien écrit. Ce n'est pas une raison pour prétendre qu'il n'était pas philosophe" (1981: 350). Kocc is known as having constantly challenged the authority of the king of the Wolof kingdom of Kayor. In one instance, Kocc openly expressed his thoughts about the excess of power on the part of the king. However, Kocc's words were recounted to the king. Thus, "le *demel* [king] ayant appris que Cothi s'était permis de tenir un discours si républicain, résolut la mort du philosophe" (Boilat, p. 347). Boilat mentions that Kocc was eventually saved from the king's wrath thanks to his intelligence and wisdom. Overall, Kocc Barma and Biram-Thiam-Demba relied only on their oral skills. Their works are oral texts that were transmitted from generation to generation and deserve to be collected and transcribed.

2. The structuring of knowledge in most West African traditional societies

belongs to the sphere of folk philosophy. The definition of a philosophy in Africa has engendered a lot of controversy among various African and foreign philosophers and intellectuals. The debate began after the publication of *La philosophie bantoue* (1949) by Placide Tempels, a Belgian missionary in the Congo. The discussion that followed Tempels' theses related to the definition of a Bantu worldview and cosmogony spearheaded what became better known as ethnophilosophy.

The idea of ethnophilosophy is built upon the premise of unanism. Hountondji argues that the aim of ethnophilosophy is,

> de définir une philosophie africaine spécifique, une vision du monde commune à tous les Africains d'hier, d'aujourd' hui et de demain, un système de pensée collectif et immuable, éternellement opposable à celui de l' Europe. (1977: 46).

Along the same lines, A. Appiah writes: "It is indeed odd to suppose, with some unanimists, that a people [Africans] should share the same beliefs on all the major issues in their lives" (1992: 105).

Mohamadou Kane warns against a uniform perception or view of African cultures and societies. In his analysis of the African folktale (which analysis we can extend to culture), he proposes instead to think in terms of "aires culturelles:"

> Il faut [donc] se dégager d'une conception par trop uniformisante du conte africain et, d'une façon générale, de la culture africaine, pour un peu plus penser en termes d'aires culturelles. (1968: 30)

Finally, Achille Mbembe, in his discussion on the *fétichisme culturel*, informs against "la fascination démesurée sur des courants d'idées portés par une vision <<fixiste>> et <<décontextualisé e>> des cultures et des sociétés africaines" (1988: 55).

To that effect, B. Davidson gives a very specific example by stating that "in Tanzania [for example], there are many languages and acute contrasts of soil, climate, habitat, or cultural tradition" (1994: 168). Further down, the same author characterizes Africa as being made of "lands of infinite variety and situation" (op.cit., p. 175-76).

From 1930 on, three prominent African intellectuals created schools of thought: Léopold Senghor defined Négritude as "l'ensemble des valeurs du monde noir." Cheikh Anta Diop went further back to antiquity in order to claim ancient Egypt as being part of the African heritage; his philosophical thoughts are generally known as Egyptianism. Finally, Kwamé Nkrumah created the philosophy of African Personality and Consciencism. What these three intellectuals have in common is that they get (or claim to) most of their inspiration from the African traditional systems of thought and literature.

There is an on-going debate on ethnophilosophy (also known as folk/philosophy) and modern philosophy. Questions such as is there an African philosophy, can African traditional and religious systems of thought be considered as philosophy are hotly debated by the following authors: H. Aguessy, "Tradition orale et structures de pensée: essai de méthodologie" (1972), A. Appiah, *In my Father's House. Africa in the Philosophy of Culture* (1992), F. Crahay, "Conceptual Take-Off Conditions for a Bantu Philosophy" (1965), C.A. Diop, *Antériorité des civilisations nègres. Mythe ou vérité historique?* (1967), J.W.C. Dougall, "Characteristics of African Thought" (1932), Y.M. Guissé, *Philosophie, culture et devenir social en Afrique noire* (1979), R. Horton, "African Traditional Thought and Western Science" (1967a, 1967b), P. Hountondji, *Sur la "philosophie africaine." Critique de l'ethnophilosophie* (1977), A. Kabou, *Et si l'Afrique refusait le développement?* (1991), L. Keita, "The Debate Continues: A Reply to Olabiyi Yai's 'Misère de la philosophie spéculative" (1981), N. Koffi, "Controversy sur l'existence d'une philosophie africaine" (1977), S. Lukes. "On the Social Determination of Truth" (1973), J. Mbiti, *The Study of African Religions and Philosophy* (1969), V.Y. Mudimbe, *The Invention of Africa. Gnosis, Philosophy, and the Order of Knowledge* (1988), A. Ndaw, *La pensée africaine* (1983), K. Nkrumah, "Consciencism" (1964), L. Senghor, *Liberté 1. Négritude et humanisme* (1964) and *Ce que je crois* (1988), B. Sine, "Esquisse d'une réflexion autour de quelques éléments de 'philosophie' wolof" (1974), A. Sylla, *La philosophie morale des wolofs* (1978), M. Towa, *Essai sur la problématique philosophique dans l'Afrique actuelle* (1971) and *L'idée d'une philosophie négro-africaine* (1979), C. Wauthier, *The Literature and Thought of Modern Africa* (1979), K. Wiredu, *Philosophy and an African Culture* (1980), O. Y. Yai, "Théorie et pratique en philosophie africaine: misère de la philosophie spéculative (Critique de P. Hountondji, M. Towa et autres)" (1978).

CHAPTER VII

Writing, Literacy, and Orality,
the use of Arabic and Clericalism.

The question of writing, literacy, and orality is multi-faceted. In this section, I will be considering the different aspects of writing in some West African traditional societies. I will not deal with the theme of the incompatibility between writing and orality or numeracy, for my informant, S. Ñan, writes in Arabic and has also the knowledge of numbers Western script. Therefore, for the purposes of this study, it is important to analyze the themes of writing and orality as complementary rather than as conflicting. To consider writing and orality in West Africa as being a simple polarity would be misleading. However, there are poets and griots who are completely illiterate and do not read or write in any language, even in their own maternal language; they rely only on the oral medium to practice their art. Likewise, there are poets and singers who know how to read and write (usually Arabic) but who still compose and perform orally in their native languages.

The following remark by E. Julien will help in understanding the balance that exists between writing and orality in most African societies:

> The art of speaking is highly developed and esteemed in Africa
> for the very material reasons that voice has been and continues to
> be the more available medium of expression, that people spend a
> good deal of time with one another, talking, debating,

entertaining. For these very reasons, there is also respect for speech and for writing as communicative and powerful social acts. (1992: 24)

A. *Writing, Literacy, and Orality.*

When it first appeared in human society, writing was often associated with mystery.[1] Even though one can find systems of writing in Africa in isolated spots, writing itself was not very widespread. Thus, one must "reconnaître que l'Afrique noire, en général, s'est tenue hors des aires historiques de l'écriture" (Iba D. Thiam 1980: 60). Some African societies did not have any writing system whatsoever.[2] In West Africa, the history of writing is intimately linked to the advent of Islam. In other parts of Africa (mostly Eastern, Central and Southern Africa, parts of Nigeria) where Islam had less impact, writing was influenced by the introduction of the Bible and Christianity.[3]

Generally speaking, Wolof bards are more versed in oral art; once in a while, one comes across a few who have a very restricted mastery of writing. This is the case of Ñan who did not go to French school; instead, he went to Qur'anic school at a tender age like the majority of young Senegalese (myself included). Ñan acquired the use of Arabic script because of his being exposed to Islam and to the Qur'an. According to my own observation, the Wolof singer does not make the distinction between orality and writing which is readily made in most of the scholarship dealing with oral literatures. Ñan finds it a normal thing to be a Muslim and his use of the Arabic script is very limited.[4] He has a logbook in which he has written the list of the rulers of the Waalo kingdom (see Appendix II) as well as the number of years they stayed in power. Ñan, like most of the Wolof griots and most Senegalese, does not speak Arabic. As for the French language, Ñan knows a few words because he was conscripted into the French Army in 1950 and spent two years in Mauritania.

Ñan is primarily an oral performer; he is a poet who composes and improvises while singing and reciting. Thus, he "writes history more with his tongue than with his hand." There are also African writers who have attended Western (mostly European) educational institutions yet they choose to write in their maternal languages. That is the case of Okot p'Bitek who wrote poetry in the Acoli language of Uganda. He has also recreated tales and poems from Acoli traditional literature in his poetry (M. Condé and M. Radouane 1977: 14-15). Others such as Thomas Mofolo or D.O. Fagunwa wrote in their maternal languages, the first one in Sesutho, the second in Yoruba.

For certain African authors, however, writing itself is not confined to letters on paper. Traditional African art is also a system of writing, for instance pictographs and epigraphy. E. Mveng characterizes that art in the following fashion:

> La civilisation négro-africaine n'est pas seulement orale; elle est aussi écrite, et son écriture, c'est notre art traditionnel. Les dessins des tissages touareg du désert, des tissages dogon du Mali, des motifs adinka du Ghana, des poids ashanti et baoulé de Côte-d'Ivoire, des bas-reliefs d'Abomey, du Bénin ou de Foumban, les motifs Abbdia du Sud-Cameroun, les scènes sculptées des Tchokwé de l'Angola, les symboles des Bakuba du Kassaï, et les graffiti des parchemins populaires d'Ethiopie, tout cela constitue un langage écrit qui raconte l'histoire et la vie de nos peuples. (E. Mveng, "Négritude et civilisation gréco-romaine," 1972, p. 50; cited in H.L. Gates, Jr., *Black Literature and Literary Theory*, 1990, p.122).

Contemporary African societies, like European societies in the transitional period of the late Middle Ages, are shifting from a predominantly oral culture to a manuscript culture but they are doing so during a time in which electronic means are rapidly being introduced for the storage of information. G.L. Bruns wonders "what happens when an oral tradition is subsumed or overlaid by a manuscript culture, such that the authority of the tradition is altered or diverted by the authority of bookish learning that textual traditions strive to maintain" (1980: 115). The following inquiry on the part of H. R. Jauss is also very pertinent:

> What is to be done when an authority, distant in time and preserved only in writing, has forfeited the immediacy of living speech or address which it had in the oral culture whence it originated when, more particularly, its doctrine or message is no longer in tune with the world view, the attitudes and morals of a later time? (1990: 54)

When a society shifts from an oral to a manuscript culture, there will be inevitably feedbacks between the written texts on the one hand and popular culture and oral lore on the other. In the case of Senegal (and most African countries), many of the oral traditions and literatures are being collected and written down. The most important aspect of that enterprise is the transcription of tales, genealogies, stories, and poems in the original language of performance. Eventually, when more people know to read and write Wolof, they will be able to read individually the transcribed and annotated oral materials in Wolof; at the same time, there will be the possibility to recreate the traditions orally by using written texts. This work will be done probably when there are no more griots as they exist now in Senegal. Additionally, most performers who want to perform orally by using written texts will obviously be literate. A. Lord writes that "singers who accept the idea of a fixed text are lost to oral tradition processes. This means death to oral tradition and the rise of a generation of 'singers' who are reproducers rather than re-creators" (1960: 137). Lord's remarks are mostly based on his study of oral traditions in Yugoslavia; however, his remarks have relevance for other traditions. He made the good point that a singer who relies on a fixed text permanently is lost to the processes of oral tradition, therefore to memorization without a visual aid. The training of the ear (aural process) is also abandoned to the advantage of the eye (visual process). One must note that some great bards were blind and thus relied solely on their memory: Homer is said to have been blind. Ancumbu Caam, the Wolof singer with whom I worked is also blind. There is an aura of mystery that is linked to the blindness of bards. A commonly held theory is that since a bard has lost his sight, he tends to develop his memory and then train his ears. However, that is not always the case. During his fieldwork among the Muslims in Yugoslavia, Lord remarks that "beggars, blind or otherwise, were not very good singers" (1960: 18).

In Senegal too, one finds professional or semiprofessional singers among the blind and they are a common sight in the streets of Dakar. This professionalism does not necessarily make good singers out of these beggars and blind people. Since Senegal is predominantly a Muslim country, it is a common custom and part of the culture to see the poor and needy begging.

To come back to the loss of the processes of oral tradition, if the process itself is lost, the oral tradition is not necessarily lost; rather, a specific kind of oral tradition is lost. In contemporary Senegal, there are cases of singers and performers who are literate and are exposed to writing and reading; however, they still compose songs orally and they improvise as well. Finally, Sèq Ñan, the Wolof singer who uses Arabic to write down a tally of names (the rulers of Waalo), can be considered as a reproducer and a re-creator at the same time. He re-enacts the knowledge he has gotten from his ancestors and, at the same time, he adds his own, thereby recreating the Wolof tradition.

B. *Clericalism, the Use of Arabic, and the Griot as a Scribe*

The history of clericalism in West Africa is intimately linked to the advent of Islam in that region. Arabic itself was a new tool that the Muslim traders brought along with them from North Africa. Thus came into existence a new class of literate clerics. J. O. Hunwick states that "it was perhaps not until the 17th century that some African languages were being written in the Arabic script and it is most likely that persons who became literate in their own languages in this way would have first become literate in the Arabic language itself" (1974: 18). Clericalism and the use of Arabic in West Africa can be analyzed under two angles: the use and function of Arabic and its influence on African languages.

Concerning the first point, Arabic responded to "the most widespread use to which the art of writing was put in West Africa, since it required little more than a rudimentary literacy: the writing of charms and talismans" (J.O. Hunwick, op. cit., p. 19). The practice that consists in using Arabic in order to write charms was consolidated by proselytism. In West Africa, the Tukulor and the Mandinka people were the chief proselytizers. About the latter, Golberry writes in his *Fragments d'un voyage en Afrique fait pendant les années 1785-86 et 1787 dans les contrées occidentales de ce continent*:

Les Mandigues sont un grand peuple de l'Afrique. Plusieurs

colonies de ce peuple se sont établies dans le pays de Bambouk et sur les bords de la Gambre [the River Gambia]. Les marchands et les marabouts de cette nation ont une grande influence sur toute cette partie de l'Afrique occidentale. Ces noirs sont instruits; ils sont simples et fins, et commerçants aussi habiles qu'infatigables . . . Ils professent avec zèle la religion de Mahomet, et cependant ils ont conservé beaucoup de pratiques de fétichisme et d'usage superstitieux." (Cited in P. Marty 1917: 369)

Proselytism and the spread of the writing of charms and talismans were mostly the results of the activities of a special class of literate and semi-literate clerics: the *marabouts*.[5] Marty adds: "Après les Maures, ils [the Mandinka] constituent le deuxième facteur de l'islamisation du Sénégal" (ibid., p. 368).

Concerning the second point, the use of Arabic helped in the writing of African languages, thus gradually establishing a semi-literate culture. On the influence of Arabic on African languages, V. Monteil remarks that it had at least one positive aspect which is that "la *fixation* par l'écriture même si la romanisation actuelle la bat en brèche, est un bienfait incontestable, faute de quoi les grandes langues véhiculaires de civilisation (swahili, haoussa, peul) seraient restées liées à la précaire oralité" (1963: 18-19 [author's emphasis]).

The clan of the *marabouts* grew from a few Tukulor, Peul, and Mandinka individuals travelling across the large open savannahs of West Africa to large organized sects and families headed by learned men.[6]

Kouyaté believes in the supremacy of the oral over the written; this leads us to the question of performance and to the aesthetics of oral traditions.

Notes to Chapter Seven

1. M. Lichtheim remarks that "when writing first appeared in [Ancient] Egypt, at the very beginning of the dynastic age, its use was limited to the briefest notations designed to identify a person or a place, an event or a possession. An aura of magic surrounded the art which was said to derive from the gods. As its use slowly grew, its first major application (if we judge by the evidence of what has survived) took the form of an *Offering List*, a long list of fabrics, foods, and ointments, carved on the walls of private tombs" (Miriam Lichtheim, *Ancient Egyptian Literature; A Book of Readings*, vol. 1, p. 3. Berkeley: University of California Press, 1975 [author' s italics]).

In his article devoted to African oral traditions and literature, H. Scheub demonstrates how the scribe in Ancient Egypt was the mediator between the oral performer and his audience. Scheub adds that, "with the advent of literature [in Ancient Egypt], the oral tradition did not die. The two media continued their parallel development: both depended on a set of similar narrative and poetic principles." ("A Review of African Oral Traditions and Literature," *African Studies Review*, 28, 2-3 (1985): p. 26).

Scheub's viewpoint is reinforced by Guy O. Midiohouan who remarks that "l'oralité et la scripturalité sont [donc] deux modes différents de communication linguistique mais ne sont pas exclusives l'une de l'autre. Elles définissent aussi deux formes de société. Cependant les sociétés de vieille tradition écrite conservent une part d'oralité" (1987: 2).

In West Africa proper, certain ethnic groups developed various writing systems. K. Hau writes: "Within a roughly triangular piece of territory in West Africa a number of writing systems have been discovered during the past hundred and fifty years belonging to peoples who have lived in the area for many centuries and whose writing symbols appear generally uninfluenced by Arabic or Roman epigraphy" ("PreIslamic Writing in West Africa," *Bulletin de l' I.F.A.N.*, 35 (1973): 6). K. Hau's study focusses mainly on the Vai script of Liberia.

See also De Moraes Farias's article on West African writing in general and on paleographic evidence and the living tradition of lettering types within the arabic calligraphies of West Africa "(The oldest extant writing of West

Africa: Medieval epigraphs from Ǝssuk, Saney, and Egef-n-Tawaqqast (Mali)," *Journal des Africanistes*, 60 (2) 1990: 65-113.

In most societies, there were a lot of restrictions imposed on writing. W. J. Ong observes that "writing is often regarded at first as an instrument of secret and magic power" (1982: 93, citing J. Goody's "Restricted Literacy in Northern Ghana," *Literacy in Traditional Societies*, 1968, p. 236). In Africa, "some societies of limited literacy have regarded writing as dangerous to the unwary reader, demanding a guru-like figure to mediate between reader and text" (W. J. Ong, loc. cit. ; citing J. Goody and I. Watt's "The Consequences of Literacy," *Literacy in Traditional Societies*, 1968, p. 13).

In the last analysis, the importance of writing in the formation of civilizations should not be overstressed. In an interesting article on world history, S. Feierman discusses the topic of writing in human civilization as the latter topic is conceived in the writings of Bennassar Bartolomé and Chaunu Pierre (*l'ouverture du monde*, XIVᵉ - XVIᵉ siècles, 1977) and Fernand Braudel (*The Mediterranean and the Mediterranean World in the Age of philip II*, 1976). Following in the steps of Braudel, Chaunu and Bennassar posit that "one of the central elements in the emergence of civilization is the existence of writing" (Feierman 1993: 177). Furthermore, Braudel, Bennassar and Chaunu have built "a hierarchical complex of elements (that are relevant to European civilizations) which together form a coherent configuration: political and economic hierarchy, towns, commerce and intercommunication, *writing*, the plough, high densities of population, and historical dynamism" (Feierman, Ibid.; [my emphasis]).

According to Feierman, the problem with this complex when applied to Africa, in the context of world histories like Braudel's or Bennassar and Chaunu's, is that the interrelations do not hold. Feierman gives the following example:

The Igbo-speaking areas of Southeastern Nigeria, [for example], had very high population densities; in recent times some parts of the region have reached 800 per square mile. People cultivated the land with hoes, had a very dense network of periodic markets (in which markets took turns with one another on four-or-eight-day cycles to make it easy for merchants to move from one to another), and had a network also of long distance trade fairs. By late in the first millenium A. D. the region was importing substantial quantities of trade goods overland from the

Mediterranean - *all this without writing* and, in most parts of Igboland, without clear forms of political hierarchy. Egalitarian councils maintained the market peace, and the agents of religious oracles communicated over long distances. Many different kinds of ritual functionaries co-existed in Igboland, each preserving one or another form of knowledge, to be transmitted orally to the next generation. Artisans practiced numerous crafts. The region was an economically dynamic one both internally and in relation to export trade. (S. Feierman Ibid., [my emphasis]

2. This is the case of the Akamba people of East Africa. J. Mbiti labels that situation as an *absence d'écriture*. He writes that "étant donné que les Akamba n'ont inventé ni ne possèdent aucun système d'écriture, la communication verbale a été le seul moyen de répandre les nouvelles alentour, les coutumes, les moralités, les jugements, promesses, décisions politiques, chants, histoires, fables, proverbes, etc." ("L'éveil de la littérature indigène de la tribu Akamba," *Présence Africaine*, 24-25, (1959): 241).

3. For instance, there were writings in Zulu or Sesotho. However, D. P. Kunene remarks that in South Africa, "the missionaries through their translations of the Bible, indirectly contributed to the beginnings of written literatures" ("African-Language Literature: Tragedy and Hope," *Research in African Literatures*, 23 (1992): 12). Bernth Lindfors considers that much of African writing is derivative. Commenting on the earliest African authors (at the beginning of the twentieth century), he concedes that "the first lengthy prose narratives in Sesuto, Yoruba, and Igbo were transparent imitations of John Bunyan's *The Pilgrim's Progress*, which was usually among the first books after the Bible to be translated into an African vernacular language or used in a simplified English edition in missionary schools" ("Oral Tradition and the Individual Literary Talent," *Studies in the Novel*, 4 (1972): 201). For more details on writings in Yoruba, see Olakunle George, "The Predicament of D.O. Fagunwa," Unpublished (1993): 1-23. On writings in Sesutho, see D.P. Kunene, *Chaka* by Thomas Mofolo. London: Heinemann, 1981. On writings in Acoli, see G.A. Heron, *Song of Lawino & Song of Ocol* by Okot p'Bitek. London: Heinemann, 1984.

It is generally assumed by various critics that Yambo Ouologvem's novel *Le Devoir de Violence* (1968) is a re-creation of the epic structure in novel form. Concerning the interaction between West African Oral Traditions and the

African novel written in French and English, the re-creation of oral techniques in the novel, the similarities, commonalities, and differences between certain Western-educated African novelists and the griot, see Eileen Julien's recent study, *African Novels and the Question of Orality* (1992).

4. The use of Arabic in the transliteration of African languages is a very old practice, referred to as *ajami*. Albert Gérard remarks that "in the eighteenth century, the needs of religious propaganda prompted learned men to use the Arabic script in order to transliterate some of the more widely spoken vernacular languages of West Africa. There thus arose several literatures of the *Ajami* type" (*Canadian Review of Comparative Literatures*, (1980): 68). Along the same lines, H. Labouret writes:

Dans les pays où l'écriture est connue, des lettrés, empruntant les caractères et la métrique arabes, ont rédigé de nombreuses *qacidas* dans leur propre langue au lieu d'écrire tout simplement en arabe. En agissant ainsi, ils veulent atteindre le grand public des illetrés. Ces poèmes, appris par les aveugles et les mendiants, sont chantés ou modulés par eux; des étudiants, des marabouts en voyage les récitent dans les mosquées devant une nombreuse assistance. Ils sont placés ainsi à la portée de tous, tandis qu'ils ne seraient accessibles qu'à une élite très restreinte s'ils étaient composés en arabe. (1941: 258)

Baron Roger makes the specific remark pertaining to writing and to the use of arabic to the effect that Senegalese were acquainted with writing, at least some of them:

Ce n'est pas que les Sénégalais ignorent entièrement l'usage de l'écriture; un bon nombre d'entre eux lisent et écrivent tant bien que mal l'arabe, qu'ils ne comprennent généralement pas (op.cit., p. 139).

W. Pichl has collected from Senegal a Wolof text transliterated in Arabic. Pichl labels the text as "von Ndiaye Thiernot, Thiès, in arabischer Schrift geschrieben" (1961: 258 bis).

5. R. Deniel remarks that "le rôle du marabout est ancien. Les Ano [Ivory Coast] recourent à lui de longue date, car ils discernent dans la consultation de ce personnage l'efficacité d'un *savoir contenu dans un livre*-- le coran -- et concrétisé par le *nansi-gi*, l'eau versée sur l'écritoire " (1976: 91 [author's

emphasis]).

The *marabouts* constitute a prominent and essential feature of Mandinka society; P. Marty (op. cit.) already stressed that factor. The following passage captures the whole essence and meaning of the *marabouts* among the Mandinka people of Mali:

> Le *Karamoko* (maître coranique) ou le *mori* (marabout) est
> · comme le griot: homme de savoir, on ne le rencontre qu' aux
> côtés des rois et des fama dont il est le conseiller. De nos jours
> encore, les descendants de ceux-là qui jouèrent un si grand rôle
> à la cour des empereurs du Mali, vivent côte à côte dans les
> anciennes résidences des *Masa* (souverain, chef): à Jaliba (Berté
> et Cissé), à Krina (griots traditionalistes), à Kaba-Kangaba (Berté,
> Haïdara) et à Keila (griots traditionalistes Diabaté et marabouts
> Haïdara). C'est encore le cas à Brazā et Salamale; à Kita, avec
> son moribugu habité par les Cissé et son *djelibugu* à quelques
> Kilomètres, etc. (Claude Meillassoux 1963: 207, footnote; citing
> an unpublished article by Yussuf Cissé, [Author's emphases]).

In Mandinka society (Mali, Guinea, and the Gambia), the *marabouts* are found primarily among the Cissé and Touré families.

Commenting on the *marabouts* and on Islam in Waalo, B. Barry writes: "En marge, et souvent à l'intérieur de cette division traditionnelle de la société [Wolof], nous assistons, du fait de l'Islam, à l'apparition d'une nouvelle classe constituée par le marabout et ses adeptes" (1985: 70).

Writing on the *marabouts* in Wolof society, Baron Roger indicates that "ils jouissent de beaucoup de considération et exercent d'autant plus d'influence dans le pays, qu'ils vendent des amulettes ou *gris-gris* et qu'ils se mêlent de médecine" (op.cit., p. 139).

On the *marabouts,* D. Boilat writes: "On entend, en général, par marabout un prêtre mahométan, mais il faut aussi comprendre dans cette catégorie tout homme recommandable par ses bonnes moeurs et pratiquant toutes les observances de la loi" (1984: 301). Further on, Boilat stresses the important function played by the *marabout* among the Wolof: "Ces hommes [*marabouts*] moralisent le peuple, donnent généralement des conseils de paix et de conciliation. Sans leur influence, les villages des Wolofs ne seraient que des réunions de brigands, de scélérats, d'assassins" (loc. cit.).

On the *marabouts* who are at the same time traders (Dyula of northern present-day Ivory Coast and Mali), see Daniel Amara Cissé, *Histoire Économique de l'Afrique noire, tome 3: le moyen age*, 1988, pp. 88-89. See also the interesting analysis on the rise of the *maraboutique* power in pre-colonial Wolof society as well as during the colonial times by Christian Coulon (*Le Marabout et le prince*, 1981, pp. 61-72).

6. One of the most famous writers and thinkers of Senegal is Cheikh Moussa Kamara, who wrote poetry as well as articles on Islamic thought and theology (see "L'Islam et le christianisme" par Cheikh Moussa Kamara. Traduction et annotations par Amar Samb, *Bulletin de l' I.F.A.N* , 35 (1973): 269-322).

Paul Marty has also extensively written on the *Maraboutique* families of Senegal: the religious sect of *Tidianisme* with Al-Hadj Omar in Fuuta, Al-Hadj Malik Sy in Tivaouane; the sect of *Mouridisme* with Amadou Bamba in Touba and other sects such as those of Cheikh BouKounta, of the Mandinka, the Diola, the Fulas (see P. Marty, *Etudes sur l'Islam au Sénégal*, Tome I, *Les Personnes*. Paris: Ernest Leroux, 1917).

On the *mourides* and Amadou Bamba (the Wolof messiah), see C. Coulon, op.cit., pp. 72-88.

On the power structure of the Senegalese Brotherhoods (*Tariqas* in Arabic), the intrabrotherhood and interbrotherhood disputes, the involvement of politicians in Brotherhood disputes during the colonial period and in the post-colonial era, see Lucy C. Behrman, *Muslim Brotherhoods and Politics in Senegal*, 1970, pp. 61-83. R. Arnaud writes: "Le vocable *mourid* désigne, d'ailleurs dans les pays musulmans autres que le Sénégal, le disciple de foi ardente qui aspire à arriver jusqu'à la divinité" (1912: 14). In his article, Arnaud also elaborates on the practice of Islam in Senegal, on the marabouts and overall on Islamic sects (cf. Arnaud, "L'Islam et la politique musulmane française en Afrique," 1912.

For a more extensive treatment of the Senegalese *Mouride* brotherhood, see Donald B. Cruise O'Brien, *The Mourides of Senegal. The Political and Economic Organization of an Islamic Brotherhood*. Oxford: Oxford University

Press, 1971.

See also the excellent analysis by Moriba Magassouba of the *Mouride* brotherhood; of its founder Serigne Bamba; the principles of the brotherhood based on faith (prayer), work, discipline, and the seeking of knowledge. (Cf. M. Magassouba, *L'islam au Sénégal. Demain les mollahs?* 1985, pp. 25-39). For a more specific and detailed analysis of the work ethic of the *Mouride* brotherhood, see Vincent Monteil, *L'islam noir*, 1980, pp. 367-376.

An important study on Senegalese writings in Arabic is that of Amar Samb, "Essai sur la contribution du Sénégal à la littérature d' expression arabe," (Thèse. Lettres. Paris IV, 1971). Lille: service de reproduction des thèses de l' Université, 1972.

See also the thorough study on Islamic clericalism among the Jakhanke people of Senegambia by Lamin Sanneh (*The Jakhanke Muslim Clerics - A Religious and Historical Study of Islam in Senegambia.* Lanham, MD: University Press of America, 1989).

On the contribution and influence of Islam on African oral literatures, African literatures in European languages, African indigenous beliefs, and African cinema, see Kenneth Harrow (ed.), *Faces of Islam in African Literature.* Portsmouth, NH. London: Heinemann Educational Books and James Currey, 1991.

CHAPTER VIII

The Transmission of Knowledge.
Creativity, Composition, and Aesthetics.
Islam and Indigenous Religious Values in West Africa.

The first section of this chapter is based on a case study, namely an interview I had with Ancumbu Caam and his son Magate; the focal point in that dialogue was how the father orally transmits his knowledge to his son.

An essential feature of knowledge in traditional West African societies is the existence of a substratum; then, Islam (and in some cases Christianity) comes to affix itself as a superstratum on that substratum. Thus, when one considers knowledge in Wolof society, one has also to take into account the memorization of the Qur'an that the poet or singer acquires at an early age. I do not mean to say that the acquisition and transmission of knowledge in Wolof society is confined solely within the spheres of Islamic thought; the memorization of knowledge, its oral performance, and its transmission were carried out long before the advent of Islam in Senegal. However, there are striking similarities in the way knowledge is acquired, memorized, and then transmitted between Wolof indigenous knowledge and Islamic knowledge.

A. *The Transmission Of Knowledge.*

In societies in which literacy is of great importance, the oral transmission of knowledge still plays an important role.[1] R. Finnegan writes:

> In both the classical and the medieval world, oral delivery (even
> of previously written forms) was the accepted medium -- and this
> does not lead us to assume that the verbal art conveyed through
> this means was therefore lacking in the artistic detachment of
> 'literature'. (1973: 121)

Concerning the societies without writing, the transmission of knowledge
is equally a concern for the members of those oral societies. In his study of
collective memory and oral transmission of knowledge, A. Leroi-Gourhan
remarks:

> Le corps de connaissances du groupe est l'élément fondamental
> de son unité et de sa personnalité et la transmission de ce capital
> intellectuel est la condition nécessaire à la survie matérielle et
> sociale (1965: 65).

It would be difficult to dissociate the transmission of knowledge from its
nature, structure, and mode of acquisition.   I distinguish two kinds of
knowledge: oral knowledge and written knowledge; the transmission of the
former is more open for it is performed within the community, in front of
audiences, whereas the latter is largely an individual enterprise. An oral poet
can teach many students at one time whereas a Qur'anic teacher would transmit
knowledge to a smaller audience or to students individually; for instance, the
teacher of Qur'anic thought does a lot of exegetical work (*jange xam-xam* in
Wolof). The oral poet or griot teaches knowledge mostly in the form of
metaphors, proverbs, and sayings. In both cases, there is an esoteric element in
the way knowledge is taught and transmitted; however, there are differences
between the two forms of transmission. A. Kabou remarks:

Les sociétés africaines précoloniales n'étaient pas toutes des sociétés sans écriture. Il semble que celle-ci ait invariablement eu, là où elle existait, un caractère ésotérique ou magique qui en interdisait la diffusion. Et, de fait, encore de nos jours, le savoir dans les villages reste confiné à des cénacles restreints, et la richesse matérielle accaparée, comme au XVI ème siècle, par une poignée "d'hommes d'affaires" ou de politiciens incapables de concevoir des systèmes permettant d'étendre ces privilèges au plus grand nombre. Ainsi, le gel progressif des acquisitions techniques s'explique, aujourd'hui comme hier, par la coagulation des mentalités, laquelle, à son tour, empêche l'émergence de discours sociaux suffisamment neufs pour déboucher sur une modification des conditions de vie des populations. (1991: 175)

These remarks are corroborated by the words of Djeli Mamadou Kouyaté in the *Sunjaata Epic* [2]

When I was recording Ancumbu Caam and his son, I addressed questions to the father. Thus, he was doing all the talking. His son Magate was sitting by him. Besides me, my father was present and he was seated between Ancumbu and Magate. At the end of the last question I put to Ancumbu and after he finished reciting the genealogy of his own family, I turned to Magate. What I wanted the son to tell me was how he was acquiring the knowledge orally from his father. I was very surprised when Ancumbu Caam answered the question that I had directed to his son. I could feel all the weight of the authority the father has upon the son. The latter can speak only when authorized to do so by the father. I gently reiterated my question to Magate. At this point, the father could also feel my insistence on having Magate speak and since it was the same question, I guess that Ancumbu did not see the necessity or the purpose of answering again. There was a brief pause and then Magate started talking. The father's silence was the permission, the "green light," for the son to speak. Magate praised his father as being a very good man and said that whenever they visited people or were in front of an audience, he, Magate, would listen to his father; if there were certain things he did not understand, he would wait until they got home before he would ask his father to explain to him the passages, words, expressions, or genealogies in question. This is basically a relationship between a good father and a good son.[3] Magate did not say more than that.

Thus, the most salient point in the transmission of knowledge in this case is the fact that, whenever the father is performing in public (and he does so very often), the son would listen carefully and would not interrupt him. Later on, when they are alone, he would ask his father to explain to him what he did not understand during the performance. Also, it is during the performance that Magate sharpens his listening and memorizing skills.

I asked Magate when he would start performing himself. His answer was that for the present, he did not need to perform. Whenever he was with his father and the latter was performing, Magate would participate more and more in the performance; for instance, he would provide his father with a name when the latter forgot it while reciting. Additionally, the older the father gets, the more his memory is failing him and Magate's presence is needed all the more; Magate also leads his father to performances as well as visits to people's houses, for the father is blind (see Appendix I, for the transcription of the interview.)

B. *Creativity, Composition, and Performance Aesthetics.*

In Senegalese oral traditions, there are different manners and techniques of composition. Various elements enter into the equation. However, there is a common thread which links those elements: poetic flexibility. The emphasis is on the poet, not on the poem. The most important function of poetic flexibility which L. White calls "poetic license" is that "it enables us to take into account the wide variety of different performances the prevailing aesthetic can encompass and to locate this broader range of poems in a more complex set of social circumstances" (L. White 1989: 37).

In a study devoted to the *chants-poèmes* of the Sereer women of the village of Fadiouth in Senegal, Raphaël N'Diaye remarks that "la création, la forme et le contenu du chant-poème sereer sont déterminés, à des degrés divers, par l'ordonnance de la structure sociale" (1986: 84). R. N'Diaye collected these songs from different women who were not griots; the circumstances in which they composed their songs varied.

The author of song 4 in N'Diaye's collection is Daba Koura Sarr; after reciting her poem-song, she declares: "J' ai crée cette oeuvre d'un seul trait. Je n'ai pas eu à arranger les mots après coup, à choisir celui-ci à la place de celui-là. Par ailleurs, j'ai gardé l'oeuvre dans ma mémoire jusqu'à ce que notre groupe ci-présent ait l'occasion de se réunir. J'ai convié mes compagnes à m' écouter et c'est alors que je leur ai révélé le chant-poème afin qu'elles l'apprennent" (N'Diaye, ibid., p. 90-91). She also composed song 5, at the end of which she declares: "Je retournais la terre de notre rizière en compagnie de ma fille Thérèse. Si je parvenais à la dépasser quelque peu, l'instant d'après, c'est elle qui l' emportait sur moi. J'en ai été émue, et c'est pourquoi j'ai crée le chant-poème, séance tenante dans le feu de l'action. Je ne l' avais pas préparé avant" (N'Diaye, p. 91-92).

The author of poem-song 8 is Anna Tening Sarr who says:

Si j'ai composé le chant-poème, c'est que je n'ai pas de frères.

Je n'ai pas de fils non plus . . . Un jour, dans le calme de ma chambre, je me mis à penser et je composais cette oeuvre . . . Le chant-poème composé, je le gardais dans ma mémoire; puis le jour où tu [R. N'Diaye] vins nous enregistrer, j'en donnais une exécution publique....Je n'ai pas eu à procéder personnellement à des retouches en le composant. Je l'ai conçu d'un seul jet et il n'a connu aucune modification ultérieure. (Cited by N'Diaye, p. 95-96)

The reason for this last remark is that these women also practice group composition. For instance, if one composes a song, one can come to the group and perform it so that the group can suggest changes and modifications before it is publicly performed.

The poem-songs of the Sereer serve here for comparative purposes in considering the nature of composition and creativity among the Wolof, and more precisely with Ñan. As I stressed earlier, the women who composed the poem-songs are not griots. However, the Sereer also have a caste system.[4] Most of their songs are spontaneously composed, others are not. Ñan the Wolof singer has inherited this epic tale and most of his art from his ancestor; the tale is old and has undergone minor changes as embellishments have been added to it by successive generations of griots. However, there is still an element of composition even though the griot who is currently reciting the epic tale is not the author who originally created it. As remarked by A. Lord, "for the oral poet the moment of composition is the performance" (1960: 13).

In each performance of the epic tale, the content varies somewhat from the previous performance. I recorded two performances of the genealogy of the rulers of Waalo. When I compare the two versions, there are differences. As an example, in line 17, Ñan said at the beginning of his sentence that Mbañ stayed in power for 17 years but he meant Naatogo Taa Yaasin; he went on to correct himself after having glanced at his logbook. However, in the second performance, he did not make the same mistake. When he got to l. 17, he uttered only the name Naatogo Taayaasin, which was the correct one.

Whenever the *Epic Tale of the Waalo Kingdom* is performed, the griot gives a fresh rendering. The boundary between old and new is then blurred. The performances would be "old wine in a new bottle."

When he is performing, the gestures the singer makes, the clothes he is wearing, the manner in which he is seated, his facial expressions, the positions in which the plucked lute is held, all these elements constitute the aesthetics of his oral performance. Thus, aesthetics in oral performance belong above all to the visual domain, to the domain of audience participation. When the epic tale is written down, many aesthetic elements are lost.

C. *Islam and Indigenous Religious Values in West Africa.*

This section will be divided into three parts: the first part will be devoted to indigenous religious beliefs in West Africa and specifically in Senegal. The term indigenous subsumes the term traditional. What is meant by traditional religions is a set of beliefs that are uninfluenced by either Christianity or Islam. The second part will deal with the advent and impact of Islam in West Africa and the way in which it influenced the traditional religious beliefs. In the last part, I shall examine syncretism and its manifestations in West Africa and among the Wolof. Even though the Wolof converted to Islam in great numbers, they have not entirely given up their traditional beliefs. Most traditional African religious systems share certain common features. R. Horton observes that "it is typical of such systems that they include, on the one hand, ideas about multiplicity of spirits, and on the other hand, ideas about a single supreme being" (1967a: 61).

Contrary to the misleading idea that African traditional religions are strictly polytheistic, monotheism also existed in those systems.[5] What some of these African traditional religious systems of thought have in common with the revealed religions, particularly with Islam, is that beliefs cannot be questioned:

> Established beliefs [in traditional cultures] have an absolute validity, and any threat to such beliefs is a horrific threat of chaos. (R. Horton 1967: 168)

These traditional religions are also said to be based on the "closed" predicament which is characterized by a lack of awareness of alternatives, by the sacredness of beliefs, and by anxiety about threats to them (Horton 1967b: 156). In contemporary Wolof and Senegalese society, traditional religions still exist; however, they are profoundly influenced and altered by Islam and Christianity.

Islam was first introduced to Fuuta by the Moors. From there, it spread to the other ethnic groups such as the Wolof. P. Marty remarks that "vers les quinzième ou seizième siècles, si l'on en croit les chroniqueurs portugais, une grande partie des peuples sénégalais avaient embrassé, au moins partiellement, l'Islamisme" (1917: 5). It is generally taken for granted that Islam was introduced to Senegal by the Moors and most of all by their *marabouts* (Marty, op. cit., p. 69-70; citing Père Labat's *Nouvelle Relation de l'Afrique occidentale*, 1728).

On the attitude of the Senegalese vis-à-vis Islam as well as the presence of Islam in West Africa is general, Marian A. Johnson writes:

Islam came early to Senegal (about 1200 A.D.) and at first was rejected but later (by the nineteenth century) became the major religion, wiping out many indigenous belief systems. Today most Senegalese belong to one of two main Muslim sects, the Mourides or the Tidjanis. Islam was the most flexible of the religions to come to West Africa, easily assimilating traditional religions and customs. Not unlike other Africans, the Senegalese have chosen to assimilate certain elements and to omit others, creating a distinctive variant of Islam (op.cit., 1989: 112).

What is peculiar about the nature of Islam as well as about the indigenous beliefs is that both kinds of religion were distributed along geographical lines but not according to ethnic lines.[6]   For instance, the *marabouts*, whether they were Moors or Tukulor, thought that they shared the same faith and that that faith transcended ethnic lines; however, in a few cases such as those of Waalo and Fuuta, the Moors tried to impose their rule violently on the local populations; consequently, there were wars between the Moors and the Black populations (Marty, op. cit., p. 69-70; citing Labat, 1728).

In his study of Islam among the Wolof, G. Nicolas notes: "Sur le plan religieux, l'influence des maîtres coraniques maures a été déterminante dans la naissance et l'évolution de l'islam Wolof.   Toutefois, un antagonisme fondamental oppose également depuis l'origine les pasteurs sahariens blancs et les cultivateurs noirs Wolof" (1978: 364).

Likewise, when it comes to the traditional religions, the Sereer and the Wolof share many similar concepts. The presence of the *marabouts* in Senegal is the most prominent feature of Islam in that area. Thus, one finds similarities between certain Islamic and indigenous beliefs. For instance, the jinns of Islam are comparable to the spirits of traditional religions. D. Ames writes: "The [Gambian] Wolof all profess Islam, but they have kept many pre-Islamic beliefs and practices, modifying some considerably to accommodate Islamic practice" (1959: 263).[7]

The attitude of certain Islamic clerics and thinkers of Senegal toward their native language (which they wrote by using Arabic script), certain traditional beliefs, and even toward Christianity denotes a spirit of tolerance. For instance, W. Soyinka makes an important remark about *Tierno Bokar*, by Hampaté Ba. Ba's study is about a Peul saint and Muslim cleric called Tierno Bokar, who taught Hampaté:

> *Tierno Bokar* is a straightforward biography. It narrates the religious apprenticeship and the growth of wisdom in an individual whose largeness of vision enables him, even while lauding the superiority of Islam over Christianity, to preach the accommodation of the rival faith within the spirit of tolerance. (W. Soyinka 1990: 77)

L. Brenner makes a similar remark in his study of West African Sufi on the spiritual search of Tierno Bokar: "Cerno Bokar's tolerant and at times almost ecumenical attitude was justified by the Muslim doctrine that all the forms of monotheism which preceded Islam were valid" (1984: 151). This spirit of tolerance is also emphasized by A. Samb writing about Cheikh Moussa Camara. When speaking about Christians, the latter would say "que Dieu les agrée!" A. Samb adds: "L' emploi de cette formule de souhait pour des prêtres chrétiens qu'on n'emploie que pour un compagnon du Prophète [Muhammad] ou un saint musulman dénote l'esprit ouvert plus que tolérant de Cheikh Moussa Camara" (1973: 290).

One of the most important doctrinal and theological works on Islam is the Persian El-Bokhârî's (810 A.D.-870 A.D.) *Çahîh'*. Bokhârî's work is based on the *h'adîths* (deeds and sayings of the prophet Muhammed). Thus, Bokhârî recounts a *h'adîth* in which the prophet enjoins his followers and the Muslims in general not to question the People of the Book ("Les Gens du Livre," i.e. Jews and Christians). Thus, in this *h'adîth* the prophet encourages tolerance vis-à-vis other revealed religions while at the same time propounding the theological position of Islam vis-à-vis the Jews and the Christians and their sacred books. (El-Bokhârî 1964: 40-41).

Conversely, the illiterate majority in Senegal still keeps many aspects of its traditional creeds even though some of these are in apparent contradiction with Islamic tenets. Moreover, Islam suppresses some of those customs and creeds that are considered to be pagan. For instance, the performing of a therapeutic healing process called *ndëp* is forbidden by Islam; however, that practice is still in vogue among the Wolof, and most of all among the Lebu. Also, swearing is forbidden by Islam; however, people do swear.[8] Also, even though the consumption of alcohol is forbidden by Islam, some Muslims do drink alcohol. In short, most West African Muslims practice an Islam that has adapted itself to the social and cultural environment.

A final remark concerning Islam is that besides considering its relationship vis-à-vis traditional African religions, one must also take into consideration the clash between Western and Islamic cultures as well as the role that Islam played during the European colonization of Africa. To that end, S. Gellar remarks that "during the colonial period, Islam was a conservative and stabilizing force in Senegalese society, content to make its peace with colonial society in exchange for cultural autonomy" (1982: 123).

302

Notes to Chapter Eight

1. At the end of the twelfth century and the beginning of the thirteenth, universities started developing in Europe; books and printed materials acquired more importance. Febvre and Martin remark: "Malgré l'importance de l'enseignement oral, les étudiants eux aussi avaient besoin d'un minimum de livres" (1958: 23). Even though books were needed by students in universities of medieval Europe, Martin and Febvre add: "Ils [the students] pouvaient prendre ce que nous appellerions des 'notes de cours', et se fier pour une part considérable à une *mémoire* que les méthodes d'enseignement en honneur au Moyen Age avaient sans nul doute considérablement *développée*" (loc. cit. [emphases added]).

Along the same lines, M. Bucaille stresses the importance of recitation concerning the Qur'an. The author notes first that the Prophet (Muhammad) and the believers following him recited the text by heart and it was also written down by the scribes in his following. He then adds: "At a time when not everybody could write, but everyone was able to recite, recitation afforded a considerable advantage because of the double-checking possible when the definitive text was compiled" (M. Bucaille op.cit., p. 127).

Even writers and historians use oral testimonies in their writings. A case in point in that of Jules Michelet in his *Histoire de la Révolution française*. Writing after the events (the 1789 Revolution) had passed, Michelet talked to old people and witnesses of those events as well as using written testimonies. Thus: "Voilà ce que j'ai trouvé, constaté et vérifié [events of the 1789 Revolution] soit par les témoignages *écrits*, soit par ceux que j'ai *recueillis* de la *bouche* des vieillards [Emphases added]" (J. Michelet 1952: 7).

2. Mamadou Kouyaté says that "le savoir doit être un secret" (cited by D.T. Niane 1960: 78). In a footnote, Niane adds: "Voici une des formules qui revient souvent dans la bouche des griots traditionalistes. Ceci explique la parcimonie avec laquelle ces détenteurs des traditions historiques dispensent leur savoir. Selon eux les Blancs ont rendu la science vulgaire; quand un Blanc sait quelque chose tout le monde le sait. Il faudrait que nous arrivions à faire changer cet état d'esprit si nous voulons un jour savoir tout ce que les griots ne veulent pas livrer" (Niane, op. cit., p. 78-79).

3. As a comparison, the case of Avdo Mededovic, the singer of the Balkan Slavic oral narrative songs, is interesting. Avdo was also a tradesman. A. Lord writes: "One of the greatest shocks of his [Avdo's] life had come when the son to whom he had given over his business and all his capital, that Avdo himself might retire peacefully to the farm, had squandered everything in riotous living. There was bitter disillusionment in his voice as he told of it. He had been brought up to honor and obey his father and to believe that 'as a man sows, so shall he reap.' Having been a good son, he felt that he deserved to have a good son" (A.B. Lord, "Avdo Mededovic, Guslar," *Journal of American Folklore*, 69 (1956): 321).

4. See R. N'Diaye, op. cit., p. 84.

R. Mauny also stresses the importance of the caste system in Sereer society: "Le griot occupe au pays sérère, comme dans une bonne partie de l'Afrique noire, le bas de l'échelle sociale" (R. Mauny, "Baobabs - cimetières à griots," (1955): 75).

See also the important article on the caste systems in West Africa by Tal Tamari, "The Development of Caste Systems in West Africa," *Journal of African History*, 32 (1991): 221-50.

5. In his analysis of the main characteristics of traditional African religions, A. N'Daw remarks that "la religion traditionnelle africaine reconnaît l'existence d'une entité suprême transcendante" (1983: 213). On the Wolof, A. Sylla notes: "De quelque côté que l'on considère le monothéisme des Wolof on en arrive à conclure qu'il est antérieur à leur contact avec l'islam" (1978: 51).

It is also important to take into account the attitude of the griot vis-à-vis Islam. To that effect, I. Leymarie-Ortiz observes that "Islam has been tolerated by the griots, despite frequent rivalries between griots and marabouts, because it has not obliterated traditional cults and customs such as polygyny. Islamic sects also appeal to some griots because they put forward social equality while giving the griots a role to perform. Members of these sects are recruited among all social strata and marriages between members of different social status are allowed" (1979: 191).

6. L. Brenner argues that "Africans in a given region share a broad pool of concepts and ideas, although the distribution of these shared concepts should be expressed in geographical and not ethnic terms" ("Religious Discourses in and

about Africa," 1989, p. 92).

Contrary to what G.L. Hazoumé says, Islam in Senegal and in West Africa was not generally practiced along ethnic lines: "L'introduction de religions étrangères (christianisme et islam) créera un espace culturel conflictuel au sein duquel les divergences spirituelles épouseront des formes ethniques" (M. MBongo, 1985; citing G.L. Hazoumé, *Idéologies tribalistes et nation en Afrique*, 1972, p. 70 and 77.)

The Wolof belong to the *Tijaania* Muslim sect as well as to *Muridism*; the latter sect was headed by Amadou Bamba from 1886 until his death in 1927 (P. Marty, op. cit., pp. 220-232). Senegalese belong to various Islamic sects but that fact does not prevent them from coexisting. They are (and were) Muslim regardless of their ethnic background.

7. The most notable example of syncretism between traditional African religions and Christianity in West Africa is that of the *deima* cult. That cult or sect was created in the 1950s by Marie Lalou among the Bete of Ivory Coast (see Denise Paulme, "Une religion syncrétique en Côte d'Ivoire: le culte *deima*," *Cahier d'études africaines*, 3 (1962): 5-90.)

The case of William Wade Harris is also very well known. Harris who is dubbed a "black prophet" was born circa 1850 in Cap Palmes, Liberia. In the second half of the nineteenth century, Harris made a commitment to spread the apostolic propaganda. Ibrahima Kaké writes:

> In 1910, Harris had a vision of the Archangel Gabriel ordering him to carry the good word to peoples practicing animistic religions...

> Everywhere he went, he commanded that everything associated with traditional religious beliefs be destroyed. He introduced himself to these terrified people as being sent by God and ordered to destroy idols; he threatened horrendous calamities to those who might try to keep even one in their house. (1994: 28)

Harris's church is a blend of African beliefs and christian tenets even though it is apparent from the above account that he was against anything that was indigenous or animistic. Harris preached in an area comprised of present-

day Liberia, Ivory Coast and Ghana (former Gold Coast). Up to today, Harris
has a strong following in Ivory Coast. However, one should not underestimate
the impact that christianity had had in Africa. Moreover, one should also take
into account the transformations that the christian doctrine has experienced (and
still continues to do so) in Africa. Peter Worsley rightly remarks that "christian
doctrine became an African weapon, sharper than any spear, since it changed
men's minds, not merely compelled their bodies" (op.cit., p. 88).

So far, the most authoritative source on religious sects (traditional
christian) in Ivory Coast is that of B. Holas. The author treats the prophetic cult
of Boto Adaï, the movement of William Harris; the religious movements of
ayéré kpli and *massa*; the Lalou movement; the indebtedness of these pseudo-
christian sects to African traditional thought (See B. Holas, *Le séparatisme
religieux en Afrique noire, l'exemple de la Côte d'Ivoire*, Presses Universitaires
de France, 1965).

Another famous syncretic sect is *Kimbanguisme*; it was created in the
1920's in Central Africa by a black priest named Kimbangu; that sect was
constantly suppressed by the Belgian colonial administration. On the founder
of that sect, G. Balandier (1955) makes the following obsevation:

> Simon Kimbangou naquit en septembre 1889, à Nkamba, au nord
> de Thysville (Congo Belge); il fut éduqué dans une Mission
> baptiste de la région et y acquit en même temps qu'un savoir
> profane une bonne connaissance de l' Ancien Testament. (p. 427)

> On lui reconnaît la capacité de guérir les malades et de ressusciter
> les morts. Son action miraculeuse se modèle sur celle du Christ
> et le village de Nkamba, principal lieu de ses miracles, reçoit le
> nom de "Nouvelle Jérusalem." (p. 428)

> L' enseignement de Simon Kimbangou intervient à un autre
> niveau: il remet de l'ordre, et provoque un début de
> rationalisation, au sein de systèmes religieux dégradés, qui ont
> permis la naissance de cultes et de croyances multiples et
> disparates; il ne retient qu' un élément fondamental, le *culte des
> ancêtres* sur lequel il s'appuie [author's emphasis] (p. 429).

See also Marie-Louise Martin, *Kimbangu. An African Prophet and his church*. William B. Ferdmans Publishing Company and Basil Blackwell, 1975. On the co-existence between African traditional religious systems and Islam in West Africa, see Jack Goody, "The Impact of Islamic Writing on the Oral Cultures of West Africa," *Cahier d' études africaines*, 11 (1971): 455-66, and Lamin Sanneh. "The Origins of Clericalism in West African Islam," *Journal of African History*, 17 (1976): 49-72.

8. I. Basgöz noticed the same phenomenon in his analysis of Turkish folk narratives. His study is based on an experiment the author has conducted in Turkey. He writes: "The Islamic religion has been considered to be the main cause of the disappearance of the obscene elements from Turkish folk literature. Our experiment did not support this opinion. The peasants among whom the strongest religious belief exist did in fact relish the obscene. The answer to this paradox will be found in an examination of the education, culture, and morality propagated by the school and not in the religion" (I. Basgösz, "The Tale-Singer and His Audience," in *Folklore Performance and Communication*, 1975, p. 148-49.)

Appendix I: Interview with Ancumbu Caam and Magate Caam

Ancumbu Caam is a griot and a master of the word. Caam is blind; he is a great storyteller and one of the few remaining in Senegal still carrying on this tradition. His son, Magate Caam, was also present as well as my father Mapaté Diop, who occasionally would give some useful information about the genealogy or the involvement of the Diop family in the history of the Waalo kingdom. Caam and his son Magate belong to the caste of the *griots,* which in turn is part of the caste system of the *Ngèño.* The Caam family is from the River Senegal region. Each noble family has *griots* who are guardians of the genealogy of the family as well as the history of the region in question, or of the country. That the *griots* are part of a living oral tradition is important to note. Similar traditions are still active in many parts of contemporary Africa. During this interview, I asked questions of Caam. He spoke in Wolof, the most widely used language of Senegal, which is his and my language.

Samba: Now, I want you to tell me about your family, your ancestors, your age. I also would like you to tell me about the process of the acquisition of knowledge as a *griot* as well as the training of the *griot* starting in his childhood.

Ancumbu Caam: Did you ask me about my childhood?

Samba: Yes.

Ancumbu Caam: Did you also ask me where I got it from?

Samba: Yes.

Ancumbu Caam: This knowledge, I got from my father. His name is Amadu Caam, Amadu Caam Asta Mbay. He taught me everything. As a child I used to sit by my father and listen to him. A knowledge acquired since childhood cannot be lost. It is like a rock standing tall. I sat by him and he used to tell about history, genealogies, families of the Waalo kingdom. He used also to tell me a lot of folktales. I was very eager to learn, that's why he was very satisfied with me. He used to pray to Allah [God] to protect me and to give me a long life. Everything I know, I learned it from him since I was a little child. Medun Njaay Sefur Caam begot my father Amadu Caam. My father died at age 80. My father told me that my grandfather Medun Njaay Sefur died at 101.

Sefur Caam begot Medun Njaay Sefur Caam. Sefur Caam died at age 103. Tanor Caam begot Sefur Caam. Tanor is from the village of Mala. He belonged to the caste of the *griots* of Barlof Cubu. Tanor died at age 102. Mbañ Samb Caam begot Tanor. Mbañ Samb died at age 103. Mban also begot Xec Maya Caam and Ngor Yande Caam. Ngor Yande lived in Caggo.

This is how I got my knowledge, I got it from this lineage. My own father Amadu Caam told me all this. I got this knowledge from him; in his turn he got this knowledge from my grandfather, my grandfather from his father, and so on.

Samba: How old are you?

Ancumbu Caam: I am 81.

Samba: Now, can you answer the following question? You can't write; how then did you learn all the things you know? Can you tell me about your training? For instance, this vast knowledge you possess, is it something you rehearse for so long that you' ll never forget it?

Ancumbu Caam: Since I was a child, once I learned an event or once my father told me a story, I would never forget it. My knowledge could only increase, it couldn't decrease for the simple reason that I was a very intelligent child. God gave me this knowledge. I didn't give it to myself. When I was very young, my father used to tell me a story twice. Sometimes, when it was a lengthy story or a difficult one to grasp, he would repeat it a third time. Once that story entered my memory, I would never forget it. God gave me this knowledge. My father also was a very kind man. He was always willing to transmit his knowledge. Besides, I was a very assiduous student. I had to perform a lot of physical chores for him, which was one way to deserve that knowledge being transmitted to me. If one wants to possess such knowledge, one should be very assiduous. Also one should seek that knowledge from one's father or one's uncle or one's older brother. If one doesn't ask one's father, one's uncle, or one's older brother, one will never possess this knowledge.

Myself, I always asked my father anything I wanted to know. Farming, singing, and playing the *xalam* are the three trades I've always learned to do well. I also used to play the *xalam*, not anymore; I raised my family thanks to farming, playing the *xalam*, and singing.

When I was growing up, once I learned something, I would never forget it. Up to today, I don't forget what I've learned 60 or 70 years ago. That knowledge is in my chest [i.e., in his memory].

Samba: Did your father follow exactly the same process with your grandfather that you did with him?

Ancumbu Caam: Oh, yes, he did exactly the same. Son always followed father. My father worked very hard in order to obtain his knowledge from his own father. He used to travel with another *griot* called Yeman. They used to go from village to village. They usually got to a village at sundown because they would be travelling the whole day. Once they got to a village, they would have supper and then go to bed. The next day, after eating their lunch, they would go out of the village, to the nearest bush. There, they would be meditating, praying [Islamic prayers], and writing [in Arabic]. They would do so the whole afternoon because once they got back to the village, they wouldn't have any more time to pray or meditate for the simple reason that they would be dancing, singing, and telling stories for days. Thus, my father used only to dance, sing, and entertain people. He had three friends, *griots* themselves. They were Malexuri, Maadi Fanta, and Lamm Por. They encouraged him to start farming. When he started farming, he liked it so much that he stopped travelling around and entertaining people. When I was young, he wanted me to work on the farm with him. Instead, I told him that I was more interested in singing tales, telling stories, and playing the *xalam*. I refused to work on the farm. My grandfather Sefur Caam asked me if I really liked what I was doing, namely reciting tales and telling stories. I told him that I did. After he got tired of trying to convince me to work on the farm, my father gave up. That was the time when he really started teaching me to sing tales, to tell stories, and to memorize historical events as well as family genealogies. My training actually started at that time. I began to find some interest in farming when I became an adult. Now my father is in heaven. May God have pity on his soul! Amen.

Samba: Where are you and your family from originally?

Ancumbu Caam: We are originally from a village called Caggo, in the Waalo region, near the River [Senegal]. Your father knows that village. But my grandfather was born in Mala Barlof, Mala Maasey which was more inland. He then came to settle [here] in Caggo. My family belongs to the sub-caste of the Barlof *griots*.

My ancestors used to go to war along with the army; they used to sing in order to give courage to our fighters. Farming was also part of the activities performed by my ancestors.

Bali, Njobo, Yaay Juup, and Fatumata Joobe were sisters. Bali bore Asta

Mbay and Faa Njaay. Faa Njaay bore Jaan, she also begot my wife. Njobo bore Bineta Njobo. Njobo went to Merina and she gave birth to a boy, Njawar Samb.

Njobo is also the mother of Anta Faali. Anta Faali is the mother of Jaan Fawa. Jaan Fawa is the mother of Mademba Nay and Yaata. Njobo is the mother of Dégen. Dégen is the mother of Saa Jawaar and Batoor. Yaay Juup didn't have any children. Fatumata Joobe is the mother of Mataar Saar Mbay. Mataar Saay Mbay begot Majigen Cur, Maganar and Awa Mbay. These ancestors are those of my father's mother, my maternal grandfather.

We belong to the clan of Dogo. Dogo was my ancestor. He left Mala and settled in Mbelgor. When he arrived in Mbelgor, he stayed there for a long time. A woman called Kumba Samb lived there. You've certainly heard of Maajor. There is an adage that says: "There is peace because Maajor has been crowned." That isn't so. Maajor was neither a ruler nor a king. That man Maajor arrived in Mbelgor at night. He was carrying many spears. From afar, he could see the fire lit by Kumba Samb. He came to Kumba Samb's compound and greeted her. She returned the greetings. He asked for water to drink. She gave him water, he drank it. Kumba Samb said to Maajor: "My dear, you must be very hungry." She didn't even wait for his answer, but gave him food right away. After that Maajor took a spear and hit the woman on the forehead. She fell on the floor and started screaming, and said that she pitied the man who was hungry and thirsty; that's why she welcomed him in her compound. She didn't die.

A few years later, Maajor was chosen as a chief and ruler of Mbelgor. He summoned all the *griots* to a meeting. They all came except Kumba Samb. He said: "Are all the *griots* present?" "Yes," answered the assembly. Maajor said: "I don't think so. I don't see Kumba Samb. Go and find her!" When Kumba came, Maajor said to her: "Do you know me?" "No," answered Kumba, "I don't know you." Maajor said: "Well, my dear, you' re becoming senile. You remember that a few years back I came to your compound and asked for water. You gave me water and food." Kumba said: "Oh yes, now I remember." Maajor said: "You performed a good deed by giving me water and food. I hurt you because of the passion of fury of my youth. Now I want to redeem myself. From today, I name you as the chief of all *griots*." Dogo made the drums and they celebrated the coronation. Since Kumba Samb was my ancestor, we are also the *griots* of the Maajor clan.

In fact, the nobles and the *griots* had common ancestors. A long time ago, the princes used to play the *xalam*. Later on, two sub-castes were created because when there was dancing and drumming, people used to make a circle and the *griot* would dance. In Wolof, to make a circle is *gèwel lèn ko* [the French word *griot* corresponds to the Wolof word *géwel*]. That's the origin of the word *géwel*.[1]

Note to Appendix I

1. In his novel *Le dernier de l'empire*, the Senegalese writer and film maker Ousmane Sembene fictionalizes the word *géwel*. In a footnote, he writes:

> Geew: rond, cercle.   C'est le mot qui a donné naissance à
> Geewël: faire le rond, cercle autour de quelqu'un - par extension
> guewel: caste des griots musiciens. (1981: 49)

Thus, Sembene concurs with the griot Ancumbu Caam to the effect that the origin of the word *géwel* (griot) is *gèew* (i.e., a circle).

Appendix II: Sèq Ñan' s List of the Rulers of Waalo

1. Facsimile

(١)

بِسْمِ اللهِ الرَّحْمَنِ الرَّحِيمِ

فَصَلْ مُوجُرْ عَبْدُ الشَّمْسِ

عَبْدُ الشَّمْسِ نَكْ مُوجُورْ عِمَّانْ

عِمَّانْ مُوجُرْ عُمَرْ، عُمَرْ مُوجُرْ بُو بَكْرَ

عُمَرْ مُوجُرْ جَاجَانْ جَانْ جَاءِ

جَاجَانْ جَاءِ نَكْ بَلَنْ وَالَ فُكِ أَنْ

أَكْ جُرُمْ بِيَنْ (16 w)   (16 ans)

٢ بَرَكْ بَرَكْ بُوخْ بَلَنْ وَالَ   (84 ans)

٣ بَرَكْ جَاكَ بَارْ بَلَنْ وَالَ   (17 ans)

١ عَمَدُ فَاضَمْ بَلَنْ وَالَ   (9 ans)

٥ لَقَنْ يُمَنِكْ بَلَنْ وَالُ   (1 an.)

٦ بَرَخَنْ يُمَنِكْ بَلَنْ وَالُ   (1 an.)

٧ جَاذَ كَ يُمَنِكْ بَلَنْ وَالُ   (1 an.)

٨ فَاضَمْ يُمَنِكْ بَلَنْ وَالُ   (1 an)

Numuo. 2

وَنَجَوَاذْ جَلَنْ وَالْوَ (١٩٨)

مِجَوَاذْ جَلَنْ وَالْوَ (١٩٨)

ضَوَ وَاذْ جَلَنْ وَالْوَ (١٩٨)

اذْ نَنَذْ وَاذْ جَلَنْ وَالْوَ (١٩٨)

يِكُو دَبِنْ يُمْ عَمَدْ جَاطِمْ بَسْ دَنْنَذْ
وَاذْ : جِبِيلْ كُورْ أَنْ بِبَكِينْ، أَيْ
(تُوكُرِيَلَمْ) جُوطِبْكَ جَلْ تِيجَلْ
تُوكُرِيَ .

شى (جَر جا كَ وِلنَ (13ـاس) مَوُم بَّجِبِ كَّدَ
جَا كَ كُمَتَ فِريُوُنَ (15ـاس) مُوُم بَّجِبِ كَّلَ
بُمُوُنَ كُضَنَ وَانَسُلَ (أَمَلَ جَلُ) (24 Heures)

4

(‫ﻧﻤﺒﺮﻩ‬ 3)

^۸ ‫ﺑﺴﺮﻡ ﺑﺠﺪﻙ ﻟﻮﺏ ﺩﻭﺏ ﺩﺑﺴﺖ ﻗﻠﺘﻰ‬
‫ﻭﺍﻟﻮ‬ (ﺩ7ans) ‫ﻣﻮﻡ ﺟﻮﺳﻞ‬

‫ﺟﻜﺨﻞ ﺑﻮﺝ ﻗﻠﺘﻰ ﻭﺍﻟﻮ‬ (ﺩ9۰) ‫ﻣﻮﻡ ﺑﺠﺒﻜﺨﻞ‬

‫ﻗﺎ ﻧﻮﻟﻮ ﺗﺞ ﻳﻴﺲ‬ (ﺩ14ans) ‫ﻣﻮﻡ ﺑﺠﺒﻜﺨﻞ‬

‫ﻋﺮ ﺑﺮﻡ ﻗﻠﺘﻰ ﻭﺍﻟﻮ‬ (ﺩ12ans) ‫ﻣﻮﻡ ﺑﺠﺒﻜﺨﻞ‬ .

‫ﻧﺞ ﺑﺮﻡ ﻗﻠﺘﻰ ﻭﺍﻟﻮ‬ (ﺩ15۰۰) ‫ﻣﻮﻡ ﺑﺠﺒﻜﺨﻞ‬

‫ﺩﺑﺴﺒﻰ ﺑﺮﻡ ﻗﻠﺘﻰ ﻭﺍﻟﻮ‬ (ﺩ۰۰19) ‫ﻣﻮﻡ ﺑﺠﺒﻜﺨﻞ‬ .

‫ﺟﻠﻜﺠﺎﺭ‬

‫ﺗﺠﺎﻙ ﻛﻤﺴﺐ ﺗﻢ ﺟﻜﺒﺮ ﻗﻠﺘﻰ ﻭﺍﻟﻮ‬
‫ﺟﺮﻡ ﺗﺠﺎﺭﺍﺵ‬ (ﺩ7ans) ‫ﻣﻮﻡ ﻧﻮﻛﺮﺑﻞ‬

‫ﻗﺮ ﺑﻴﺖ ﻗﻠﺘﻰ‬ (ﺩ5۰۰) ‫ﻣﻮﻡ ﻧﻮ ﻧﺮﺑﻞ‬

‫ﺗﺠﺎﻙ ﻛﻤﺴﺐ ﻛﻨﺠﺪﻙ ﻛﻠﻮﺕ ﻗﻠﺘﻰ ﻭﻻ‬
‫ﻛﺪﺍﻥ ﺍﻙ ﺑﺮﻭﻡ‬ (ﺩ۰۰15) ‫ﻣﻮﻡ ﻟﺮ ﻧﺰﺑﻞ‬

318

5

إِجَا كُمُنِيَمْ نَانْ سَكَّ جَلْتَ وَالَتَ وَالْ (22 ans)
مُومْ تُوكْرِيلَ

بَاجَاكَ كُوتِبَانْ جَلْتَ وَالْ (13 ans)
مُومْ لُوكْرِيلَ

بَنْجِمْ تَاِنُوكُ جَلْنَ وَالُ (1 an)
مُومْ لُوكْرِيلَ

يَصَمْ سُومْ جَاكَ جَلْتَ وَالْ (17 ans)
مُومْ لُوكْرِيلَ

رَمْ بَجِبِكَ عَبْدَالِ جَلْتَ وَالْ (17 ans)
مُومْ لُوكْرِيلَ

رَمْ كُودِى جْرَانْ جَلْتَ وَالْ (70 ans)
بُومْ لُوكْرِيلَ

6

Numero 5

وهجرتا كوتناي جلّي (3ans) مُوم لوكبريل

بهجربتّ يكرّل هلّي (8ans) مُوم بجبالخل

نجاكّ دارفوتّ جلّي (7ans) مُوم بلجكّل

نانكو جرنجالّ كلّي (5ans) مُوم لوكبريل

ماتُولّ برمر جلّي (11ans) مُوم لوكبريل

اجربتّ نجاكّ جلّي (14ans) مُوم لوكبريل

نانكو جرنجالّ قلّي (11ans) مُوم لوكبريل

بجركو كجون جلّي (ans) مُوم جوشل

11جركوكجون جلّي (3ans) مُوم جوشل

11جربلّ لكن جمّ (7ans) مُوم لوكرّل

11جركوتدام قلّي (2ans) مُوم بجبكّل

15جرعيشّ البوّا (12ans) مُوم جوشل

Numero 6

هنا أولاد فرداري وَلَتَن (44 ans) صوم لوكبربلا

لاترجاك وَلَتَن (6 ans) صوم لوكبربلا

مرم بجك عزم بحر (33 ans) صوم بجبكل

جاك أرم بكر علتن والسور (27 ans) صوم بجبخل

بالوكوآزم بكر علتن (33 ans) صوم بجبخل

مرم كودى مرتيوب قلتن (9 ans) صوم بجبخل

مر بتنز بك رين قلتن (8 ans) صوم بجبخل

مرم أنت هوب قلتن (10 ans) صوم بجبخل

جالك لمفت فرناي قلتن (5 ans) صوم بجبخل

وكل بات نى نوم علتن (12 ans) صوم بجبخل

مرم بك رين قلتن (9 ans) صوم بجبنخل

مر بنتن عادم سال قلتن (12 ans) صوم بجبخل

8

Numero 7

خروف قرد ارو جلتی (300) صوم لو تخربل
مّبتوّم مالك عتت دارو (1500) صوم لو تخربل
مبتوّم مالك عتت دارو مو بترتب مبع بواد
مو سبی الت بلدبرب ج (1854)

2. *Translation of the Facsimile into English*

In the name of God, Most Gracious, Most Merciful,[1]

Qusay begot Abu Samsi
Abu Samsi begot Imaar
Imaar begot Umar. Umar begot Bubakar
Bubakar Umar begot Njaajaan Njaay
1. Njaajaan Njaay ruled Waalo for sixteen years (16 years)
2. Barak Barka ruled Waalo (24 years)
3. Barak Caaka Mbaar ruled Waalo (17 years)
4. Amadu Faatuma ruled Waalo (9 years)
5. Lafna Yumayga ruled Waalo (1 year) [2]
6. Farakuna Yumayga ruled Waalo (1 year)
7. Caparga Yumayga ruled Waalo (1 year)
8. Faatuma Yumayga ruled Waalo (1 year)
9. Mbañ Wadde ruled Waalo (1 year)
10 Fija Wadde ruled Waalo (1 year) [3]
11. Daffa Wadde ruled Waalo (1 year)
12. Dunda Wadde ruled Waalo (1 year)
From Amadu Faatuma to Dunda Wadde: They are [i, e., the people between Amadu Faatuma and Dunda] males and females. They are Logars [a title]. They ruled one after the other. [4]
13. Tan Fara Njaak ruled (13 years) [5]
14. Njaak kumba Xuri Mboj (15 years) [6]
15. Mboy Kumba Waslu (did not sit on the throne) (24 hours)
16. Yérim Mbañik Koy Joy Joos, ruled Waalo (7 years). He is a Joos
17. Cukli Mboj ruled Waalo (9 years). He is a Tèjèk [7]
18. Naatogo Tañ Yaasin (17 years). He is a Tèjèk
19. Fara Yérim ruled Waalo (12 years). He is a Tèjèk
20. Mbañ Yérim ruled Waalo (15 years). He is a Tèjèk
21. Dembaané Yérim ruled Waalo (12 years). He is a Tèjèk [8]
22. Njaak Kumba Samb Jakèr ruled Waalo for seven years (7 years). He is a Logar
23. Fara Xot ruled (5 years). He is a Logar
24. Njaak Kumba Kijiki Kuluka ruled Waalo for fifteen years (15 years). He is a Logar
25. Njaak Kumba Nan Saku ruled Waalo (22 years). He is a Logar
26. Njaak Ko Jaay ruled Waalo (13 years). He is a Logar

27. Mbañ Naatogo ruled Waalo (1 year). He is a Logar
28. Mam Jok Jaak ruled Waalo (17 years). He is a Logar
29. Yérim Mbañik Abdaali ruled Waalo (17 years). He is a Logar
30. Yérim Kodu Njuraan ruled Waalo (70 years). He is a Logar
31. Fara Takko Taay ruled (3 years). He is a Logar
32. Fara Pénda Tigérélé ruled (8 years). He is a Tèjèk
33. Njaak Daaru Xocc ruled (7 years). He is a Tèjèk
34. Naatogo Fara Njaak ruled (5 years). He is a Logar
35. Naatogo Yérim ruled (11 years). He is a Logar
36. Fara Pénda Njaak ruled (14 years). He is a Logar
37. Naatogo Fara Njaak ruled (11 years). He is a Logar
38. Fara Ko Joos ruled (8 years). He is a Joos
39. Fara Ko Joob ruled (3 years). He is a Joos
40. Fara Pénda Lakar Jam (7 years). He is a Logar
41. Fara Ko Ndaam ruled (2 years). He is a Tèjèk
42. Fara Aysa Naalèw (12 years). He is a Joos
43. Naatogo Fara Daaro (44 years). [9] He is a Logar
44. Bar Caaka ruled (64 years). He is a Logar
45. Yérim Mbañik Aram Bakar (33 years). He is a Tèjèk [10]
46. Njaak Aram Bakar ruled Waalo (27 years). He is a Tèjèk
47. Naatogo Aram Bakar ruled (33 years). He is a Tèjèk
48. Yérim Kodu Fara Ngoné ruled (12 years). [11] He is a Tèjèk
49. Fara Pénda Tak ruled (8 years). He is a Tèjèk
50. Yérim Anta Joob ruled (10 years). He is a Tèjèk
51. Njaak Kumba Xur Yaay ruled (5 years) [12]
52. Kuli bata San Joj ruled (12 years). He is a Tèjèk
53. Yérim Mbañik Tak ruled (2 years). He is a Tèjèk
54. Fara Pénda Haad Masal ruled (12 years). He is a Tèjèk
55. Xarfa Xari Daaro ruled (3 years). He is a Logar [13]
55. Ma Mboj Maalik Aysa Daaro (15 years). He is a Logar [14]
Ma Mboj Maalik Aysa Daaro is the last Barak to sit on the throne. His reign coincided with the coming of Faidherbe (1854).

Notes to the Translation of the Facsimile

1. This is a traditional Islamic invocation. In the performance, the singer starts by invoking his own name. I think that this differenciation on the part of the singer is linked to his own attitude vis-à-vis the questions of orality and writing.

2. In the performance, Barak Barka Jèri is between Amadu Faatuma and Lafna Yumayga. However, he is not on this list.

3. Aljuma Wadde is mentioned in the performance between Fija and Dunda but is not on the script.

4. In the performance, Ñan states that the people that are between Barak Barka Jèri and Dunda Wadde ruled for nine years. He also mentions that they were crowned at Njaasèw where Njaajaan first appeared. There, each one of them was bathed before the crowning but died a year later, as a consequence of that bath. Ñan does not write the above statement on the facsimile.

5. This person is not mentioned in the performance.

6. This name is not in the performance.

7. This name corresponds to line 16 of the performance.

8. This character corresponds to line 20 of the performance.

9. In the performance, Ñan adds Daxès to this name.

10. In the performance (line 44 to line 46), Ñan mentions the title Tèjèk as he does in this list. He does not mention all the titles in a consistent manner in the facsimile and in the performance.

11. One year in the performance.

12. Fifteen years in the performance.

13. Corresponds to line 59 of the performance.

14. In the performance, Ñan adds the name Maram Caw to Ma Mboj Maalik Aysa Daaro.

3. *Transcription in Roman Characters of Sèq Ñan's Performance*

Man, Sèq Ñan, maay xalamal Xalifa Joob si kër baayam Mapaaté Joob, fii si Rosso-Sénégal; baayam si Baraak yi la bok. Wax naa né Waalo moy fi nga xamné fa la buur njëkè fēñ. Njaajaan nak, sériif la, Lamtoro la, Barak la. Waalo nak, amna jurom béni tèmèri at ak ñaar fuk ak jurom (625). Njaajaan, ma nga judò Mudèri Jaawara. Boba, ñunk ko wowè Mamadu Aydara. Waalo amna jurom fuki Barak ak jurom ñaar (57); ñu mom Waalo jurom bén tèmèri at ak ñaar fuk ak jurom (625) Fédérbe soga sancce Ndar si mil wii saan sénkaan kat (1854).

Njaajaan Njaay, Qusay moy maamam.

Qusay mo jur Abu Samsi.

Abu Samsi mo jur Imaar.

Imaar mo jur Umar.

Umar mo jur Bubakar Umar.

Bubakar Umar mo tocc Gana.

Bubakar Umar mo tuubël Abraham Sal sa Mudèri Jaawara.

Abraham Sal mayé domam Fatumata sal Bubakar.

Njaajaan judo si sëy bobu.

1. Njaajaan Njaay, fuki at ak jurom béne la mom Waalo (16).

2. Barak Barka, ñaar fuki at ak ñénte la falu Waalo (24).

3. Barak Caaka Mbaar, Fuki at ak jurom ñaar la falu Waalo (17).

4. Amadu Faatuma, jurom ñénti at la falu Waalo (9).

5. Baraak Barka Jèri,

6. Lafna Yumayga,

7. Ak Farakuna Yumayga,

8. Ak Caparga Yumayga,

9. Ak Faatuma Yumayga,

10. Ak Mbañ wadde,

11. Ak Fija Wadde,

12. Ak Aljuma Wadde,

13. Ak Dunda Wadde.

Ñoñu, jurom ñénti (9) Barak yi. Mom nañu Waalo jurom ñénti at (9). Ku si né, béne at nga am si nguur gi, saay. Ñom xèxu ñu. Si mbirum Njaasèw lañu dèwé. Ku si né, Njaasèw lañ la falé, fi Njaajaan njëkè fèñé. Ku si né, bu sa wuxtu nguur jotè, dañu lay yobu Njaasèw, sanga la fa; sangu bobu fèbar la. Bu béne at matè, nga saay si nguur gi. Ku si né, mom nga Waalo béne a.

14. Taañ Yaasin, mom na Waalo ñaar fuki at (20).

15. Yérim Mbañik Ko Ndooy Démba, mom na Waalo jurom ñaari at (7).

16. Coli Mboj Tukili Mboj, mom na Waalo jurom ñénti at (9).

17. Mbañ...Heuh ! Naatogo Taa Yaasin, mom na Waalo fuki at ak jurom ñaar (17).

18. Fara Yérim, falu na Waalo fuki at ak ñaar (12).

19. Mbañ Yérim, falu na Waalo fuki at ak jurom (15).

20. Démbaané Yérim, falu na Waalo fuki at ak ñaar (12).

21. Njaak Kumba Amtaak Jakèr, falu na Waalo fuki at ak ñaar (12).

22. Njaak Kumba Amtaak Jakèr, falu na Waalo jurom ñaari at (7).

23. Fara Xèt, falu na Waalo juromi at (5).

24. Njaak Kumba Am Cinjing, gor la, falu na Waalo fuki at ak jurom (15).

25. Njaak Kumba Amndaal Sangu, falu na Waalo ñaar fuki at ak ñaar (22).

26. Njaak Kor Njaay, falu na Waalo fuki at ñént (14).

27. Mbañ Naatogo, mom na Waalo béne at (1).

28. Ma Mboj Njaak, mom na Waalo fuki at ak Jurom ñaar (17).

29. Yérim Mbañik Abdaali, falu na Waalo jurom ñaar fuki at (70).

30. Fara Takko Taay, falu na Waalo ñéti at (3).

31. Fara Pénda Tigérélé, falu na Waalo juromi at (5).

32. Barak Caaka Daaro Xoc, falu na Waalo jurom ñaari at (7).

33. Naatogo Fara Njaak, falu na Waalo juromi at (5).

34. Naatogo Yérim, falu na Waalo fuki at ak jurom (15).

35. Fara Pénda Njaak, falu na Waalo fuki at ak ñént (14).

36. Ngañ Fara Njaak, falu na Waalo fuki at ak béne (11).

37. Fara Kor Jol Jos, falu na Waalo jurom ñéti at (8).

38. Fara Kor Joob Jos, falu na Waalo ñéti (3).

39. Fara Pénda Lanaar Dém, falu na Waalo jurom ñaari at (7).

40. Fara Kor Ndaama, falu na Waalo ñaari at (2).

41. Fara Aysa Naalèw, falu na Waalo fuki at ak ñaar (12).

42. Daaro Daxèk Daaro, falu na Waalo kaaran katran (44).

43. Bar Caaka Logar, falu na Waalo jurom béne fuki at ak ñént (64).

44. Yérim Aram Bakkar, Tèjèk la, falu na Waalo fanwèri at ak ñét (33).

45. Naatogo Aram Bakkar, Tèjèk la, falu na Waalo fanwèri at ak ñét (33).

46. Njaak Aram Bakkar, Tèjèk la, falu na Waalo ñaar fuki at ak jurom ñaar (27).

47. Yérim Anta Joob Jos, falu na Waalo béne at (1).

48. Yérim Anta Joob, falu na Waalo fuki at (10).

49. Yérim Kodu Fara Ngoné, falu na Waalo béne at (1).

50. Njaak Kumba Xura Mboj, falu na Waalo fuki at ak jurom (15).

51. Mboy Kumba Xédé. Mboy Kumba Xédé mii nak, laa lèn wox né la ñu
    waral fas, yobu ka Ndèr.

Mu jaar Bëdde; bi mu jaarè Bëdde, Sirabawar mi, Mboy Kumba Xédé, baaxul ndax

da fa xèxak Njaak Kumba Mboj, réy ka ba paré, jigènam jogé Mbayaan, mu réy ka ca biir bayaga ga. Ki daal, déful lubaax. Ñu nèxal naar bu ño wox Saalmon, daa di jël wurus bu baré, daa di jël xaalis bu baré, daa di ko jox Saalmon, ni ko: "Bu ngonè, danu takke fas wii, mu wara bofi Ndèr. Mu né: "Waaw." Mu jala sa wala gëlé, dém sa taatu ngéte ga. Mu war fas wa ba égge sa diggu bëdde ba. Bi nga xamné ndigeli mi ngi laal ndox mi, mu tëgge sox sa bop ba, tocc ndaalu bop ba. Samay maam ñom nak wëy: "Mboy Kumba Xédé xuusul bëdde, Njaalu ya la tak." Mom dé amul pal.

52. Njaak Kumba Xur Yaay, falu na fuki at ak jurom (15). Mom mo rampalaasé [remplacé] Mboy Kumba Xédé mi amul pal.

53. Fara Pénda Tigérélé, Tèjèk, fuki at ak jurom (15).

54. Daaro Kumba Xur Yaay momèt, jurom béne at la mom Waalo (6).

55. Kura Mbaba Sën Mboj, juromi at (5).

56. Barak Saayobé Mboj, jurom béni at (6).

57. Fara Faata Mborso, jurom ñéti at (8).

58. Yérim Mbañik Tigirélé, ñaari at la mom Waalo (2).

59. Xërfa Xar Daaro, ñéti at la mom Waalo (3).

60. Fara Pénda Aram Sal, fuki at ak ñaar la falu Waalo (12).

61. Ma Mboj Maalik Aysa Daaro Maram Caw, fuki at ak jurom (15).

Mo dajèk Fédérbe si mil wiisaan séngkaat kat (1854).

4. *Translation of Ñan's Performance*

I, Sèq Ñan, am playing the xalam for Xalifa (Samba) Diop in the house of his father Mapaté Diop in Rosso-Sénégal. His father belongs to the royal ruling house of the barak. I say that Waalo is the country where kings first appeared. Njaajaan himself is a holy man, a lamtoro, and a barak. The kingdom of Waalo had been in existence for 625 years. Njaajaan was born in Muderi Jaawara. Then, he was called Mamadu [short for Muhammad] Aydara. All together, Waalo had 57 baraks. They ruled Waalo for 625 years before Faidherbe created Saint-Louis in 1854.

Njaajaan Njaay, Qusay is his ancestor.

Qusay begot Abu Samsi.

Abu Samsi begot Imaar.

Imaar begot Umar.

Umar begot Bubakar Umar.

Bubakar Umar destroyed Gaana. [1]

Bubakar Umar converted Abraham Sal [2] at Muderi Jaawara.

Abraham Sal married his daughter Fatumata Sal to Bubakar.

Njaajaan was born of that union.

1. Njaajaan was the first ruler of the empire of Waalo. He sat on the throne for 16 years.

2. Barak Barka replaced him. He sat on the throne of Waalo for 24 years.

3. Barak Caaka Mbaar ruled Waalo for 17 years.

4. Amadu Fatuma sat on the throne of Waalo for nine years.

5. Barak Barka Jèri,

6. Lafna Yumayga,

7. And Farakuna Yumayga,

8. And Caparga Yumayga,

9. And Fatuma Yumayga,

10. And Mbañ Wadde,

11. And Fija Wadde,

12. And Aljuma Wadde,

13. And Dunda Wadde.

Those were the nine Baraks. They ruled Waalo for nine years. Nine years. Each one of them ruled for one year. Those rulers didn't wage any war. They died during the events of Njaasèw. Each one of them was crowned at Njaasèw where Njaajaan first appeared. When one's turn to be crowned was up, he was brought to Njaasèw where Njaajaan first appeared. There, each one of them was bathed for, that bath made one diseased. [3]

14. Taañ Yaasin replaced them. He ruled Waalo for 20 years.

15. Yérim Mbañik Ko Ndooy Démba replaced him. Seven years.

16. Coli Mboj Tukili Mboj ruled Waalo for nine years.

17. Mbañ... Eh [4] Naatogo Taa Yaasin ruled Waalo for 17 years.

18. Fara Yérim sat on the throne of Waalo for 12 years.

19. Mbañ Yérim sat on the throne of Waalo for 15 years.

20. Démbaané Yérim sat on the throne of Waalo for 12 years.

21. Njaak Kumba Amtaak Jakèr sat on the throne of Waalo for 12 years.

22. Njaak Kumba Amtaak Jakèr ruled Waalo for seven years.

23. Fara Xèt sat on the throne of Waalo for five years.

24. Njaak Kumba Am Cinjing, he is a noble, sat on the throne for 15 years.

25. Njaak Kumba Amdaal ruled Waalo for 22 years.

26. Njaak Kor Njaay ruled Waalo for 14 years.

27. Mbañ Naatogo ruled Waalo for 1 year.

28. Ma Mboj Njaak ruled Waalo for 17 years.

29. Yérim Mbañik Abdaali ruled, sat on the throne of Waalo for 70 years.

30. Fara Takko Taay ruled Waalo for three years.

31. Fara Pénda Tigérélé sat on the throne of Waalo for five years.

32. Barak Caaka Daaro Xoc ruled Waalo for seven years.

33. Naatogo Fara Njaak ruled Waalo for five years.

34. Naatogo Yérim sat on the throne of Waalo for 15 years.

35. Fara Pénda Njaak sat on the throne of Waalo for 14 years.[5]

36. Ngañ Fara Njaak sat on the throne of Waalo for 11 years.

37. Fara Kor Jol Jos sat on the throne of Waalo for eight years.

38. Fara Koor Joob Jos sat on the throne of Waalo for three years.

39. Fara Pénda Lanaar Dém sat on the throne of Waalo for seven years.[6]

40. Fara Kor Ndaama sat on the throne of Waalo for two years.

41. Fara Aysa Naalèw ruled Waalo for 12 years.

42. Daaro Daxèx Daaro sat on the throne of Waalo for 44 years.

43. Bar Caaka Logar sat on the throne for 64 years.

44. Yérim Aram Bakkar, he is a Tèjèk, sat on the throne for 33 years.

45. Naatogo Aram Bakkar, he is a Tèjèk, sat on the throne for 33 years.

46. Njaak Aram Bakkar, he is a Tèjèk, sat on the throne for 27 years.

47. Yérim Anta Joob Jos sat on the throne for one year.[7]

48. Yérim Anta Joob sat on the throne for ten years.

49. Yérim[8] Kodu Fara Ngoné sat on the throne for one year.

50. Njaak Kumba Xura Mboj sat on the throne for fifteen years.[9]

51. Mbooy Kumba Xédé, I told you that Mbooy Kumba Xédé took part in a
battle. He was mounted on a horse and was taken to Ndèr.[10] He went
through Bëdde. When he arrived at Bëdde, he fought Njaak Xura Mbooy, and
killed him. Njaak's sister came, and he killed her too. That was a great
mistake. A Naar [11] called Saalmon was called in. Sirabawar took a lot of gold
and silver and gave them to Saalmon. He was told that, by early evening, a
horse would be ready to depart for Ndèr. He agreed. He crossed the river [12] and

went to the other side. He took the horse knee-deep, among the reeds, in a small lake. After that, he shot [at Njaak Xura] and opened his skull. My grandfather used to say: "Njaak Xura never crossed the lake." It is said that he [Njaak Xura] never sat on the throne. He never made it to Ndèr. Njaak Kumba Xur Yaay sat on the throne for 15 years.[13] He replaced Njaak Kumba Xédé. The latter never sat on the throne. He was a Joos.

52. Njaak Kumba Xur Yaay sat on the throne for 15 years. He replaced Mboy Kumba Xédé who wasn't crowned.

53. Fara Pénda Tigérélé, he is a Tèjèk, sat on the throne for 15 years.

54. Daaro Kumba Xur Yaay sat on the throne for six years.

55 Kura Mbaba Sën Mboj, five years.

56. Barak Saayobé, six years.

57. Fara Faata Mborso, eight years.

58. Yérim Mbañik Tigérélé ruled Waalo for two years.

59. Xërfa Xar Daaro sat on the throne for three years.

60. Fara Pénda Aram Sal sat on the throne for 12 years

61. Ma Mboj Maalik Aysa Daaro was the last Brak, 15 years. He died in 1854. His reign coincided with the coming of Faidherbe. [14]

334

Notes to the Translation of Ñan's Performance

1. The Empire of Ghana.

2. The reference is to the conversion of Abraham Sal to Islam.

3. The Wolof singer means that there was some kind of bad spell or magic in the water. In the popular mind, there is always a possibility of harming a person from a distance, by various means such as charms or incantations.

4. The singer meant to say Naatogo, instead he mentioned the name (Mbañ) that he had already uttered.

5. Many rulers bear the same first name Fara Pénda.

6. This line is not on the Arabic script.

7. The name on the next line is similar to this one but Jos has been added to this name.

8. Many rulers bear this same first name.

9. Five years on the Arabic script.

10. Ndèr was the capital of Waalo; the Brak resided there.

11. Naar is the term used in Wolof in order to designate the Moors of Mauritania (see note to line 965, chapter III). Saalmon is the equivalent of Solomon, or Suleyman.

12. The River Senegal.

13. Njaak Kumba Xura is different from Njaak Kumba Xur Yaay.

14. Faidherbe was the French governor who consolidated the French presence in Senegal in the middle of the nineteenth century.

From 1854 to 1885, a French military expedition went from Saint-Louis to Waalo in order to put an end to the wars that the Moors were waging against the local Wolof and Tukulor populations. The aim of that expedition was also to pacify the whole region of Waalo and place it once and for all under strict French colonial rule. Yoro Dyao's expertise and help was sought by the French governor of Sénégal. Dyao was evaluated in these terms by the French military officers: "Yoro-Diao, homme de bonne famille, [qui] s'était déclaré pour nous et nous avait servi de guide" (*Annales Sénégalaises*, 1885, p. 20 [Author not mentioned]). On Dyao's brother, Fara-Penda (Dyao designated him to work with the French), he was complimented in the following fashion: "Il [Fara-Penda] nous rendit les plus grands services en ralliant petit à petit les gens du Oualo et rétablissant les villages, tout en soutenant une lutte acharnée contre les Maures" (loc. cit.).

In his discussion of the Wolof states and kingdoms in the 19th century, Y. J. Saint-Martin highlights the upheavals brought to those kingdoms by the French occupation. The author notes the annexation of Kayor in 1865 but also the annexation of Waalo "devenu <<tout français>> depuis 1855, selon Faidherbe. Magré les palinodies de quelques chefs nommés par les Français, c'est le pays Wolof tout entier qui est secoué en profondeur" (Saint-Martin op.cit., p. 575).

5. *Study of Ñan's Performance*

This is an attempt to reconstitute the genealogy of the rulers of Waalo as sung and performed by the Wolof singer, Sèq Ñan. This reconstitution is not an easy task for, as an example, there are problems of chronology and of concordance between the performed version and the tally of names written in Arabic by Ñan.

There are other versions of this genealogy which constitute a paradigm within the framework of Wolof historiography. A glance at the various versions[1] shows more similarities than discrepancies between them. The personal stamp of the singer on the genealogy is not that important whereas the mark of the Wolof singer on the epic tale is paramount.

In his study devoted to two griots of Senegambia, E. Makward compares two Senegalese griots: Anchou Thiam and a female griot called Haja M'Bana Diop; both griots are from Waalo. As pointed out by the author, Thiam is faithful to tradition and to the accuracy of past events in Waalo whereas Diop takes more liberty in the way she recites those events. Makward makes the following point:

> M'bana Diop is indeed a singer and a composer of songs, and not a reciter of poems. In *Ndyaadyan Ndyaay*, she does not narrate the career of the legendary first king of the Wolof, as a more traditional griot would do. She only refers to a few very well known legendary or semi-legendary facts about Ndyaadyan Ndyaay. (1990: 30)

Ancumbu Caam, the griot who told me how he was transmitting his knowledge to his son Magate, is the opposite of M'Bana Diop. Ancumbu is much closer to Anchou Thiam whereas Ñan is much closer to M'Bana Diop but they are not quite the same for, even though Ñan is striving towards a better and more modern standard of living, he is not involved in politics. Makward adds that M'Bana attended the convention of the Union Progressiste Sénégalaise, the political party of the former president of Sénégal, Léopold Senghor (1990: 34). Makward also stresses the fact that M'Bana enjoys a higher economic status than Anchou (she has an air-conditioner in her living-room, a refrigerator, and a television set; she also made the holy pilgrimage to Mecca). The reason why it is important to dwell on the economic status of these griots is that this strategy will help in countering a misunderstanding about Wolof genealogies. Makward also states that M'Bana told him that "mere memorization of genealogies is a minor art form among the Wolof" (p. 28). Basically, M'Bana Diop can be considered as a griot who fits the characterization of J. Irvine: "Many *griots* sing for both sides [of the audience] and so must maintain versions of the genealogy that are favorable to each" (1978: 665).

There are two kinds of genealogies among the Wolof: poetic genealogies and historical genealogies. In a study devoted to a Wolof oral praise song, G. Joseph considers that the poem he is analysing is a poetic genealogy (1979: 145). Joseph makes the important distinction by noting that "in contrast to history, poetic genealogies proceed according to the whims of the singer" (op. cit., p. 148). The performer of poetic genealogies may sing a genealogy according to the link he or she has with the subject being sung or according to the gifts and rewards he or she is expecting.

In the case of Ñan, memorization of the genealogy of the rulers of Waalo is important for the performance. He even took the expedient of writing down the genealogy and the number of years each ruler was in power in Arabic script in order to minimize the mistakes he might be prone to make when reciting it.

In his study of the kingdom of Waalo, B. Barry devoted a chapter to the reconstitution of the chronology of the rulers (or baraks) of the kingdom. However, Barry carried out his reconstitution on the basis of written intermediary sources whereas in the present study, the reconstitution is done directly from an oral performance. From time to time, while reciting, the singer would glance at his tally of names in order to corroborate or to double check what he was singing. Barry stresses the difficulty of reconstituting the genealogy of the kingdom of Waalo (1985: 317).

What is the aim in reconstituting the genealogy of the rulers of Waalo and historical genealogies in general ? Are the people mentioned in the genealogy real or fictional ? When one considers all the studies devoted to the kingdom of Waalo, the historical evidence demonstrates that most (if not all) the rulers have actually existed.

On the historical significance of genealogies in African studies, J. Bazin writes:

> We are faced with two possibilities. One is that we obtain, often with only great difficulty, a list of names which has a performative value associated with the very recitation of the list - such as that which the legitimate authority must enunciate during a given village or lineage ritual - that provides a document which is very likely to be authentic but from which it is very difficult if not impossible to extract genealogical information. The other form is that by which we obtain access to genealogical knowledge already constituted, but having as its function the legitimation of an acquired situation, more relevant perhaps to present-day tensions than to the facts of the past, and thus functioning like myths of origin. (1986: 63)

The following remarks will deal with the nature of the relationship between the various people involved in this genealogy. Equally important is the bond that exists between the people (their genealogy) and the soil, namely their environment, the country, Waalo. The relationship between the soil, the rulers, and the ruled in Waalo is symbolized by the fact that the barak, after coming to the throne, made to noble families a customary payment of a dozen slaves (*dyög*) as rent for the land, proof that, although the land did not belong to him, he had the right to dispose of it (A. Bara Diop 1968: 50). The Wolof identified themselves with the land (*suuf* in Wolof, or *terroir* in French). In the study of pre-colonial, traditional African societies, one must take into account the role that nature in general and the land in particular play in traditional African thought as well as in social and political systems. The symbiosis between nature and man in those societies was very complex. An example of how nature was the foremost element that influenced all aspects of life in most traditional African societies is the Yoruba Ijala chant as described by S.A. Babalola (1966: 124). In the context of nature, the Ijala chant fulfilled social and poetic functions. The period being described in the Ijala chant as well as in the Wolof tale coincides with the late European middle ages and up to the period when West Africans came into contact with Europeans. Needless to say, because of the strong presence of nature and the closeness of man to it, there was a strong mystical appraisal of nature that is reflected in most of the myths and tales of origin. Besides being a deep mystery to man, nature was also a provider of food, it was the agent that sustained life and assured survival. Additionally, the bond between the land and man was not based on ownership. This can be explained partially by the fact that there was (and still is) abundant uncleared land and also the African continent was (and still is) underpopulated. In a passage devoted to the Baoule people of present-day Ivory Coast, T. Weiskel observes that "land tenure in traditional Baoule agriculture is concerned with rights to cultivate a given plot rather than ownership *per se* " (1973: 137). Weiskel also gives the example of the Mbuti Pygmies of Zaïre, Central Africa, where "the notion of exploiting nature is foreign to their mode of thinking for nature is not conceived of as an alien object upon which they operate" (ibid., p. 125).

In present-day Africa, there are sweeping changes when it comes to land ownership, which gradually became the norm only with the advent of writing and the contact of Africans with Europeans. Notarized land titles and leases increased and reversed the customs of the non-ownership of land in most parts of Africa. Thus, in most parts of present-day Africa, land ownership is a reality just as in many other parts of the world. However, it is more widespread in urban areas than in rural areas.

Nature as described by the Wolof singer in the tale is very different from the present-day situation. I remember my father telling me of how the vegetation was more lush and how the River Senegal held more fish when he was growing up in the 1920's as compared to the 1980's. I could detect a tone of nostalgia and regret in his voice when he was comparing the state of the land and, generally speaking, nature in his childhood with its state then. However, that idyllic and quasi-edenic state of nature of bygone days is very different from what is found today. This decline was a combination of the progressive desiccation of trees, a growing desertification, the uncontrolled action of man on the land (fires, cattle grazing, the extensive commercial farming also known as agri-business, and the widespread use of pesticides...), as well as persistent drought in the northern part of Senegal as well as in most parts of present-day

West Africa. During the harmattan season which is also the dry season (October to May), there is a hot wind that blows sand from the Sahara desert into Senegal. Thus, a good portion of arable land is progressively lost to the desert each year.

The stress here is placed on the inalienable aspect of land and soil. The Wolof made a distinction between the owner of the land and the person who exploited it. The former could not alienate the land while the latter had all the rights, not only to exploit the land, but also to enjoy the fruits of his labor. However, a small portion of the harvest was paid to the owner of the land. This system resembles latifundium but the two institutions are different.

Besides considering the structure of the genealogy itself, I will also discuss the function of the genealogy within Wolof society as well as the notion of kinship. I will consider the elements of inference, of telescoping, of compression, and of feedback. These concepts influence the manner in which the genealogy is recited by the singer. Therefore, they affect performance.

The caste system had been in existence for a long time among the Wolof. J. Irvine observes that:

> Wolof genealogy must be seen in the context of a society much concerned with distinctions of rank and relations of patronage, and in which prevailing ideology links both of these to birth and family. (1978: 653)

A few aspects are specific to Wolof genealogy in particular and to most African genealogies in general. There are two aspects on which one can put a stress: age differences and age sets. Age differences constitute the rule while the age sets category is the exception. D. Paulme writes:

> Within the family there is no equality; instead relations between real brothers are always in terms of an elder -- that is superior -- and a younger brother. (1973: 78)

Most traditional societies had a political system based on gerontocracy. However, there are many variations within the structures of kinship. A more detailed analysis of this Wolof genealogy would show how complex the kinship system is in Wolof society.

Three types of relationship are distinguished in human society: consanguinous, marital, and filial (see C. Lévi-Strauss 1958: 56).

Islam has considerable impact on this Wolof genealogy. The singer, Ñan starts his recitation by saying that Qusay is Njaajaan Njaay's ancestor. Also, the first line of his arabic facsimile is the Islamic invocation of Allah: "In the Name of Allah, the Most Gracious, the Most Merciful." The following chart is a genealogy of the prophet's family as established by A. Rahim (*Islamic History*, 1981):

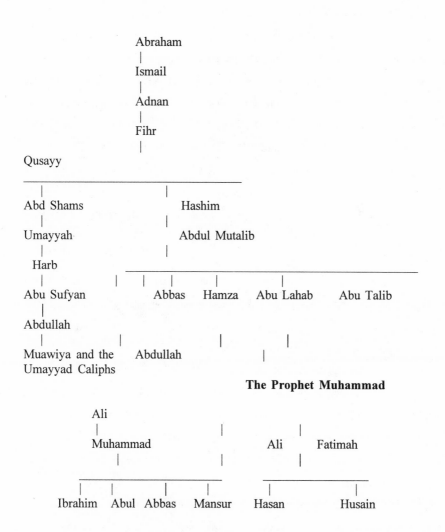

The fact that Njaajaan is linked by consanguinity to the Prophet Muhammad according to Sèq Ñan would confer enormous prestige not only

upon the hero himself but upon the barak of Waalo who are his descendants. A few key discrepancies separate the list above from that of Ñan. The latter does not mention Qusay's descent from Abraham. He starts with Qusay. However, he does mention Abu Samsi (or Abd Shams). The line of descent from Qusay and Abu Samsi through Imaar, Umar, and Bubakar Umar is not mentioned in Rahim's genealogy. From there (Bubakar Umar in Ñan's list), the name of Njaajaan comes into play. The relationship between Njaajaan and Bubakar Umar is one of consanguinity for, the latter begot the former.

As I explained elsewhere (see the Introduction), the reason why the Wolof singer is tying his Wolof genealogy to that of the prophet is to give prestige to the Wolof genealogy. This strategy also provides a grounding for the Wolof genealogy.

In his study of the northern Somali of East Africa, I. M. Lewis (1962: 40) highlights the link the Somali make between their genealogy and that of the prophet. The Somali genealogy is exclusively traced through the agnatic line. The strong patrilineal nature of the Somali system of kinship can be explained partly by the nomadic, shifting way of life. The same system organized around patriarchy is found among many nomadic peoples; because of an insecure and hostile environment (desert, raids, invasions), the males are the ones who provide protection to the clan or tribe.

Conversely, in most pre-colonial African societies, the cognatic aspect is more emphasized. This emphasis can also be partly explained by the sedentary, agricultural and stable way of life as well as many rituals associated with femininity, motherhood, birth, and the life cycle. As a general remark, "the matriarchal system proper [in Africa] is characterized by the collaboration and harmonious flowering of both sexes, and by a certain preeminence of woman in society, due originally to economic conditions, but accepted and even defended by man" (C. A. Diop 1974: 145).

As an example, there is the tribal life of the Gikuyu people of Kenya; in their foundation myth, Gikuyu, the mythical founder of Gikuyu society invited young men to marry his daughters but "he would give his consent only if they agreed to live in his homestead under a matriarchal system" (J. Kenyatta 1965: 7).

In Wolof society, the emphasis is placed on matrilineality. The avuncular aspect (relationship between a man and his sister's children) is also very much valued. Lévi-strauss argues that a kinship system that stresses the avuncular aspect is the simplest system of kinship. He then adds:

> L'avunculat, pour être compris, doit être traité comme une relation intérieure à un système, et que c'est le système lui-même qui doit être considéré dans son ensemble, pour en apercevoir la structure. Cette structure repose elle-même sur quatre termes (*frère, soeur*, père, fils) unis entre eux par deux couples d'oppositions corrélatives, et tels que, dans chacune des deux générations en cause, il existe toujours une relation positive et une relation négative. (Lévi-Strauss 1958: 56 [emphases added])

The importance of the maternal uncle is indeed very important in most African traditional societies. The following remark made by J. Kenyatta on the Gikuyu can also be applied to the Wolof:

> The mother's brother, who is called *mama* [author's emphasis] (my or our uncle), is the only one in the family group who enjoys that title. For *there is no uncle on the father's side*, because those who might be called uncle, according to European system of kinship, are called "fathers" in the Gikuyu society. *The uncle's relation with his sister's children is that of fatherly love and*

affection. He has a certain influence over the children (1965: 18 [emphases added])

In my own family, my mother's brothers had a lot of influence over my siblings and me. Conversely, my father's brothers were just like "fathers" to us and had no influence whatsoever. However, as I pointed out earlier, Islam has greatly modified the features of Wolof genealogy.

The following remarks made by G. Duby on kinship and the nobility in the eleventh and twelth centuries in Northern France apply also in many ways to Islamic genealogy:

> L'individu [in France] se sent pris [au contraire] dans un groupe familial de structure beaucoup plus stricte, axé sur la filiation agnatique, et d'orientation verticale: il se sent membre d'un lignage, d'une race où *de père en fils* se *transmet un héritage*; l'aîné des garçons assume la direction de cette maison, et l'histoire de celle-ci peut s'écrire sous la forme d'un arbre enraciné dans la personne de l'ancêtre fondateur, qui se trouve à l'origine de toute la puissance et de toute l'illustration de la race. L'individu est devenu lui-même un prince; il a pris une conscience d' héritier . (Duby 1988: 164-65 [emphasis added])

Then Duby emphasizes the

> *règles successorales qui favorisent les fils aux dépens des filles,* les plus âgés aux dépens des puînés, et *qui valorisent* donc à la fois *la branche paternelle et l' aînesse.* (Duby, op. cit., p. 165 [emphases added])

In the epic tale, we have the following examples in which the mother's first name is affixed to the first name of the son as a matronymic: Amadu Fatuma; Taañ Yaasin; Njaak Kumba; and Fara Pénda. Most of the names in the genealogy are built on the same pattern. E. Makward underscored "the traditional Wolof reference to one's mother in naming" (1990: 38).

A closer analysis of the genealogy of the rulers of the kingdom of Waalo shows the pre-eminence of the son of the ruler's sister in a collateral succession. Speaking about the succession to the throne of Cayor (or Kayor), another Wolof kingdom, D. Boilat writes:

> Cette succession au trône, en ligne collatérale n'est point particulière au royaume du Cayor: on la retrouve dans celui du Walo, dont le roi porte le titre de *brak* [author's emphasis]; mais on y suit une marche différente. C'est toujours *le premier fils de la soeur aînée du roi défunt*, ou, pour mieux dire, le premier enfant (car ici point de loi salique qui interdise le trône aux femmes) de la soeur aînée du roi ou de la reine défunte *qui lui succède quand il est majeur*. (1984: 291-92 [emphases added]).

A major difficulty pertaining to Ñan's genealogy is the establishment of the correct kinship between the rulers. Although the succession is not from father to son but rather from maternal uncle to nephew, the Wolof singer does not elaborate on the name of the rulers' sisters.

The strict chronological accuracy of the genealogy is not of great concern to Ñan. For instance, on line 29, Yérim Mbañik Abdaali is said to have been on the throne for 70 years; this seems to be a very long reign. However, this is not impossible for it depends at what age the rule begins. If Yérim began his reign at age 15, he would have had to live to age 85, which is not beyond belief. However, there is no indication as to a legal minimum age to begin to rule.

The lack of a written record of births did not prevent most of pre-colonial and colonial societies from keeping, at least in the memory, the age of the people. In his demographic study of the Peul Bandé of southeast Senegal (Sénégal oriental), G. Pison writes on the Bande's system of age estimation based on pluviometry and on circumcision (1980: 187-95). The count of the seasons was another way of estimating people's age. Since there are only two seasons (one dry and one wet), it was relatively easy to estimate a person's age. Thus, the custom was to say that so and so had twenty or thirty rainy seasons. Events such as floodings, droughts, and locust invasions were also used as ways of estimating a person's age.

What bearing do elements such as inference, influence, compression, and telescoping have on this Wolof genealogy? What all these concepts have in common is that they all relate to the sphere of performance.

In an article entitled "L'utilisation des données ethnographiques comme sources de l'histoire" (p.79), J. Vansina suggests the use of the technique of inference in the field of oral traditions. Inference is a technique that consists in comparing the present ethnographic data (what I collected in Senegal, for instance) to other historical sources. Then, one would have to compare specific points drawn from each side: from the sources made up of other historical proofs and the present collected source. One should also pay attention to the possibility that one event or point from the present data (or vice versa) came from the other source.[2]

There are four other known transcribed versions of the rulers of Waalo (Barry 1985: 311-16):

-List of Capitaine Azan (1861) who had collected two versions: the first one from Fara-Pénda and the second one from Demba-N'Diaye.

-List of Yoro Dyao published by Rousseau (1929).

-List of the 52 Baraks of Waalo (1186-1855), performed by Amadou Wade, translated into French in 1943 by Bassirou Cissé, and annotated by Vincent Monteil.

-List of the Baraks as performed by Samba Ndienne Bara, collected in 1944 by Boubou Sall, and published in French by Félix Brigaud.

In this genealogy, there is an extraneous material, the Qur'an and the incorporation of Arab genealogies into the Wolof genealogy. The tally of names was written down by the performer himself; he did so by recalling the genealogy from his memory. There is an influence on the tally of names from a written, fixed form, namely the Qur'an, on this Wolof genealogy as performed by Sèq Ñan.

The Bible (Old and New Testaments) had considerable influence in Africa, mostly in Southern and Eastern Africa. Consequently, the people of those parts of Africa have incorporated the Bible into their traditions. In countries such as Kenya, Zimbabwe, and South Africa, a combination of the Bible and white settlements has contributed to the destruction of local African traditions. The peoples there did not have the shield that those in West Africa had, in spite of colonialism and of other foreign ideologies and religions such as Islam and Christianity. It seems as if the peoples of East and Southern Africa have in many cases developed an amnesia vis-à-vis their own traditions. Most of the peoples who live in that part of the African continent have not totally assimilated the European way of life (like other peoples in other parts of the continent) and yet their indigenous traditions have been erased, if not totally, at least in great part. My comparison does not mean that West Africa is better off than East Africa. Both areas have experienced colonialism and a loss of personality and identity. However, West Africa has been less affected when it comes to the loss of indigenous traditions.

Telescoping, the compression of historical events that occured over a long stretch of time into a short period, is a tendency of oral traditions in general and of Wolof oral history. D. Henige defines two causes:

> Telescoping may occur through the faulty collective memories of the transmitters of the list. This is especially true in societies where such transmission is not an official function and where sanctions are not imposed for error. (1973: 371)

He then adds:

> A [less] conscious and therefore [less] obvious, form of telescoping is to compress an entire epoch into a generation or a reign of a single ruler. (Henige, op. cit., p. 375)

In some African societies, there is a person officially designated within the court to keep the royal genealogy and to recite it. In Wolof society, this is not the case. Any griot who is knowledgeable about genealogies can recite them. However, there are devices that are set up in order to counter telescoping. One of these is to have a head of the household whose genealogy is being sung check on the singer. That is the case among the Xhosa of Southern Africa, where there exists that kind of device as observed by J. Opland: "Heads of households also know the poems treating their departed ancestors, which are recited on ritual or ceremonial occasions in order to initiate communication between the living and the dead" (1980: 19).

In Wolof society, we must distinguish two subjects of genealogies: family genealogies (in which the genealogies of the commoners are included) and royal or noble genealogies. Family genealogies tend to be shorter whereas historical (or royal) genealogies tend to be longer. J. Irvine makes the following remark on Wolof genealogies:

> Some few non-*griot* elders, male and female, can produce partial genealogies for their own families, or they may offer an opinion on a *griot's* performance. But the elders are invariably weak on matrilateral ties, and they are likely to disclaim responsibility for knowing or for recounting the more distant relationships. When nobles do discuss genealogy among themselves, the discussion is usually limited to fairly close relationships among living individuals, in which the genealogical background is not more that two or three generations deep. (1978: 656)

J. Irvine's remark is pertinent when applied to family genealogy in which one must take into account the importance of the extended family. What J. Irvine is referring to as partial genealogies is probably tied to the fact that it is difficult to include hundreds and hundreds of people that are not direct descendents of the main person being considered in the genealogy. Those additional names constitute offshoots branching from the basic genealogical tree. Since matrilineality is very strong within Wolof society, most heads of households are rather strong in their knowledge of matrilateral ties; the sister, her brother, and the son of the sister constitute the basic core of kinship among the Wolof of Senegal.

Royal genealogies tend to be more rigid and more stable than family genealogies for, in the case of family genealogies, the living individuals are included and, in Senegal, almost every other day, one "discovers" a cousin, an aunt, an uncle, a nephew, a niece, a great-grand-parent, or a distant relative one did not know about. Therefore, from the date of that "discovery", these newly found relatives must be included in new genealogies, in addition to the persons who were already in them.

In the case of the royal genealogy as performed by Ñan, my father, (Mapaté Diop, the head of the household), was present. Since the whole performance (the epic tale and the genealogy), took two days, with some interruptions, I was very impressed by the fact that once in a while my father, who seemed to be dozing, would suddenly wake up from his apparent sleep and would interrupt the singer, for the latter had made a mistake. Then, my father would start from where Ñan had made the mistake and would correct it. This interruption on my father's part would sometimes last for an hour because he would go into many details of kinship ties; my father's elaboration would also include kinship ties between ancestors and living individuals. The griots themselves, namely Caam and Ñan, have told me that my father was indeed very knowledgeable about genealogies and about the history of Waalo as a whole. Therefore, not only did they consult him sometimes but they were very careful not to distort the genealogy, to telescope parts of it, or to compress it in his presence.

When I was growing up in Dakar, some relatives from Waalo used to visit us. Thus, I heard and witnessed countless conversations bearing on kinship between my parents and those visitors. The aim of those conversations was to verify the accuracy of certain events of the past as well as to compare and contrast genealogical data and kinship ties.

Many heads of noble families within Wolof society are like my father. They usually learn their genealogy from their parents. I asked my father how he had learned to memorize these genealogies. He answered me that, as a boy, he used to listen to his father and mother when they were talking about kinship ties. Blood ties are very important among the Wolof and particularly among the inhabitants of Waalo. It is generally considered as a good sign that a person from a noble family should know about his or her genealogy. On my part, I recorded our family genealogies for the simple reason that I could not learn orally from my father, for the setting was very different. I was born in Dakar and grew up in an urban setting.

It is also taken for granted that genealogy and kinship ties are not solely a monopoly of the griot, even though a noble person would not deign to play a musical instrument for this practice belongs entirely to the griot. However, as a general rule, the griot who is attached to the noble family is in charge of keeping the genealogy as well as transmitting it. The function played by heads of noble households like my father during a performance can be referred to as a "safety-valve." The head of household does not prevent the singer from reciting the genealogy, but at the same time he makes sure that the singer does not distort it or compress it either. This "safety-valve" can be considered as a precaution against telescoping or distortion linked to a faulty collective memory.

Nowadays, there are griots who make up false genealogies in order to satisfy a rich man or woman even though that man or woman is considered as belonging to a lower category of social stratification. E. Makward (1990: 32 and passim) alluded to this phenomenon, which people in Senegal readily qualify as being a "coming up even" on the part of the *nouveaux riches* or the *parvenus*, or simply persons who belong to a caste but became rich and influent.

Thus, in Senegal, a *nouveau riche* is compelled to have a glittering false genealogy fabricated for him or her.[3]

Notes to the Study of Ñan' s Performance

1. H. Azan collected two versions of the list of rulers of Waalo: one from Fara-Penda and one from Demba-N'Diaye (1864a: 339-40); see also V. Monteil's list (1966: 37-8) as recited by Amadou Wade. B. Barry (1985: 311-16) lists all the existing versions of genealogies of Waalo. Besides Monteil and Azan, Barry cites the version collected by Félix Brigaud from Boubou Sall in 1944 and a version collected by R. Rousseau (1929) from Yoro Dyao; actually, that list was written by Yoro Dyao in his famous *Cahiers de Yoro Dyao*).

2. Besides S. Ñan's performance of the genealogy of the rulers of Waalo and his Arabic facsimile, there are other transcribed lists of the rulers of Waalo: Azan (1864), Rousseau (1929), F. Brigaud (1962), and V. Monteil (1966).

3. In March of 1993, I received a personal communication from Edris Makward (Professor in the Department of African Languages and Literatures at the University of Wisconsin at Madison) to the effect that Ancumbu Caam is likely to be the same person as Ancu Thiam. Both Ancumbu and Makward's griot come from the same village (Caggo). Both have sons called Magate and live in the suburbs of Dakar. Makward and I are conducting further inquiries into this identification.

BIBLIOGRAPHY

(This bibliography contains references that are both cited in this study and that were consulted in the course of this study).

ACHEBE, Chinua. *Hopes and Impediments*. Selected Essays. New York: Doubleday, 1989.

ADAMS, Adrian. *La terre et les gens du fleuve - Jalons, balises*. Paris: L'harmattan, 1985.

AGBLEMAGNON, N'Sougan F. *Sociologie des sociétés orales d'Afrique noire. Les Eve du Sud-Togo*. Paris: Éditions Silex, 1984.

AGUESSY, Honorat. "Tradition orale et structures de pensée: Essai de méthodologie." *Cahiers d'histoire mondiale*, 14 (1972): 270-97.

AKIWOWO, Akinsola A. "Contributions to the Sociology of Knowledge from an African Oral Poetry." In *Globalization, Knowledge and Society: Readings from International Sociology*. Martin Albrow and Elizabeth King. London: eds., SAGE Publications in association with the International Sociological Association/ISA, 1990. Pp. 103-117.

ALI, Yusuf. *The Holy Qur'an*. Text, Translation, and Commentary by Y. Ali. Brentwood, Maryland: Amana Corp., 1983.

AMEGBLEAME, Agbeko S. "La poésie ewe: structures formelles et contenu." *Revue de littérature et d'esthétique négro-africaines*, 3 (1981): 89-109.

AMES, David. "Belief in 'Witches' among the Rural Wolof of the Gambia." *Africa*, 29 (1959): 263-73.

AMIN, Samir, ed. *Modern Migrations in Western Africa*. Studies presented and discussed at the Eleventh International African Seminar, Dakar, April 1972. London: Published for the International African Institute by Oxford University Press, 1974.

AMIN, Samir. Preface to *Le Royaume du Waalo*, by Boubacar Barry. Paris: Éditions Karthala, 1985.

AMSELLE, Jean-Loup, ed. *Les migrations africaines. Réseaux et processus migratoires*. Paris: François Maspero, 1976.

AMSELLE, Jean-Loup, ed. "Ethnies et espaces: pour une anthropologie topologique." In *Au coeur de l'ethnie - ethnies, tribalisme et état en Afrique.* Paris: Éditions de la découverte, 1985. Pp. 11-48.

ANOZIE, Sunday O. *Structural Models and African Poetics. Towards a Pragmatic Theory of Literature.* London: Routledge & Kegan Paul Ltd, 1981.

ANYIDOHO, Akosua. "Linguistic Parallels in Traditional Akan Appelation Poetry." *Research in African Literatures,* 22 (1991): 67-81.

APPIAH, Anthony K. *In my Father's House. Africa in the Philosophy of Culture.* Oxford: Oxford University Press, 1992.

ARMAH, Ayi, K. "Fiction As Criticism of Fiction. Larsony". *First World,* 1 (1977): 50-5.

ARNAUD, Robert, "L'islam et la politique musulmane française en Afrique." *Renseignements Coloniaux et documents du comité de l'Afrique française,* (1912): 3-20.

AYOADE, John A. A. "Tradition and political development in Africa." In *Symposium Leo Frobenius II.* Bonn: Deutsche UNESCO-Kommission, 1980. Pp. 157-75.

AZAN, H. "Notice sur le Oualo." *Revue Maritime et Coloniale,* 9 (1863a): 395-422.

----------------."Notice sur le Oualo." *Revue Maritime et Coloniale,* 9 (1863b): 607-655
.

----------------."Notice sur le Oualo." *Revue Maritime et Coloniale,* 10 (1864a): 327-360.

----------------."Notice sur le Oualo." *Revue Maritime et Coloniale,* 10 (1864b): 466-498.

AZUONYE, Chukwuma. "The Romantic Epic of the Anambra Igbo: An Introductory Survey." *Uwandi Igbo-Journal of Igbo Life and Culture,* 1 (1984): 4-16.

BA, Hampaté, and CARDAIRE, M. *Tierno Bokar, le sage de Bandiagara.* Paris: Présence Africaine, 1957.

BA, Hampaté, and DIETERLEN, G. *Koumen. Texte initiatique des Pasteurs Peul.* Paris. La Haye: Published by Mouton & Co for École Pratique des Hautes Études-Sorbonne, 1961.

BA, Ibrahim. Personal communication. Dakar, Senegal. June 19, 1993.

BABALOLA, S.A. *The Content and Form of Yoruba Ijala.* Oxford: Clarendon Press,1966.

BAKHTIN, M.M. *The Dialogic Imagination*, Michael Holquist, ed. Translated by Caryl Emerson and M. Holquist. Austin: Texas University Press, 1990.

BALANDIER, Georges. *Sociologie actuelle de l'Afrique noire.* Paris: Presses Universitaires de France, 1955. Rpt. 1963.

----------------------------. *Anthropologie politique.* Paris: Presses Universitaires de France, 1967.

BARBER, Karin. "Interpreting Oríki as History and as Literature." In *Discourse and its Disguises-The Interpretation of African Oral Texts*, edited by Karin Barber and P.F. de Moraes Farias, eds. Birmingham University, England: Centre of West African Studies, 1989. Pp. 13-23.

--------------------. "Post-colonial Criticism and Yoruba Popular Culture." Unpublished paper on file at Northwestern University: The Institute for Advanced Study and Research in the African Humanities, Evanston, Illinois. 17 pp.

BARON ROGER, Jacques François. *Recherches philosophiques sur la langue ouolofe.* Paris: Librairie orientale de Dondey-Dupré, 1829.

BAROU, Jacques. "Immigrés africains devant la caméra." *Journal des africanistes*, 60 (1990): 141-151.

BARRY, Boubacar. *Le Royaume du Waalo.* Paris: Éditions Karthala, 1985.

BASGÖZ, Ilhan. "The Tale-Singer and His Audience." In *Folklore Performance and Communication*, edited by Dan Ben-Amos and Kenneth S. Goldstein. The Hague. Paris: Mouton, 1975. Pp. 143-203.

BATHILY, Abdoulaye. *Les portes de l' or: le royaume de Galam, Sénégal, de l' ère musulmane au temps des négriers, VIIIe-XVIII siècle.* Paris: L' Harmattan, 1989.

BAUMANN, D. and WESTERMANN, D. *Les peuples et les civilisations de l'Afrique.* Paris: Payot, 1957.

BÉDIER, Joseph, ed. *La Chanson de Roland.* Paris: Union Générale d'Éditions, 1929. Rpt. 1982.

BEHRMAN, Lucy C. *Muslim Brotherhoods and Politics in Senegal.* Cambridge, MA: Harvard University Press, 1970.

BEN-AMOS, Dan. "Toward a Definition of Folklore in Context." *Journal of American Folklore*, 84 (1971): 3-15.

BÉRENGER-FÉRAUD, Laurent-Jean-Baptiste. "Étude sur les griots des peuplades de la Sénégambie." *Revue d'anthropologie*, 5 (1882): 266-79.

----------------------------. *Recueil de contes populaires de la Sénégambie.* Paris: Leroux, 1885.

BERNAL, Martin. *Black Athena. The Afroasiatic Roots of Classical Civilization*, vol.1. New Brunswick, N.J.: Rutgers University Press, 1987.

BIBLE, The Holy. "Genesis." Revised Standard Version. Iowa Falls, Iowa: World Bible Publishers, 1971.

BIEBUYCK, Daniel, and MATEENE, Kahombo. *The Mwindo Epic.* Berkeley and Los Angeles: University of California Press, 1969.

BLOCH, Howard R. *Etymologies and Genealogies. A Literary Anthropology of the French Middle Ages.* Chicago: University of Chicago Press, 1983.

BOILAT, David. *Esquisses sénégalaises.* Paris: Éditions Karthala, 1984.

BOMBA, Victoria. "Traditions about Ndiadiane Ndiaye, first *Buurba* Djolof." *Bulletin de l' Institut Fondamental d' Afrique Noire*, 39 (1977): 1-35.

BRENNER, Louis. "'Religious Discourses in and about Africa." In *Discourse and its Disguises-The Interpretation of African Oral Texts*, edited by Karin Barber and P.F. de Moraes Farias. Birmingham University, England: Centre of West African Studies, 1989. Pp. 87-105.

----------------------. *West African Sufi. The Religious Heritage and Spiritual Search of Cerno Bokar Saalif Taal*. London: C. Hurst & Company, 1984.

BRIGAUD, Félix. "Histoire traditionnelle du Sénégal. Le royaume du Waalo." *Études sénégalaises*, 9 (1962): 63-92.

BROWN, Calvin S. "The Relations between Music and Literature as a Field of Study." *Comparative Literature*, 22 (1970): 97-107.

BRUCKNER, Pascal. *Le Sanglot de l' Homme Blanc. Tiers-monde, Culpabilité, Haine de Soi*. Paris: Éditions du Seuil, 1983.

BRUNS, Gerald L. "The Originality of Texts in a Manuscript Culture." *Comparative Literature*, 32 (1980): 113-129.

BUCAILLE, Maurice. *The Bible, the Qur'an and Science*. Translated from the French by Alastair D. Pannell and the Author. Indianapolis, IN: American Trust Publications, 1978.

BUGUL, Ken. *Le baobab fou*. Dakar: Les Nouvelles Éditions Africaines, 1983.

CALAME-GRIAULE, Geneviève. "The Spiritual and Social Role of Women in Traditional Sudanese Society." *Diogenes*, 37 (1962): 75-87.

--. "Stylistic Study of a Dogon Text." In *French Perspective in African Studies*, edited by Pierre Alexandre. Oxford: Published by Oxford University Press for International African Institute, 1973. Pp. 26-39.

CALVET, Louis-Jean. *Linguistique et colonialisme. Petit traité de glottophagie*. Paris: Payot, 1974.

CAMARA, Laye. *L'Enfant noir*, edited by Joyce A. Hutchinson. Cambridge: Cambridge University Press, 1966.

-------------------- *Le Maître de la Parole. Kouma Lafôlô Kouma*. Paris: Plon, 1978.

CAMARA, Sory. *Gens de la parole. Essai sur la condition et le rôle des griots dans la société Malinké*. La Haye: Mouton & Co, 1976.

CASSIRER, Ernst. *The Philosophy of Symbolic Forms*. Vol. 2: *Mythical Thought*. New Haven and London: Yale University Press, 1975.

CHALIAND, Gérard. Introduction to *Les Damnés de la terre*, by F. Fanon. Paris: Gallimard, 1962. Rpt 1991.

CHAN, Marie. "Chinese Heroic Poems and European Epic." *Comparative Literature*, 26 (1974): 142-168.

CHINWEIZU, ONWUCHEKWA, Jemie, MADUBUIKE, Ihechukwu. *Toward the Decolonization of African Literature*, vol. 1. Washington D. C.: Howard University Press, 1983.

CISSÉ, Daniel Amara. *Histoire économique de L'Afrique noire. Tome 3 lemoyen age*. Abidjan - Paris: Presses Universitaires et Scolaires d'Afrique (PUSAF) and L'Harmattan, 1988.

CISSÉ, Youssouf Tata and KAMISSOKO, Wa. *La grande geste du Mali - Des origines à la fondation de l'empire*. Paris: Editions Karthala and Association Arsan, 1988.

CLIFFORD, James. *The Predicament of Culture*. Cambridge: Harvard University Press, 1988.

CONDÉ, Maryse, and RADOUANE, Mokhtar. "La création littéraire." In *Patrimoine culturel et création contemporaine en Afrique et dans le monde arabe*, sous la direction de Mohamed Aziza. Dakar. Abidjan: Les Nouvelles Éditions Africaines, 1977. Pp. 13-32.

CONNELLY, Bridget. "Etymology as Genealogy: On Generation(s) and

Transmission(s)." In *Arab Folk Epic and Identity*, by B. Connelly. Berkeley: University of California Press, 1986. Pp. 225-74.

CONRAD, David C. "Islam in the Oral Traditions of Mali: Bilali and Surakata." *Journal of African History*, 26 (1985): 33-49.

"CONQUÊTE DU OUALO." In *Annales Sénégalaises de 1854 à 1885*. Paris: Maisonneuve Frères et Ch. Leclerc. Pp. 5-22.

COOLEN, Michael T. "The Wolof Xalam Tradition of the Senegambia." *Ethnomusicology*, 27 (1983): 477-98.

COQUERY-VIDROVITCH, Catherine. "Recherches sur un mode de production africain." *La pensée*, 144 (1969): 61-78.

CORNEVIN, Robert. *Histoire des peuples de l'Afrique noire*. Paris: Éditions Berger-Levrault, 1960.

COULON, Christian. *Le marabout et le prince* (Islam et pouvoir au Sénégal). Paris: A. Pedone, 1981.

CRAHAY, Franz. "Conceptual Take-Off Conditions for a Bantu Philosophy." *Diogenes*, 52 (1965): 55-78.

CREED, Robert P. "The Singer Looks At His Sources." *Comparative Literature*, 14 (1962): 44-52.

CRUISE O'BRIEN, Donald B. *The Mourides of Senegal. The Political and Economic Organization of an Islamic Brotherhood*. Oxford: Clarendon Press, 1971.

CURTIN, Philip D. "Precolonial African History." In *AHA Pamphlets, 501*. Washington, D.C.: American Historical Association, 1964. Pp. 3-66.

----------------------. "Field Techniques for Collecting and Processing Oral Data." *Journal of African History*, 9 (1968): 367-85.

----------------------- *Economic Change in Precolonial Africa. Senegambia in the Era of the Slave Trade*. Madison: The University of Wisconsin Press, 1975.

364

----------------------. "Africa: Traders and Trade Communities." In *Cross-Cultural Trade in World History*, by P.D. Curtin. Cambridge: Cambridge University Press, 1984.

DAO, James. "The Ashanti King of North America." *San Francisco Sunday Examiner & Chronicle* (Sunday June 7, 1992). P. 4.

DAVIDSON, Basil. *The Growth of African Civilisation. West Africa 1000-1800.* London: Longman, 1965.

----------------------. *The Search for Africa. History, Culture, Politics.* New York, Toronto: Random House and Random House of Canada Limited, 1994.

DENIEL, Raymond. *Une société paysanne de Côte-d'ivoire: les Ano. Traditions et changements.* Abidjan: INADES, 1976.

DHINA, Amar. *Grandes figures de l'Islam.* Alger: Entreprise nationale du livre, 1986.

DIABATÉ, Massa M. *Janjon et autres chants populaires du Mali.* Paris: Présence Africaine, 1970.

---------------------. M. *Kala Jata.* Bamako: Editions populaires, 1970.

---------------------. *Le boucher de Kouta.* Paris: Hatier, 1982.

DIABATÉ, Moussa (Massa?) M. "Kele Monson Diabaté, The Greatest Mandingo Griot of His Generation." *Afrique Histoire* (No date): 43-45.

DIAGNE, Ahmadou Mapaté. "Un pays de pilleurs d'épaves - Le Gandiole." (Obtained from an incomplete source of reference).

DIAGNE, Pathé. "Royaumes sérères-Les institutions traditionnelles du Sine Saloum." *Présence africaine*, 54 (1965): 142-72.

----------------------. *Pouvoir politique traditionnel en Afrique occidentale-Essais sur les Institutions politiques précoloniales.* Paris: Présence africaine, 1967.

----------------------. "Langues africaines, développement économique et cultures nationales." *Notes Africaines*, 129 (1971): 2-19.

----------------------. "De la démocratie traditionnelle. Problèmes de définition." *Présence Africaine*, 97 (1976): 18-42.

DIAKITÉ, Tidiane. *L' Afrique malade d' elle-même*. Paris: Éditions Karthala, 1986.

DIALLO, Liliane. "Aux origines du Wubri-Tênga et de Guilongou (Burkina-Faso), d'après une tradition orale recueillie dans ce village." *Genève-Afrique*, 23 (1985): 9-36.

DIAWARA, Mamadou. *La Graine de la Parole*. Stuttgart: Franz Steiner Verlag, 1990.

DIENG, Bassirou. "La représentation du fait politique dans les récits épiques du Kayor." *Bulletin de l'Institut Fondamental d'Afrique Noire*, 42 (1980): 857-86.

DIKE, Onwuka K. and EKEJIUBA, Felicia I. "Change and Persistence in Aro Oral History." *Journal of African Studies*, 3 (1976): 277-96.

DILLEY, Roy. "Performance, Ambiguity and Power in Tukulor Weavers' Songs." In *Discourses and its Disguises*, edited by K. Barber and P.F. de Moraes Farias. Birmingham, England: C.W.A.S., Birmingham University, 1989. Pp. 138-51.

DIOP, Abdoulaye-Bara. "La tenure foncière en milieu rural wolof (Sénégal): historique et actualité." *Notes Africaines*, 118 (1968): 48-52.

----------------------. *La société wolof-Les systèmes d'inégalité et de domination*. Paris: Éditions Karthala, 1981.

DIOP, Alioune Oumy. *Le Théatre Traditionnel au Sénégal*. Dakar: Les Nouvelles Editions Africaines, 1990.

DIOP, Cheikh Anta. "Étude linguistique ouolove." *Présence Africaine*, 5 (1949): 848-53.

366

----------------------. *L'Afrique noire précoloniale.* Paris: Présence africaine, 1960.

----------------------. *L' antériorité des civilisations nègres. Mythe ou vérité historique?* Paris: Présence Africaine, 1967.

----------------------. "Introduction à l'étude des migrations en Afrique centrale et occidentale. Identification du berceau nilotique du peuple sénégalais." *Bulletin de l'Institut Fondamental d'Afrique Noire*, 35 (1973): 769-92.

----------------------. *The African Origin of Civilization. Myth or reality.* Translated from the French by Mercer Cook. Chicago: Lawrence Hill, 1974.

----------------------. *Parenté génétique de l'égyptien pharaonique et des langues négro-africaines.* Dakar-Abidjan: Les Nouvelles Éditions Africaines et IFAN, 1977.

----------------------. "Origin of the ancient Egyptians." In *General History of Africa (II) Ancient Civilizations of Africa*, edited by G. Mokhtar. Paris: UNESCO, 1981. Pp. 27-57.

----------------------. *Civilisation ou Barbarie. Anthropologie sans complaisance.* Paris: Présence Africaine, 1981.

----------------------. *The Cultural Unity of Black Africa-The Domains of Patriarchy and of Matriarchy in Classical Antiquity.* Translated from the French by Présence Africaine. Chicago: Third World Press, 1990.

DIOP, Momar Coumba and DIOUF, Mamadou. *Le Sénégal sous Abdou Diouf.* Paris: Karthala, 1990.

DIOUF, Mamadou. *Le Kajoor au XIX⁰ siècle - Pouvoir ceddo et conquête coloniale.* Paris: Karthala, 1990.

DOUGALL, James W.C. "Characteristics of African Thought." *Memorandum*, 10 (1932): 5-30.

DOZON, Jean-Pierre. "Les Bété: une création coloniale." In *Au coeur de l'ethnie. Ethnies, tribalisme et état en Afrique.* Paris: Éditions de la découverte, 1985. Pp. 49-85.

DUBY, Georges. "Structures de parenté et noblesse dans la France du nord aux XIe et XIIe siècles." In *La société chevaleresque*, by G. Duby. Paris, Flammarion, 1988 Pp. 143-66.

DUGGAN, Joseph. "Social Functions of the Medieval Epic in the Romance Literatures." *Oral Tradition*, 1 (1986): 728-66.

----------------------. "Medieval Epic as Popular Historiography: Appropriation of Historical Knowledge in the Vernacular Epic." *Grundriss der Romanischen Literaturen Des Mittelalters*, vol. XI, tome 1. Heidelberg: Carl Winter Universitätsverlag, 1986. Pp. 285-310.

DUGUAY-CLÉDOR, Amadou. *La bataille de Guîlé*. (1931). Abidjan-Dakar-Lomé: Les Nouvelles Editions Africaines, Rpt. 1985.

DUMESTRE, Gérard. *La geste de Ségou*. Paris: Armand Colin, 1979.

DUMONT, Pierre. "Les dictionnaires wolof-français et les mots d'origine française." *Notes Africaines*, 43 (1974): 80-4.

DUNDES, Alan. "Texture, Text, and Context." *Southern Folklore Quarterly*, 28 (1964): 251-65.

DUPIRE, Marguerite. "Obscenité et société: virelangues Serer (Sénégal)." *Research in African Literatures*, 10 (1979): 75-89.

DURAND, Bernard. *Histoire comparative des institutions*. Dakar-Abidjan-Lomé: Nouvelles Éditions Africaines and Faculté des Sciences Économiques et Juridiques, Université de Dakar, 1983.

EAGLETON, Terry. *Literary Theory. An Introduction*. Minneapolis: University of Minnesota Press, 1983.

EL-BOKHÂRÎ, Abou 'Abdellah Mohàmmed ben Isma'îl ben Ibrahîm. *L'authentique tradition musulmane*. Translated from the Arabic (into French) by G. H. Bousquet. Paris: Grasset and Fasquelle, 1964.

ELIADE, Mircea. *Aspects du mythe*. Paris: Gallimard, 1963.

ENO BELINGA, Samuel Martin. "La musique traditionnelle d'Afrique Noire." In *Colloque sur l'Art nègre*. Paris: Société Africaine de Culture et Présence Africaine, 1971.

EISENSTADT, S.N. "Post-Traditional Societies and the Continuity and Reconstruction of Tradition." *Daedalus* (1973): 1-27.

--------------------------. *Comprendre la littérature orale africaine*. Issy les Moulineaux: Les Classiques Africains, 1978.

FALL, Yoro. "Les Wolof au miroir de leur langue: quelques observations." Jean-Pierre Chrétien and Gérard Prunier, eds., *Les ethnies ont une histoire*. Paris: Editions Karthala and ACCT, 1989. Pp. 117-123.

FANON, Frantz. *Les damnés de la terre*. Paris: Gallimard, 1962. Rpt. 1991.

FEBVRE, Lucien et MARTIN, Henri-Jean. *L'apparition du livre*. Paris: Albin Michel, 1958.

FEIERMAN, Steven. "African Histories and the Dissolution of World History." Robert H. Bates, V. Y. Mudimbe, and Jean O'Barr, eds., *Africa and the Disciplines. The Contribution of Research in Africa to the Social Sciences and Humanities*. Chicago and London: The University of Chicago Press, 1993. Pp. 167-212.

FINNEGAN, Ruth. "Literacy versus Non-literacy: The Great Divide? Some Comments on the Significance of 'Literature' in Non-literate Cultures." In *Modes of Thought. Essays on Thinking in Western and Non-Western Societies*, edited by Robin Horton and Ruth Finnegan. London: Faber, 1973. Pp. 112-44.

----------------------. "Transmission in Oral and Written Traditions: Some General Comments." In *Literacy and Orality. Studies in the Technology of Communication*. New York: Blackwell, 1988. Pp. 139-74.

FOLEY, John M. *The Theory of Oral Composition. History and Methodology*. Bloomington: Indiana University Press, 1988.

FRYE, Northrop. *Anatomy of Criticism*. New York: Atheneum, 1969.

FURNISS, Graham. "Typification and Evaluation: A Dynamic Process in Rhetoric." In *Discourse and its Disguises. The Interpretation of African Oral Texts*, edited by K. Barber and P.F. de Moraes Farias. Birmingham, England: Centre of West African Studies, Birmingham University, 1989. Pp. 24-33.

GADEN, Henri. "Légendes et coutumes sénégalaises. Cahiers de Yoro Dyao." *Revue d'Ethnographie et de Sociologie*, (1912): 119-37.

----------------------. *Proverbes et maximes Peuls et toucouleurs*. Paris: Institut D'ethnologie, 1931.

GAMBLE, David. "The Wolof of Senegambia. Together with Notes on the Lebu and the Serer." In *Ethnographic Survey of Africa. Western Africa Part 14*, edited by Daryll Forde. London: International African Institute, 1957.

GARDNER, John, and Maier John. *Gilgamesh*. Translated from the Sî-leqi-unninnî version. New York: Vintage Books. Random House, 1985.

GATES, Henry Louis, Jr., ed. *Black Literature and Literary Theory*. New York and London: Routledge, 1990.

GELLAR, Sheldon. *Senegal-An African Nation Between Islam and the West*. Boulder, Colorado, Hampshire, England: Westview Press and Gower Publishing Co., 1982.

GELLNER, Ernest. "Post-Traditional Forms in Islam: The Turf and Trade, and Votes and Peanuts." *Daedalus* (1973): 191-206.

GEORGE, Olakunle. "The Predicament of D.O. Fagunwa." Unpublished paper on file at Northwestern University: The Institute for Advanced Study and Research in the African Humanities. Evanston, Illinois. 23 pp.

GÉRARD, Albert. "The Study of African Literature: Birth and Early Growth of a New Branch of Learning." *Canadian Review of Comparative Literature* (Winter 1980): 67-92.

GIKANDI, Simon. "Ngùgi's Conversion. Writing and the Politics of Language." *Research in African Literatures*, 23 (1992): 131-44.

GLINGA, Werner. *Literatur in Senegal. Geschichte, Mythos und gesellschatliches Ideal in der oralen und schriftlichen literatur.* Berlin: Dietrich Reimer Verlag, 1990.

GOODY, Jack. "The Impact of Islamic Writing on the Oral Cultures of West Africa." *Cahier d'Études Africaines*, 11 (1971): 455-66.

GRAVAND, Henri. *Visage africain de l'église-une expérience au Sénégal.* Paris: Éditions de l'Orante, 1961.

---------------. "Fondements historiques et anthropologiques de la nation sénégalaise." In *Symposium Leo Frobenius II.* Bonn: Deutsche UNESCO-Kommission, 1980. Pp. 46-55.

GRIAULE, Marcel. "L'alliance cathartique." *Africa*, 18 (1948): 242-258.

GUERNIER, Eugène. *L'apport de l'Afrique à la pensée humaine.* Paris: Payot, 1952.

GUISSE, Youssouph M. *Philosophie, culture et devenir social en Afrique noire.* Dakar: NEA, 1979.

HALE, Thomas A. *Scribe, Griot, and Novelist. Narrative Interpreters of the Songhay Empire.* Gainesville: University of Florida Press/Center for African Studies, 1990.

HARROW, Kenneth W. ed. *Faces of Islam in African Literature.* Portsmouth, NH. London: Heinemann Educational Books and James Currey, 1991.

HAU, Kathleen. "Pre-Islamic Writing in West Africa." *Bulletin de l' Institut Fondamental d'Afrique Noire*, 35 (1973): 1-44.

HEIDEL, Alexander. *The Babylonian Genesis.* Chicago: The University of Chicago Press, Phoenix Books, 1942.

HENIGE, David. "Oral Tradition and Chronology." *Journal of African History*, 12 (1971): 371-89.

--------------------. "The Problem of Feedback in Oral tradition: Four Examples from the Fante Coastlands." *Journal of African History* 14 (1973): 223-35.

----------------------. *Oral Historiography*. London: Longman, 1982.

HERON, G.A. Introduction to *Song of Lawino & Song of Ocol*, by Okot p'Bitek. London: Heinemann, African Writers Series, 1984.

HERSKOVITS, Melville J. "Traditions et bouleversements de la culture en Afrique." *Présence Africaine*, 34-35 (October 1961-Janvier 1962): 124-31.

HISKETT, Mervyn. *The Sword of Truth. The Life and Times of the Shehu Usuman Dan Fodio*. New York: Oxford University Press. 1973.

HOLAS, B. *Le séparatisme religieux en Afrique noire - L'exemple de la côte d'Ivoire*. Paris: Presses Universitaires de France, 1965.

HOMBURGER, Léon. *Les langues négro-africaines et les peuples qui les parlent*. Paris: Payot, 1957.

HOPKINS, J.F.P. (Translator, editor, and annotator), LEVTZION, N. (editor and annotator). *Corpus of early Arabic Sources for West African history*. Cambridge, England: Cambridge University Press, 1981.

HORTON, Robin. "African Traditional Thought and Western Science. (Part I)." *Africa*, 37 (1967a): 50-71.

----------------------. "African Traditional Thought and Western Science. (Part II)." *Africa*, 37 (1967b): 155-87.

----------------------. Stateless Societies in the History of West Africa." *In History of West Africa*, vol. 1. Edited by J. F. A. Ajayi and M. Crowder. New York: Columbia University Press, 1971. Rpt 1976.

HOUNTONDJI, Paulin J. *Sur la "philosophie africaine". Critique de l'ethnophilosophie*. Paris: François Maspéro, 1977.

HUNWICK, J.O. *Literacy and Scholarship in Muslim West Africa in the Pre-Colonial Period*. Nsukka: University of Nigeria Press, 1974.

HUTTON, Patrick H. "The Problem of Oral Tradition in Vico's Historical Scholarship." *Journal of the History of Ideas*, 53 (1992): 3-23.

IBN-HAUCAL. "Description de l'Afrique." Traduite de l'arabe par M. le baron Mac Guckin De Slane. *Journal Asiatique*, 13 (1842):153-96.

IJOMA, Okoro J. "Igbo Origins and Migrations." *ụwa ndị Igbo. Journal of Igbo Life and Culture*, 2 (1989): 68-74.

INNES, Gordon. *Sunjata. Three Mandinka Versions*. London: S.O.A.S., 1974.

IRELE, Abiola. *The African Experience in Literature and Ideology*. Bloomington: Indiana University Press, 1990.

IRVINE, Judith. "When is Genealogy History? Wolof Genealogies in Comparative Perspective." *American Ethnologist*, 5 (1978): 651-73.

IYASERE, Solomon O. "Oral Tradition in the Criticism of African Literature." *The Journal of Modern African Studies*, 13 (1975): 107-19.

JACKSON, Thomas H. "Orality, Orature, and Ngugi wa Thiong'o." *Research in African Literatures*, 22 (1991): 5-15.

JAKOBSON, Roman. "Closing Statement: Linguistics and Poetics." In *Style in Language*, edited by Thomas A. Sebeok, ed. New York: The Technology Press of M.I.T. and John Wiley & Sons, 1960. Pp. 350-77.

-------------------------. "What Is Poetry?" In *Language in Literature*, edited by Krystyna Pomorska and Stephen Rudy. Cambridge, Massachusetts: The Belknap Press of Harvard University Press, 1987. Pp. 368-78.

JANMOHAMED, Abdul R. *Manichean Aesthetics. The Politics of Literature in Colonial Africa*. Amherst: The University of Massachusetts Press, 1988.

JAUSS, H.R. "Theory of Genres and Medieval Literature." In *Toward an Aesthetic of Reception*, by R. Jauss. Minneapolis: The University of Minnesota Press, 1982.

----------------. "The Theory of Reception: A Retrospective of its Unrecognized Prehistory." In *Literary Theory Today*, edited by Peter Collier and Helga G. Ryan, eds. Ithaca, New York: Cornell University Press, 1990. Pp. 53-73.

JOHNSON, Marian Ashby. "An American in Africa: Interviewing the Elusive Goldsmith." *International Journal of Oral History*, 10 (1989): 110-130.

JOSEPH, George. "The Wolof Oral Praise Song for Semu Coro Wende." *Research in African Literatures*, 10 (1979): 145-78.

JULIEN, Eileen. *African Novels and the Question of Orality*. Bloomington: Indiana University Press, 1992.

JUNOD, H. P. "Langues vernaculaires et véhiculaires en Afrique." *Genève-Afrique*, 2 (1963): 21-45.

KABA, Lansiné. "Islam, Society and Politics in Pre-colonial Baté, Guinea." *Bulletin de l' Institut Fondamental d' Afrique Noire*, 35 (1973): 323-44. .

KABOU, Axelle. *Et si l'Afrique refusait le développement?* Paris: Éditions l' Harmattan, 1991.

KAKÉ, Ibrahima. "L'histoire, une dimendion de l'unité." *Présence Africaine*, 49 (1964): 64-79.

----------------. "Harris, le prophète des lagunes éburnéennes." *Balafon* (le magazine de bord d'Air Afrique), 115 (Avril-Mai 1994): 26-28.

KAMARA, Cheikh Moussa. "L' Islam et le christianisme." *Bulletin de l' Institut Fondamental d'Afrique Noire*, 2 (1973): 269-322.

KAMIAN, B. "Est-il possible d'enrichir l'historiographie africaine en puisant dans le passé traditionnel et islamique?" In *Perspectives nouvelles sur l'histoire africaine*. Paris: Présence africaine, 1971. Pp. 102-10.

KANE, Mohamadou. *Les contes d'Amadou Koumba. Du conte traditionnel au conte moderne d'expression française*. Dakar: Université de Dakar-Faculté des Lettres et des Sciences Humaines, 1968.

KEITA, L. "The Debate Continues: A Reply to Olabiyi Yai's 'Misère de la philosophie spéculative'." *Présence Africaine*, 120 (1981): 35-45.

KENYATTA, Jomo. "Tribal Origin and Kinship System." In *Facing Mt. Kenya, by Jomo Kenyatta*. New York: Random House, Vintage Books, 1965. Pp. 3-20.

KESTELOOT, Lilyan, DUMESTRE, Gérard, TRAORÉ, J. B. *La prise de Dionkoloni*. (Performed by Kabinè Sissoko). Paris: Armond Colin, 1975.

KESTELOOT, Lilyan; DIENG, Bassirou ; SALL, Lampsar "L'histoire, le mythe et leurs mystères dans la tradition orale africaine. Ndiadiane Ndiaye et la fondation des royaumes wolof." *Annales de la Faculté des Lettres et Sciences Humaines de Dakar*, 13 (1983): 53-74.

KESTELOOT, Lilyan, and DIENG, Bassirou. *Du Tieddo au Talibé - Contes et mythes wolof II*. Paris, Dakar: Présence Africaine, Agence de Coopération Culturelle et Technique and Institut Fondamental d'Afrique Noire, 1989.

KESTELOOT, Lilyan. "Le mythe et l'histoire dans la formation de l'empire de Ségou." *Bulletin de l' Institut Fondamental d' Afrique Noire*, 40 (1980): 578-681.

-------------------------. "Méthodologie de la recherche et de l'analyse du récit oral." *Afrique et Language*, 26 (1986): 57-64.

-------------------------. *Anthologie négro-africaine. La littérature de 1918 à 1981*. Alleur, Belgique: Marabout, 1987.

-------------------------. "The African Epic." *African Languages and Cultures*, 2 (1989): 203-14.

KI-ZERBO, Joseph. Interview with Michel Amengual. *Une histoire de l'Afrique est-elle possible?* Entretiens radiodiffusés animés par Michel Amengual. Dakar-Abidjan: Les Nouvelles Editions Africaines, 1975.

KOFFI, Niamekey. "Controverse sur l'existence d'une philosophie africaine." *Revue de Littérature et d' Esthétique Négro-africaines*, 1 (1977): 145-62.

KONTE, Lamine. "The *griot*, singer and chronicler of African Life." *Unesco Courier* (April 1986): 21-25.

KUNENE, Daniel P, trans. *Chaka*, by Thomas Mofolo. London: Heinemann, 1981.

------------------------. "African-Language Literature: Tragedy and Hope." *Research in African Literatures*, 23 (1992): 7-15.

KUNENE, Mazisi. "Problems in African Literature." *Research in African Literatures*, 23 (1992): 27-44.

LABOURET, Henri. *Paysans d'Afrique occidentale*. Paris: Gallimard, 1941.

LANTERNARI, Vittorio. *Les mouvements religieux de liberté et de salut des peuples opprimés*. Traduit de l'italien par Robert Paris. Paris: François Maspéro, 1979.

LAPIDUS, Ira M. "Islam in Africa." In *A History of Islamic Societies*, by I. Lapidus. Cambridge: Cambridge University Press, 1988. Pp. 489-508.

LARSON, Charles. *The Emergence of African Fiction*. Rev. ed. Bloomington. London: Indiana University Press, 1972.

LASNET, Alexandre. "Ouolofs." In *Une mission au Sénégal*. Paris: Augustin Challamel, 1900. Pp. 111-35.

LAURENCE, Margaret. *Long Drums and Cannons. Nigerian Drama tists and Novelists 1952-1966*. London: Macmillan, 1968.

LEROI-GOURHAN, André. *Le geste et la parole.   Vol. 2 Mémoire et technique*. Paris: Albin Michel, 1965.

LEVTZION, Nehemia. "The Early States of the Western Sudan to 1500." In *History of West Africa*, vol. 1. Edited by J.F.A. Ayayi and Michael Crowder. New York: Columbia University Press, 1971. Rpt 1976. Pp. 114-51.

LÉVI-STRAUSS, Claude. *Anthropologie structurale*. Paris: Librairie Plon, 1958.

------------------------------. *The Savage Mind.* Translated from the French *La pensée sauvage* . Chicago: University of Chicago Press, 1966.

LEWICKI, Tadeusz. "Quelques extraits inédits relatifs aux voyages des commerçants et des missionnaires Ibàdites nord-africains au pays du Soudan occidental et central au moyen âge." *Folia Orientalia,* 2 (1960): 1-27.

LEWIS, I. M. "Historical Aspects of Genealogies in Northern Somali Social Structure." *Journal of African History,* 3 (1962): 35-48.

LEYMARIE-ORTIZ, Isabelle. "The Griots of Senegal and Change." *Africa,* 3 (1979): 183-197.

LEZOU, Gérard D. "La légende de la reine Pokou: exploitation littéraire en Côte d'Ivoire." *Revue de littérature et d'esthétique négro-africaines,* 2 (1979): 39-48.

LICHTHEIM, Miriam. *Ancient Egyptian Literature. A Book of Readings,* vol. 1: *The Old and Middle Kingdoms.* Berkeley: University of California Press, 1975.

LINDFORS, Bernth O. "Oral Tradition and the Individual Literary Talent." *Studies in the Novel,* 4 (1972): 200-17.

LORD, Albert B. "Avdo Mededovic, Guslar." *Journal of American Folklore,* 69 (1956): 320-30.

--------------------. *The Singer of Tales.* Cambridge: Harvard University Press, 1960.

LUGARD, Frederick John Dealtry. *The Dual Mandate in British Tropical Africa.* Edinburgh and London: William Blackwood & Sons, 1926.

LUKACS, Georg. *The Theory of the Novel.* Cambridge, Massachusetts: MIT Press, 1990.

LUKES, Steven. "On the Social Determination of Truth." In *Modes of Thought. Essays on Thinking in Western and Non-Western Societies,* edited by R. Horton and R. Finnegan. London: Faber & Faber, 1973. Pp. 230-48.

LY, Abdoulaye. "Le marché ouest-africain." In *La compagnie du Sénégal*, by Abdoulaye Ly. Paris, Présence Africaine, 1958. Pp. 279-89.

MAGASSOUBA, Moriba. *L'islam au Sénégal. Demain les mollahs?* Paris: Karthala, 1985.

MAGEL, Emil A. "The Role of the *Gewel* in Wolof Society: The Professional Image of Lamin Jeng." *Journal of Anthropological Research*, 37 (1981): 182-91

MAKWARD, Edris. "Two Griots of Contemporary Senegambia." In *The Oral Performance in Africa*, edited by Isidore Okpewho. Ibadan: Spectrum Books Ltd., 1990. Pp. 23-41.

MALINOWSKI, Bronislaw. *The Dynamics of Culture Change. An Inquiry into Race Relations in Africa*. New Haven: Yale University Press, 1961.

MARTIN, Marie-Louise. *Kimbangu. An African Prophet and his Church*. William B. Ferdmans Publishing Company and Basil Blackwell, 1975.

MARTY, Paul. *Études sur l' islam au Sénégal*. Paris: Ernest Leroux, 1917.

MATEENE, Kahombo. "Essai d'analyse stylistique de l'épopée de Mwindo (baNyanga du Zaïre)." *Cahiers de Littérature Orale*, 16 (1984): 59-79.

MATHEWS, R.D. "Parochialism and the Past." *The Journal of Commonwealth Literature*, 6 (1969): 100-5.

MAUNY, Raymond. "Baobabs-cimeti ères à griots." *Notes Africaines*, 67 (1955): 72-76.

MAZRUI, Alia. *The African Condition. A Political Diagnosis*. London: Heinemann, 1982.

--------------------. *The Africans-A Triple Heritage*. Toronto, Boston: Little, Brown and Company, 1986.

MBEMBE, Achille. *Afriques indociles. Christianisme, pouvoir et Etat en société post coloniale*. Paris: Karthala, 1988.

MBITI, John. "L'éveil de la littérature indigène de la tribu akamba." *Présence Africaine*, 24-25 (1959): 231-48.

------------. *The Study of African Religions & Philosophy*. London: Heinemann, 1969.

MBONGO, Nsame. "Problèmes théoriques de la question nationale en Afrique." *Présence Africaine*, 136 (1985): 31-67.

MEILLASSOUX, Claude. "Histoire et institutions du *Kafo* de Bamako d'après la tradition des Niaré." *Cahiers d'études africaines*, 4 (1963): 186-227.

MIDIOHOUAN, Guy Ossito. *Oralité, Scripturalité, langue et littérature en Afrique*. Conférence organisée par le centre cultural soviétique. Cotonou: Mars 1987.

MILLER, Christopher L. *Theories of Africans. Francophone Literature and Anthropology in Africa*. Chicago: The University of Chicago Press, 1990.

MONNIER, Laurent. "Note sur les structures politiques de l'ancien royaume de Kongo avant l'arrivée des Portugais." *Genève-Afrique*, 5 (1966): 7-35.

MONOD, J.-L. *Histoire de l'Afrique Occidentale Française*, d'après les travaux de Maurice Delafosse. Paris: Librairie Delagrave, 1931.

MONTEIL, Vincent. "La décolonisation de l'Histoire." *Preuves*, 142 (1962): 3-12.

----------------------. "Sur l'arabisation des langues négro-africaines." *Genève-Afrique*, 2 (1963): 12-19.

----------------------. "Esquisses sénégalaises." *Initiations et Études Africaines*, 21 (1966): 26-69.

----------------------. "Le Dyolof et Al-Bouri Ndiaye." *Bulletin de l' Institut Fondamental d'Afrique Noire*, 28 (1966): 595-636.

----------------------. "Un cas d'économie ostentatoire: Les griots d'Afrique Noire." *Économies et sociétés*, 2 (1968): 773-91.

--------------------. *L'Islam noir. Une religion à la conquête de l'Afrique.* Paris: Éditions du Seuil, 1980.

MORAES FARIAS, Paulo F., de. "Praise as Intrusion and as Foreign Language: A Sunjata Paradigm Seen from the Gesere Diaspora in Béninois Borgu." Unpublished paper on file at Northwestern University: The Institute for Advanced Study and Research in the African Humanities, Evanston, Illinois. 40 pp.

--------------------. "The oldest writing of West Africa: Medieval epigraphs from Ǝssuk, Saney, and Egef-n-Tawaqqast (Mali)." *Journal des Africanistes*, 60 (2) 1990: 65-113.

MOURALIS, Bernard. *Les contre-littératures.* Paris: Presses Universitaires de France, 1975.

MUDIMBE, Valentin.Y. *Entre les eaux. Dieu, un prêtre, la révolution.* Paris: Éditions Présence Africaine, 1973.

------------------------. *The Invention of Africa. Gnosis, Philosophy, and the Order of Knowledge.* Bloomington, London: Indiana University Press & James Currey, 1988.

------------------------. *Parables & Fables. Exegesis, Textuality, and Politics in Central Africa.* Madison: The University of Wisconsin Press, 1991.

NAIPAUL, V.S. *Among the Believers. An Islamic Journey.* New York: Vintage Books, 1982

NDAW, Alassane. *La pensée africaine.* Dakar: Les Nouvelles Éditions Africaines, 1983.

N'DIAYE, Raphaël. "Chants-poèmes de femme sereer: Techniques de création." *Présence Africaine*, 141 (1986): 83-101.

NDOYE-MBENGUE, Mariama. "Pour une poésie orale léboue (Sénégal)." *Notes Africaines*, 174 (1982): 45-47.

NGIJOL, Pierre. "La critique littéraire africaine dans la littérature traditionnelle orale." In *Le Critique africain et son peuple comme producteur de civilisation.* (Colloque de Yaoundé, Avril 1973). Paris: Présence africaine, 1977. Pp. 95-104.

NGUGI Wa Thiongo. *Writers in Politics. Essays.* London: Heinemann Educational Books Ltd, 1981.

NGWABA, Francis, E. "The English Novel and the Novel in English: Points of Contact and Departure." In *Modern Essays on African Literature. Studies in the African Novel*, vol. 1. Edited by Samuel O. Asein and Albert O. Ashaolu. Ibadan: Ibadan University Press, 1986. Pp. 6-26.

NIANE, D.T. *Soundjata ou l'épopée mandingue.* Paris: Éditions Présence Africaine, 1960.

----------------. "Le Mali et la deuxième expansion manden." *In Histoire générale de l'Afrique. L'Afrique du XIIe au XVIe siècle*, vol. 4. Paris, Unesco/NEA, 1985. Pp. 141-196.

NICOLAS, Guy. "Une forme atténuée du potlatch en pays hausa (République du Niger: le Dyubu)." *Economies et sociétés*, 2 (1967): 151-214.

--------------------. "Développement rural et comportement économique traditionnel au sein d'une société africaine." *Genève-Afrique*, 8 (1969): 18-35.

--------------------. "Enracinement ethnique de l'Islam." *Cahiers d' Études Africaines*, 18 (1978): 347-77.

NKETIA, J.H. *Funeral Dirges of the Akan People.* Gold Coast: University College of the Gold Coast, Achimota, 1955.

NKRUMAH, Kwame. "Consciencism." *Présence africaine*, 21 (1964): 8-32.

NYANG, Sulayman S. "Ten Years of Gambia's Independence: A Political Analysis." *Présence Africaine*, 104 (1977): 28-45.

OKION OJIGBO, Anthony. "Traditional Yoruba Political System." *Cahier d' Études Africaines*, 13 (1973): 275-92.

OKPEWHO, Isidore. "Analytical Boundaries in the Oral Narrative." *Bulletin de l' Institut Fondamental d' Afrique Noire*, 42 (1980): 822-56.

------------------------. "Does the Epic Exist in Africa? Some Formal Considerations." *Research in African Literatures*, 8 (1977): 171-200.

OLIVER, Roland and FAGE, J. D. "Northern and Western Africa during the Great Age of Islam." In *A Short History of Africa*, by R. Oliver & J. D. Fage. Harmondsworth, England: Penguin Books Ltd, Penguin African Library, 1975. Pp. 67-92.

ONG, Walter J. *Orality and Literacy. The Technologizing of the Word*. London and New York: Methuen, 1982.

OPLAND, Jeff. *Anglo-Saxon Oral Poetry. A Study of the Traditions*. New Haven and London: Yale University Press, 1980.

-------------------. *Xhosa Oral Poetry. Aspects of a Black South African Tradition*. Cambridge: Cambridge University Press, 1983.

OUOLOGUEM, Yambo. *Le Devoir de violence*. Paris: Éditions du Seuil, 1968.

OWOMOYELA, Oyekan. *Visions and revisions. Essays on African Literatures and Criticism*. New York and San Francisco: Peter Lang, 1991.

PARKER, Bettye J. "An Interview with Ngugi Wa Thiong'o." *First World*, 2 (1979): 56-59.

PAULME, Denise. "Blood Pacts, Age Classes and Castes in Black Africa." In *French Perspectives in African Studies*, edited by Pierre Alexandre. London: Published for the International African Institute by the Oxford University Press, 1973. Pp. 73-95.

---------------------. "Une religion syncrétique en Côte d'Ivoire: le culte *deima.*" *Cahiers d' Études Africaines*, 9 (1962): 5-90.

PERSON, Yves. "Chronologie du royaume Gun de Hogbonu." *Cahiers d'Études Africaines*, 15 (1975): 217-38.

PISON, Gilles. "Pluviométrie et estimation des âges. Méthode d'estimation des âges des Peul Bandé du Sénégal oriental." *Archives Suisses d' Anthropologie Générale*, 44 (1980): 187-95.

PRIGENT, Michel. Préface to *Les intellectuels et la démocratie*. Paris: Presses Universitaires de France, 1980.

PROPP, Vladimir. *Morphology of the Folktale*. Austin: University of Texas Press, 1990.

PULLEYBANK, Douglas. "Niger-Kordofanian Languages." Bernard Comrie, ed., *The World's Major Languages*. Oxford: Oxford University Press, 1990. Pp. 959-70.

RAHIM, A. *Islamic History*. Lagos, Nigeria: Islamic Publications Bureau, 1981.

REHFISCH, Farnham. "Competitive Gift Exchange among the Mambila." *Cahiers d' Études Africaines*, 9 (1962): 91-103.

RHODES, Willard. "Toward a Definition of Ethnomusicology." *American Anthropologist*, 58 (1956): 457-63.

ROBIN, J. "D'un royaume amphibie et fort disparate. Essai sur l'ancien royaume Sénégalais du Walo." *African Studies*, 5 (1946): 250-56.

ROBINSON, David. *The Islamic Regime of Fuuta Tooro*. Michigan State University: African Studies Center, 1984.

----------------------. "La question des sources dans le *Jihàd* d'Al-Hajj Umar." *Revue Française d' Histoire d' Outre-mer*, 72 (1985): 405-34.

ROUGET, Gilbert. "A propos de la forme dans les musiques de tradition orale." *Les Colloques de Wégimont*. Bruxelles: Elsevier, 1956. Pp. 132-143.

ROUSSEAU, R. "Le Sénégal d'autrefois. Étude sur le Toubé. Papiers de Rawane Boy." In *Bulletin du Comité d' Études Historiques et Scientifiques de l'Afrique Occidentale Française* (1931): 334-65.

--------------------. "Le village ouolof (Sénégal)." *Annales de Géographie*, 235 (1933): 88-94.

RUCH, E. A. and ANYANWU, K. C. *African Philosophy. An Introduction to the Main Philosophical Trends in Contemporary Africa*. Rome: Catholic Book Agency-Officium Libri Catholici, 1984.

RYLE, Herbert. *The Book of Genesis*. Text and Commentary by H. Ryle. Cambridge: Cambridge University Press, 1921.

SAAD EL-DIN, Mursi. "The place of oral tradition in the modern world (A case study of Egypt)." *La tradition orale source de la littérature contemporaine en Afrique*. Colloque International organisé par l'ICA et le PEN International avec le concours du PNUD et de l'UNESCO, à Dakar (Sénégal) du 24 au 29 Janvier 1983. Dakar-Abidjan-Lomé: Les Nouvelles Editions Africaines, 1984.

SAID, Edward W. *Orientalism*. New York: Vintage Books, 1979.

--------------------. *Beginnings. Intention and Method*. New York: Columbia University Press, 1985.

SALMEN, Walter von. "Źur sozialen Schichtung des berufsmusikertums im Mittelalterlichen Eurasien und in Afrike." *Les Colloques de Wégimont-Ethnomusicologie II*. Paris: Société d'édition <<Les Belles Lettres>>, 1960. Pp. 23-32.

SAINT-MARTIN, Yves-Jean. *Le Sénégal sous le second Empire*. Paris: Karthala, 1989.

SAMB, Amar. "Essai sur la contribution du Sénégal à la littérature d' expression arabe." Lille: Service de reproduction des thèses de l' Université, 1972.

----------------. *L'Islam et l'histoire du Sénégal*. Dakar: Éditions Hilal, 1974.

----------------. "Réflexion sur les croyances Wolof à travers les expressions linguistiques." *Notes Africaines*, 43 (1974): 77-80.

SAMB, Assane Marokhaya El-Hadji. *"Cadior Demb"-Essai sur l'histoire du*

Cayor. Abidjan-Dakar-Lomé: Les Nouvelles Editions Africaines, 1981.

SANNEH, Lamin. "The Origins of Clericalism in West African Islam." *Journal of African History*, 17 (1976): 49-72.

----------------------. *The Jakhanke Muslim Clerics. A Religious and Historical Study of Islam in Senegambia.* Lanham, MD: University Press of America, 1989.

----------------------. "'They Stooped to Conquer': Vernacular Translation and the Socio-Cultural Factor." *Research in African Literatures*, 23 (1992): 7-15.

SARTRE, Jean-Paul. *Situations philosophiques.* Paris: Gallimard, 1990.

SCHAEFFNER, André. "Situation des musiciens dans trois sociétés." *Les Colloques de Wégimont Ethnomusicologie II.* Paris: Société d'édition <<Les Belles Lettres>>, 1960. Pp. 33-49.

SCHEUB, Harold. "A Review of African Oral Traditions, and Literature." *African Studies Review*, 28 (1985): 1-72.

SEKONI, Ropo. "The Narrator, Narrative-Pattern and Audience Experience of Oral Narrative-Performance." In *The Oral Performance in Africa*, edited by I. Okpewho. Ibadan: Spectrum Books Limited, 1990. Pp. 139-59.

SELIGMAN, Charles G. *Races of Africa.* London: Thornton Butterworth, 1930.

SEMBENE, Ousmane. *Le dernier de l'empire.* Roman sénégalais - Tome 2. Paris: L'Harmattan, 1981.

SENGHOR, Léopold Sédar. *Liberté 1. Négritude et humanisme.* Paris: Éditions du Seuil, 1964.

----------------------. *Elégies majeures* suivi de *Dialogue sur la poésie francophone.* Paris: Seuil, 1979.

----------------------. *Ce que je crois.* Paris: Éditions Grasset et Fasquelle, 1988.

SEYDOU, Christiane. "Jeu de pions, jeu des armes-Le Combat singulier dans l'épopée peule." *Cahiers de littérature orale*, 32 (1992): 63-93.

SHELTON, Austin. *The African Assertion. A Critical Anthology of African Literature*. New York: The Odyssey Press, 1968.

-----------------------. "The Problem of Griot Interpretation and the Actual Causes of War in Sondjata." *Présence Africaine*, 66 (1968): 145-52.

SILLA, Ousmane. "Persistance des castes dans la société wolof contemporaine." *Bulletin de l'Institut Fondamental d' Afrique Noire*, 28 (1966): 731-70.

SIMO, Dr "La spécificité culturelle dans la littérature." *Revue de Littérature et d' Esthétique Négro-africaines*, 6 (1985): 15-27.

SIMPSON, Ekundayo. "Bilinguisme et création littéraire en Afrique." *Présence Africaine*, 111 (1979): 44-59.

SINE, Babacar D. "Esquisse d'une réflexion autour de quelques éléments de 'philosophie' wolof." *Présence Africaine*, 91 (1974): 26-48.

SINE, Babacar D., and BOUGHALI, Mohamed. "La création intellectuelle." In *Patrimoine culturel et création contemporaine en Afrique et dans le monde arabe*, sous la direction de Mohamed Aziza. Dakar. Abidjan: Les Nouvelles Éditions Africaines, 1977. Pp. 207-214.

SITOE, Bento. "Translation: Languages and Cultures in Contrast." *AH*, 9 (1990): 1-13.

SMITH, M. G. "The Social Functions and Meaning of Hausa Praise-Singing." *Africa*, 27 (1957): 26-45.

SNOWDEN, Frank M. Jr. *Blacks in Antiquity. Ethiopians in the Greco-Roman Experience*. Cambridge: The Belknap Press of Harvard University Press, 1970.

SOH, Siré Abbâs. *Chroniques du Fouta sénégalais*. (Translated from the Arabic and annotated by Maurice Delafosse and Henri Gaden). Paris: Ernest Leroux, 1913.

SOW, Ibrahima. "Réflexions sur les injures et les paroles obscènes au Sénégal." *Bulletin de l'I.F.A.N.*, 46, 3-4 (1986-87):343-78.

SOYINKA, Wole. *Art, Dialogue and Outrage. Essays on Literature and Culture*. Ibadan: New Horn Press, 1988.

--------------. *Myth, Literature, and The African World*. Cambridge: Cambridge University Press, 1990.

SUGRANYES DE FRANCH, Ramòn. "L'apologétique de Raimond Lulle vis-à-vis de l'Islam." *Cahiers de Fanjeaux (18). Islam et chrétiens du Midi XIIe-XIXe s.).* Fanjeaux, Toulouse, France: Edouard Privat, 1983.

SYLLA, Assane. *La philosophie morale des Wolofs*. Dakar: Éditions Sankoré, 1978.

TAMARI, Tal. "The Development of Caste Systems in West Africa." *Journal of African History*, 32 (1991): 221-250.

THARPE, Coleman W. "The Oral Storyteller in Hawthorne's Novels." *Studies in Short Fiction*, 16 (1979): 205-14.

THIAM, Iba Der. "La tradition orale: source privilégiée de l'histoire africaine." In *Symposium Leo Frobenius II*. Bonn: Deutsche UNESCO-Kommission, 1980. Pp. 56-80.

TODOROV, Tzvetan. *Les genres du discours*. Paris: Éditions du Seuil, 1978.

THOMAS, Louis V. "Réflexions sur un problème d'actualité: urbanisation et développement." *Notes Africaines*, 131 (1971): 72-81.

THOMPSON, Donald T. "The Joking Relationship and Organized Obscenity in North Queensland." *American Anthropologist*, 37 (1935): 460-90.

THOMPSON, Stith. *Motif-index of Folk-literature: A Classification of Narrative Elements in Folktales, Ballads, Myths, Fables, Mediaeval Romances, Exempla, Fabliaux, Jestbooks, and Local Legends* (revised and enlarged edition). Bloomington: Indiana University Press, 1989.

TONKIN, Elizabeth. "Oracy and the Disguises of Literacy." In *Discourse and its Disguises. The Interpretation of African Oral Texts*, edited by K. Barber and P.F. de Moraes Farias. Birmingham, England: Birmingham University, Centre of West African Studies, 1989. Pp. 39-48.

TOWA, Marcien. *Essai sur la problématique philosophique dans l'Afrique actuelle.* Yaoundé, Éditions Clé, 1971.

---------------------. *L'idée d'une philosophie négro-africaine.* Yaoundé: Éditions Clé, 1979.

---------------------. "Conditions d'affirmation d'une pensée philosophique africaine moderne." *Présence Africaine*, 117-118 (1981): 341-53.

UHLIG, Claus. "Forms of Time and Varieties of Change In Literary Texts." *Comparative Literature*, 37 (1985): 289-300.

U TAM'SI, Tchicaya. "Les Langues sans écriture." *Présence Africaine*, 52 (1964): 162-66.

---------------------. *Ces fruits si doux de l'arbre à pain.* Paris: Éditions Seghers, 1987.

VANSINA, Jan. "Recording the Oral History of the Bakuba -.I Methods." *Journal of African History*, 1 (1960): 43-51.

---------------------. "Recording the Oral History of the Bakuba - II Results." *Journal of African History*, 1 (1960): 257-70.

---------------------. "A Comparison of African Kingdoms." *Africa*, 32 (1962): 324-35.

---------------------. *Oral Tradition. A Study in Historical Methodology.* London: Routledge & Kegan Paul, 1965.

---------------------. "Lutilisation de données ethnographiques comme sources de l'histoire." In *Perspectives nouvelles sur l'histoire africaine.* Paris, Présence Africaine, 1971.

----------------------. *Les anciens royaumes de la savane*, 2nd ed. Kinshasa: Presses Universitaires du Zaïre, 1976.

----------------------. *Oral Tradition as History*. London: James Currey, 1985.

WACHSMAN, Klaus P. "Problems of Musical Stratigraphy in Africa." *Les Colloques de Wégimont. Ethnomusicologic III*. Paris: Société d'édition <<Les Belles Lettres>>, 1964. Pp. 19-22.

WAUTHIER, Claude. *The Literature and Thought of Modern Africa*. English translation from the French by Shirley Kay. Washington D.C.: Three Continents Press, 1979.

WEISKEL, Timothy C. "Nature, Culture and Ecology in Traditional African Thought Systems." *Cultures*, 1 (1973): 123-44.

WHITE, Landeg. "Poetic Licence: Oral Poetry and History." In *Discourse and its Disguises. The Interpretation of African Oral Texts*, edited by K. Barber and P.F. de Moraes Farias. Birmingham, England: Birmingham University, Center of West African Studies, 1989. Pp. 34-38.

WIREDU, Kwasi. *Philosophy and an African Culture*. Cambridge: Cambridge University Press, 1980.

WORSLEY, Peter. *The Third World* (second edition). Chicago: The University of Chicago Press, 1977.

WRIGHT, Bonnie L. "The Power of Articulation." In *Creativity of Power. Cosmology and Action in African Societies*, edited by W. Arens and Ivan Karp. Washington D.C.: Smithsonian Institution Press, 1989. Pp. 39-57.

WRIGHT, Derek. "Orality in the African Historical Novel: Yambo Ouologuem's *Bound to Violence* and Ayi Kwei Armah's *Two Thousand Seasons*." *The Journal of Commonwealth Literature*, 23 (1988): 91-101.

WRIGHT, Donald R. *Oral Traditions from the Gambia. Vol. 1 Mandinka Griots*. Ohio University: Center for International Studies - Papers in International Studies, Africa Series, 37, 1979.

YANKAH, Kwesi. *The Proverbs in the Context of Akan Rhetoric - A Theory of Proverb Praxis.* New York: Peter Lang, 1989.

YAI, Olabiyi B. "Théorie et pratique en philosophie africaine: misère de la philosophie spéculative (Critique de P. Hountondji, M. Towa et autres)." *Présence Africaine,* 108 (1978): 65-91.

------------------. "Issues in Oral Poetry: Criticism, Teaching and Translation." In *Discourse And Its Disguises. The Interpretation of African Oral Texts,* K. Barber and P.F. de Moraes Farias, eds. Birmingham, England: Birmingham University, Center of West African Studies, 1989. Pp. 59-69.

ZANETTI, Vincent. "Le griot et le pouvoir, une relation ambiguë." *Cahiers de musiques traditionnelles,* 3 (1990): 161-172.

ZEMP, Hugo. "La légende des griots malinké." *Cahier d'études africaines,* 6 (1966): 611-42.

ZEMPLENI-RABAIN, J. "Expression de l'agressivité et processus de médiation dans la socialisation de l'enfant wolof (Sénégal)." *Africa,* 44 (1974): 151-62.

AFRICAN STUDIES

22. Segun Gbadegesin (ed.), **The Politicization of Society During Nigeria's Second Republic, 1979-1983**

23. Tukumbi Lumumba-Kasongo, **Nationalistic Ideologies, Their Policy Implications and the Struggle for Democracy in African Politics**

24. Getachew Metaferia and Maigenet Shifferraw, **The Ethiopian Revolution of 1974 and the Exodus of Ethiopia's Trained Human Resources**

25. George Cotter, **Proverbs and Sayings of the Oromo People of Ethiopia and Kenya with English Translations**

26. J. W. T. Allen, Roland Allen, N. Q. King, Jan Knappert, et al. (eds.), **A Poem Concerning the Death of the Prophet Muhammad / Utendi Wa Kutawafu Nabii**

27. Salah M. Hassan, **Art and Islamic Literacy Among the Hausa of Northern Nigeria**

28. Samuel S. Simbandwe, **A Socio-Religious and Political Analysis of the Judeo-Christian Concept of Prophetism and Modern Bakongo and Zulu African Prophet Movements**

29. Pyare L. Arya, **Structure, Policies and Growth Prospects of Nigeria**

30. Sheikh Batu Daramy, **Constitutional Developments in the Post-Colonial State of Sierra-Leone 1961-1984**

31. Abiodun Goke-Pariola, **The Role of Language in the Struggle for Power and Legitimacy in Africa**

32. Marjorie H. Stewart, **Borgu and its Kingdoms: A Reconstruction of Western Sudanese Polity**

33. Abdalla Uba Adamu, **Reform and Adaptation in Nigerian University Curricula 1960-1992: Living on the Credit Line**

34. Thomas M. Shaw, **The Fulani Matrix of Beauty and Art in the Djolof Region of Senegal**

35. Toyin Falola, A. Ajayi, A. Alao, B. Babawale, **The Military Factor in Nigeria 1966-1985**

36. Samba Diop, **The Oral History and Literature of the Wolof People of Waalo, Northern Senegal: The Master of the Word (Griot) in the Wolof Tradition**

37. Rina Okonkwo, **Protest Movements in Lagos, 1908-1930**

38. Felton Best (editor), **Black Resistance Movements in the United States and Africa, 1800-1993**

39. Jeffrey C. Stone, **A Short History of the Cartography of Africa**

40. H.L. Pretorius, **Historiography and Historical Sources Regarding African Indigenous Churches in South Africa**